The Radical Writings of Jack Nusan Porter

The Radical Writings of Jack Nusan Porter

Compiled with an introduction
by Jack Nusan Porter

Preface
by Shaul Magid

BOSTON
2020

Library of Congress Cataloging-in-Publication Data

Names: Porter, Jack Nusan, author. | Magid, Shaul, 1958- writer of preface.

Title: The radical writings of Jack Nusan Porter / compiled with an
  introduction by Jack Nusan Porter ; preface by Shaul Magid.
Description: Boston : Academic Studies Press, 2020. | Includes
  bibliographical references.
Identifiers: LCCN 2020029923 (print) | LCCN 2020029924 (ebook) | ISBN
  9781644694633 (hardback) | ISBN 9781644694640 (paperback) | ISBN
  9781644694657 (adobe pdf) | ISBN 9781644694664 (epub)
Subjects: LCSH: Jewish radicals. | Zionism.
Classification: LCC HX550.J4 P67 2020 (print) | LCC HX550.J4 (ebook) |
  DDC 320.54095694--dc23
LC record available at https://lccn.loc.gov/2020029923
LC ebook record available at https://lccn.loc.gov/2020029924

Book design by Lapiz Digital Services.
Cover design by Ivan Grave.

Publisher by Cherry Orchard Books, imprint of Academic Studies Press.
1577 Beacon St.
Brookline, MA 02446
press@academicstudiespress.com
www.academicstudiespress.com

Dedicated to all of my "radical" teachers, especially
Morris U. Schappes, long-time editor of *Jewish Currents*,
who nurtured and mentored me over the years.

Where there is no vision, the people perish.
— Biblical proverb

Contents

Other Books by Jack Nusan Porter

Student Protest and the Technocratic Society (Adams Press, 1971)

Jewish Radicalism (Grove Press/Random House, 1973)

The Sociology of American Jews: A Critical Anthology (University Press of America, 1980)

The Jew as Outsider (University Press of America, 1981, 2014)

Confronting History and Holocaust (University Press of America, 1983, 2014)

Genocide and Human Rights (University Press of America, 1982, 2012)

Sexual Politics in Nazi Germany: The Persecution of the Homosexuals and Lesbians During the Holocaust (The Spencer Press, 2011)

Women in Chains: Sourcebook on the Agunah (Jason Aronson, 1995)

Is Sociology Dead? Social Theory and Social Praxis in a Postmodern Age (University Press of America, 2008)

The Genocidal Mind: Sociological and Sexual Perspectives (University Press of America, 2006)

Predicting Genocide and Terrorism (with Trevor Jones, in progress)

Preface

In June 1962, the newly formed Students for a Democratic Society completed the Port Huron Statement that launched what became known as the New Left, a broad-based movement mostly of young Americans who subjected America to a systemic critique of politics, economics, racial, social, and military practices. The year 1962 was an auspicious year in that it preceded major Civil Rights legislation and the escalation of the conflict in Vietnam by only a year or two and followed only two years after the FDA approved the birth control pill in June 1960.

The New Left was in part a break from the old left, or Roosevelt's liberalism, arguing that the inequities, injustices, and military imperialism of America in the Cold War era ran counter to America's principles of freedom and equality. In a way, it was a movement to save America by undermining it. This gave birth to the Free Speech Movement in Berkeley during the 1964-65 academic year, the rise of Black Nationalism in 1966, and the students protests and riots in 1968. By the end of the 1960s, early Baby Boomers were making their voices heard in an America that was becoming increasingly unsettled and unstable.

In those tumultuous years, the term "radical" was often worn as a badge of honor, a statement of conviction and a belief that there were no good incremental solutions to systemic problems. To be a radical meant to stand on the forefront of a progressive critique of American liberalism, as conservatism, emerging with Barry Goldwater's failed 1965 run against Lyndon Johnson, had not yet become a political force to be reckoned with at least until the end of the 1960s with the election of Richard Nixon and the rise of the Moral Majority.

American Jews were disproportionately represented in the New Left. Some were "red diaper babies," children of socialists or communists from a pre-war era, some were radicalized through a variety of political and cultural portals, from the Beat's literary movement of the 1950s, to civil rights, to rock and roll and LSD. But something happened to many New Left Jews around 1966. Stokley Carmichael (later Kwame Ture), one of the leaders of SNCC, gave a speech on June 16, 1966 in Greenwood, Mississippi, that launched the Black Nationalist movement. In that speech he argued that the movement needed to be by blacks and for blacks and essentially marginalized the many whites who risked their lives for the cause of civil rights, from the Freedom Riders of 1961 to those who marched in Selma in 1965. And it included many Jews who played leadership roles in organizations like the NAACP.

Carmichael's speech in 1966 was followed the next year with the Six-Day War in Israel in June 1967. That September, at the New Politics Conference in Chicago, the conference members adopted a position opposing "Zionist colonialism" in response to the war and its consequences, what would become known as "the occupation." Black Nationalists had adopted that they called "Third-Worldism," a doctrine that viewed oppression of people of color worldwide as part of their agenda of black liberation. Palestinians were included in that agenda.

This move alienated many Jews from the New Left who viewed this anti-Israel proposal as unfair, unjustified, and immoral. Over the course of the next few years many young Jews, radicalized by New Left politics, abandoned the movement and began to re-think their own Jewish identities. Many were also critical of Israel's politics, many were not, and Israel was not really the center of their new-found identity but rather the occasion for a re-assessment of Judaism in a radicalized frame.

The result was the rise of a plethora of new Jewish publications, student newspapers, organizations such as "The Jewish Liberation Project" "The Radical Zionist Agenda," "The Brooklyn Bridge Coalition," "Havurat Shalom" and the "Radical Jewish Student Union." Journals such as *Genesis 2*, (Boston) *The Jewish Radical* (Berkeley), *Response* (Boston), *Voice of Micha* (Washington, DC) *Hashofar* (Cleveland), and *Columbia Jewish Free Press* (NYC) disseminated radical political essays, poetry, literature, and artwork. These Jews were moving from "Jewish radicals to radical Jews," a phrase coined by Arthur Waskow in his 1971 book *The Bush is Burning: Radical Judaism Faces the Pharaohs of the Super State*. Alienated from the New Left but committed to radical politics, many of these young Jews, called "New Jews" (the title of a 1971 book edited by James Sleeper and Alan Mintz), began to make inroads into American Jewry by attacking the complacency and materialism of the American Jewish establishment of the 1960s. Jewish Federations, large suburban synagogues, and quiescent responses to the war and issues such as Soviet Jewry, became subject to verbal and sometimes even physical attack by this new generation of New Jews.

By 1973 this movement had gained considerable notoriety in the American Jewish landscape. Communities such as Havurat Shalom in Somerville, MA, The House of Love and Prayer in San Francisco, The Manhattan Havurah in NYC, and Fabrengen in Washington DC were lay-led Jewish experimental communities founded on the principles of New Leftism. In that year Jack Nusan Porter and Peter Dreier published an anthology entitled *Jewish Radicalism*. A volume whose cover had the stenciled fist used by the Black Panthers and later The Jewish Defense League, with a Jewish Star enshrined inside the fist.

Published by Grove Press, the volume was typical of its time. The paperback costs $2.75 (the hardcover slightly more). The volume was dedicated to "The men and women of the radical movement, both here in the United States and abroad," with the famous saying of Hillel the Elder, "If I am not for myself who will be for me?"

Jewish Radicalism was one of the first, and arguably the best anthology of Jewish radical thought of that period. Nusan Porter continued to publish essays and books subsequent to his editing *Jewish Radicalism*. In this volume, *The Radical Writings of Jack Nusan Porter*, we present a collection of Nusan Porter's writings spanning over three decades. It addresses the major issues that exercised radical Jews from the 1960s to the present. Nusan Porter writes about Zionism and its discontent, radicalism, race relations, activism, and even his secret affiliation with the JDL while he was a progressive radical Jew.

We are more than half a century past that intense and creative moment in American Jewish history. Much has happened. And yet in some way much stays the same. Racism still exists, the Israeli occupation still exists, sexism still exists, classism still exists, the battle between Jewish liberalism and Jewish progressivism still exists, and now a more recent Jewish (neo)conservatism has become part of the American Jewish landscape. The Occupy Wall Street movement was a brief moment whose after-shocks are beginning to be felt in the rise of Bernie Sanders, the rise of a new Jewish socialism in the revival of *Jewish Currents* magazine, and the rise of Jewish Social Justice movements. A new generation of Jewish millennials and Gen

Zers have pushed through the decades fed by the Reagan era to flex their newly found radical muscle in a variety of new agendas, projects, and programs. Gender, which was not at the forefront of the earlier Jewish radicals, at least until the early to mid-1970s, is now front and center, accompanied by a broader conversation about gender identity that extends far beyond questions of rights and equality.

It is for this reason that *The Radical Writings of Jack Nusan Porter* is appropriate for our time. While for some readers the essays may seem dated, in some way they remain very relevant. In post-Reagan America "radicalism" has become a pejorative term, a way to discredit an interlocutor. I hope *The Radical Writings of Jack Nusan Porter* will help change that. May a new generation of aspiring radicals be inspired by the old guard to find their own way. And may you succeed.

Shaul Magid
May 22, 2020
Thetford Center, Vermont

Introduction: The Roots of Jewish Radicalism

The Rationale

Why are Jews radicals? Why do they work against their class interests? This has nonplussed Republican experts for decades. The percentages may vary from 60-90%, but Jews are always way over 50% for Democrats and progressives. The reasons are many and go back to Jewish history. I summarize them below, based on the late historian Robert S. Wistrich in his masterful book, *Revolutionary Jews from Marx to Trotsky*, in his opening chapter, "Jews and Socialism":

1. Jews are outsiders;
2. Jews have the prophetic tradition;
3. Jews care about the oppressed, the disabled, the widowed, and the orphaned;
4. Jews go against their class interests; in Marxian terms, they live like capitalists yet vote like proletarians.

The History: 1881-1914

The grandparents and great-grandparents of today's radicals came to America from Russia and Poland for the most part. True, there were smaller numbers of German and Sephardic Jews, but the vast majority of American (and world Jewry) came from Eastern Europe and brought with them a variety of radical ideologies (Marxism, Socialism, Communism, Bundism, Labor Zionism), as did many other Europeans (Italians such as Sacco and Vanzetti, Greeks, Scandinavians, Germans).

They came to the impoverished urban centers—Jews are urban people; they did not go to the mines and forests of Maine or Pennsylvania or to the wild west of Colorado or Wyoming or Texas, but to urban centers like New York, Philadelphia, Chicago, Cleveland, and Milwaukee—the Lower East Side of Manhattan, the West End of Boston, the South Side of Chicago, the "Inner City" of Milwaukee.

Their language was Yiddish, not Hebrew or German, and they began to "organize." In 1907, the United Hebrew Trades comprised 74 affiliated unions and 50,000 members. By 1914, it had soared to 104 unions and over 250,000 members. The Jewish unions were the backbone of the Socialist Party of America, which had its own Yiddish-speaking wing.

The radical Yiddish press—communist, anarchist, socialist, Zionist, anti-Zionist, Bundist, religious or secular—was all widely read and influential. The largest publication was Abraham Cahan's *The Jewish Daily Forward*, which reached over 200,000 readers in 1916.

Yiddish writers such as Shalom Asch, Isaac Bashevis Singer, and Shalom Aleichem were widely read. Yiddish theater flourished. Today there is an English-language newspaper, *The Forward*, and a small Yiddish *Forward*. Only Orthodox Jews have larger Yiddish-speaking readers and press.

Socialist mayors were elected in Milwaukee as early as 1916 and as late as 1951 (Frank Zeidler). They were called "sewer socialists," more interested in fixing the roads and bridges than engaging in "permanent revolution," and they were beloved. Madison, Wisconsin, has a socialist (and Jewish) mayor to this day, Paul Soglin.

After the Russian Revolution: 1917-1939

After the successful revolt by Communists in the Soviet Union, communism grew all over the world, and with it, Jewish participation. In fact, many of the early Communist leaders—Leon Trotsky, Lazar Kaganovich, and even Vyacheslav Molotov's wife—were renegade Jews. In fact, Marxism became known as a substitute religion for secular Jews and non-Jews, with Marx as God and Lenin as Moses the Prophet.

Sociologist Nathan Glazer estimated that fully one-third of the American Communist Party was Jewish—or about 15,000; and if you added "fellow travelers"—admirers, spouses and friends—easily ten times that. Communists were active in all aspects of American life and especially in trade unions, from teachers to longshoremen.

Communism was also very attractive to intellectuals, both literary and cinematic. New York, Chicago, and Los Angeles had large numbers of Communist members, especially in the movie industry. Walt Disney was shocked when his illustrators of Minnie and Mickey and Donald Duck walked out on strike, desiring higher wages and better health benefits.

The Decline of the Old Left: 1939-1959

Several events traumatized and confused the Old Left:

1. *The Molotov-Ribbentrop Pact of 1939.* The so-called Hitler-Stalin Pact was a tremendous blow to the morale of the Communist and Socialist parties. How could Stalin make "peace" with this fascist?
2. *The Establishment of the State of Israel.* While the Soviet Union did recognize the nascent state in 1948-1949, the honeymoon was short-lived as they moved onto support for the Arab League. This left the Old Left fumbling for a rationale. Should they be Zionists and supporters of Israel or toe the party line against Israel? Many compromised by supporting Israel but rejecting Zionism as defined as Israel being the center of Jewish life. America, England, or whatever diaspora country they were in would be the center of their lives, but they would support Israel financially, politically, and emotionally.
3. *The Hard Line of the Communist Party.* This was the famous struggle between the Stalinist Left that hewed to a tough Communist line and the Trotskyite and other offshoots that desired a softer, more flexible line. In many ways it was the difference between a strict religious cult (Stalinism) and a more flexible approach to life.
4. *A Powerful Anti-Left Suppression.* This included Communists and Socialists losing their jobs, being blackballed, jailed, and even murdered. This movement was called McCarthyism, named after Senator Joe McCarthy, ironically from the progressive state of Wisconsin.

The Silent Years: The 1950s

Best epitomized by such movies as *Rebel Without a Cause* and *Invasion of the Body Snatchers*, the 1950s were a time of defensiveness, caution, isolationism and conformity and were filled with anti-Communist jingoism. Red-baiting, homophobia, racism, fear of the atomic bomb, and anti-Semitism all merged together, and at times led by such hypocrites and self-loathing men as Roy Cohn, who was both Jewish and gay. Cohn, who ironically bridged the generation to Donald Trump, led the charge against "commie Jews" and "fags." People wanted "normalcy" and quiet. With increased affluence, people left the ghettos of the inner cities and moved to the suburbs. People tried to keep a low profile.

Yet the 1950s teemed with resentment—African-Americans, rebels, hipsters, rock-and-roll. Things were going to burst.

The Radical Years: 1963-1971

It took a while, and it came as a surprise, but after John F. Kennedy, Malcolm X, Martin Luther King Jr., and Robert F. Kennedy were assassinated, the ghettos exploded and, soon after, the campuses exploded into riot and protest.

What was the difference between the Old Left and the New Left?

What were the divisions within the New Left between hippies, Yippies (Youth International Party members), and radicals? Between blacks and whites? Women and men? Gays and straights?

Why were there so many Jews in the radical movements?

All of these questions I have tried to answer in this book, through my essays from the '60s and '70s.

Post-1967: The Rise of Jewish Radical Movements

Why did specifically Jewish radical movements arise in 1967, after the Israeli-Arab Six-Day War? That was the crucial year. They arose as a reaction to the growing anti-Israel and anti-Semitic sentiments of black and white radical groups such as the Black Panthers, the Nation of Islam, and Students for a Democratic Society (SDS). I collected the writings of such newborn Jewish radical groups in my classic book *Jewish Radicalism*, which came out in 1973.

What exactly did these radical Jewish movements do?

Freedom Seders, Soviet Jewish Rallies, Trees for Vietnam, the rise of Jewish studies, collectives, *chavurot*, new forms of prayer and traditions, more democracy in the Jewish community, new roles for women and gays—all of these were examples of the new times. Basically, these Jewish groups were transforming the Jewish community just as their non-Jewish counterparts were transforming the rest of the nation.

The Conservative Reaction: Post-1967

There is an old Yiddish expression: *Az es Christlizich, iz Yiddlezich.* Roughly it means, "As the Christians do, so too will the Jews." That is, as non-Jews respond to events, eventually Jews would do the same, and often in the same manner.

Just as the "hard-hat" working-class Americans, the so-called "Silent Majority," arose in the late '60s in reaction to the rise of radical movements, so too did right-wing Zionist and neo-conservative Jews arise. They quietly did their thing, and while it took a decade or two they eventually showed their strength with the election of Ronald Reagan, and then, thirty-six years later, of Donald Trump. Liberals and the radicals were asleep at the wheel and were caught by surprise by this conservative reaction.

Just as the radical Left arose in the post-June 1967 period, after the victory in Israel, with strong opposition to Israel's "arrogance" and "colonization" of the West Bank, Golan Heights, Sinai, and Gaza, so too did a radical Right arise in Israel (*Likkud*) and in the United States (Jewish Republicans) to oppose the general Left and the Jewish Left. While most Jews saw Israel's 1967 victory as a great event that "saved" Israel from destruction by Arab armies, some saw the opposite—the beginning of the occupation of the West Bank and the "oppression" of the Palestinian people.

Three things happened to me on June 5, 1967, that had a profound effect on my life.

One, I had graduated with a B.A. from the University of Wisconsin–Milwaukee and was accepted to the sociology Ph.D. program at Northwestern University in Evanston, Illinois. I became a radical sociologist.

Two, I took my first and only "acid trip" at a graduation party on the East Side of Milwaukee. It had a profound effect on my mind, so profound that I told myself it would be my last "trip"—it was simply too powerful. I'm glad I did, or else I would not be here to write these memoirs. I would have been dead or strung out.

Three, the Israeli-Arab Six-Day War began June 5 with Israel's surprise attack to the Arabs, the destruction of their airfields, and their surge across the "green line" into Sinai and the West Bank. Never had there been so much jubilation and so few deaths. I remember my father and others wanting to send their sons and daughters to Israel to fight. Never had so much money been collected for Israel. It was a heady time.

But, as noted, there was an almost immediate reaction from the radical Left condemning Israel. This was the beginning of anti-Zionism and anti-Israel sentiment on campuses. It was at the time of the 1967 Six-Day War that I and a few others at Northwestern University founded the Jewish Student Movement, a radical Jewish movement that was progressive—we supported the black civil rights movement, we opposed the war in Vietnam, and we fought against poverty and wild capitalism, but we also supported Israel's right to exist.

This middle way was often difficult and set us up against other radicals who happened to be Jewish. Out of this tension came my book *Jewish Radicalism* and my many other articles on Jewish student activism, racism, and the war in Vietnam (several of them found in this book).

But disaffection with the Left had begun. Norman Podhoretz, in his many books including *Doings and Undoings*, *Breaking Rank*, and my favorite, *Ex-Friends*, showed how the "Old Left" split into two camps—Stalinists who supported Stalin despite his pact with Hitler in 1939 (the Molotov-Ribbentrop Pact) and his anti-Semitism (the Doctor's Plot, the killing of Jewish intellectuals, etc.), and Trotskyites who opposed Stalin and wanted continuous revolution.

This was the first major split within the Communist Party. The second split came when Podhoretz, Irving Kristol, and to some extent Nathan Glazer, Daniel Bell, Martin Peretz, and others opposed the New Left and their literary "fellow travelers" (Norman Mailer, Allen Ginsberg, William Burroughs).

In so doing they also opposed the Jewish Left such as our group. This opposition was carried out in the pages of *Commentary* magazine but also in *The New Republic* under Martin Peretz and Leon Wieseltier. The opposition to the Left and the Jewish Left has become more sophisticated and continues to this day. One of the best examples of this neo-con critique is Jonathan Neumann's 2018 book *To Heal the World? How the Jewish Left Corrupts Judaism and Endangers Israel*.

This is a brilliant book in many ways, one of the few that dares attack and criticizes in a cogent and disciplined way, using traditional Jewish sources, Jewish Left thinkers such as Michael Lerner and Art Green, as well as groups like Breira, New Jewish Agenda, and Jewish Voice for Peace.

The title of the book is important. The question mark in the title says that "healing the world"—in Hebrew, *tikkun olam*—is actually *not* emphasized in the Bible. Neumann uses religious and political history as well as Biblical exegesis to debunk this idea and shows how the Bible was twisted by Jewish radicals and liberals to support a left-wing agenda.

Moreover, he believes Judaism based solely on *tikkun olam*, on social justice projects, leads to assimilation. It is not a firm basis for Jewish continuity. Example: despite all of the social justice projects in synagogues across the country, the intermarriage rate continues to soar. It is now over 70%. In short, all of these liberal projects, from climate control to helping immigrants, do nothing to stop the slow road to Jewish extinction as a people, according to Neumann.

Furthermore, *tikkun olam* also endangers Israel. Our first priority, Neumann says, must be a concern for the safety, security, welfare, and survival of the Jewish community here in the West and in Israel, not Native Americans, Darfurians, transgender people, Palestinians, and other "oppressed." This is the old Jewish struggle between particularism and universalism. Who should I be for?

It is at the heart of Hillel the Elder's famous injunction: "If I am not for myself, who will be for me? But if I am only for myself, what am I? And if not now, when?" (*Ethics of the Fathers, I, 14*). It is a never-ending struggle to balance one's needs with those of others.

Today's Radicals

My generation, with few exceptions (David Horowitz, for example), has continued to promote progressive causes. Though confused and battered by Israel's and this country's turn to the Right, we have not sold out. But what about the younger generation of Jews, the so-called millennials, those born since 1980 or even 2000? Are they still radical?

Neo-con Norman Podhoretz was confused, frustrated, and mystified that so few Jews followed him. In fact, he wrote a book called *Why Are Jews Liberal?* And we now have a Jewish guy named Bernie Sanders, an outspoken socialist and Jew, running for President and reaching crowds of 25,000 or more in the year 2020. The majority of Jews will always be progressive, liberal and radical. The numbers may fluctuate, but it will always be that way. We may even have a Jewish socialist President of the United States. Who could have imagined it?

Sources

Buhle, Mari Jo, Paul Buhle, and Dan Georgakas (eds.). *Encyclopedia of the American Left*. Chicago and London: St. James Press, 1990. A comprehensive history and sociology of the American Left from abortion to *Di Zukunft* (a Yiddish-language newspaper founded in 1890 and still in existence).

Farber, David. *The Age of Great Dreams: America in the 1960s*. New York: Hill and Wang, 1994. Written by a Barnard College historian, this is a lucid and thoughtful account.

Gitlin, Todd. *The Sixties: Years of Hope, Days of Rage*. New York: Bantam Books, 1987. Written by a sociologist and former SDS leader, this is an honest account of the radical '60s.

Guttmann, Allen. *The Jewish Writer in America*. New York: Oxford University Press, 1971. (See especially pp. 134-177, on "Jewish Radicals.") The uniqueness of Guttmann's book is that he is one of the few to describer and analyze literary, rather than political, radicals, people like "proletarian" writers such as Abraham Cahan, Michael Gold, Howard Fast, Paul Goodman, Norman Mailer, and Allen Ginsberg. A very important book.

Liebman, Arthur. *Jews and the Left*. New York: John Wiley, 1979. According to Morris U. Schappes, this book is a "tremendously informative, often illuminating and extensive sociological study" (*Jewish Currents*, September 1979, pp. 18-20, and Liebman's response in the January 1980 issue, p. 38). For a very different and naturally critical review, see Bernard K. Johnpoll in *Commentary*, September 1979, pp. 92-94. Another critical review is by Brandeis professor Stephen J. Whitfield in *Transaction/Society*, July/August 1980, pp. 83-86, but at least they took the time and space to review it. The book is nearly 700 pages long.

Miller, James. *Democracy in the Streets: From Port Huron to the Siege of Chicago*. Cambridge, Mass.: Harvard University Press, 1994. Written by a professor of political science, this is an accurate and original account of the rise of the New Left.

Neumann, Jonathan. *To Heal the World? How the Jewish Left Corrupts Judaism and Endangers Israel*. New York: St. Martin's Press, 2018.

Newfield, Jack. *The Prophetic Minority: A Probing Study of the Origins and Development of the New Left*. New York: Signet Books, 1966. Written before the rise of the radical Jewish movement by a veteran journalist, this book was one of the first and possibly the best single volumes on the rise of the New Left.

Podhoretz, Norman. *Ex-Friends*. San Francisco: Encounter Books, 2000. The subtitle is "Falling Out with Allen Ginsberg, Lionel and Diana Trilling, Lillian Hellman, Hannah Arendt, and Norman Mailer." This is his wistful, not spiteful, polemic against his former leftist friends and contains rare accounts of his encounters with these literary lights as well as a brilliant (and he is indeed a brilliant writer—I love his construction of sentences) redaction of the radical Left, Old and New. Also see his other books: *Making It, Breaking Ranks, Doings and Undoings*, and *Why Are Jews Liberals?*

Porter, Jack Nusan, and Peter Dreier (eds.). *Jewish Radicalism: A Selected Anthology.* New York: Grove Press and Random House, 1973. My classic movement anthology on Jewish radicals and radical Jews.

_____(ed.). *The Sociology of American Jews: A Critical Anthology.* Lanham, Md.: University Press of America, 1978. Inspired by Morris Schappes' history of American Jewry from a socialist point of view (though the word "socialist" was taboo then, and even in my generation; I used the word "critical" or "radical"), this was, as Marshall Sklare told me, the first time the words "sociology of American Jewry" were used in a title. See especially the essays on Vietnam and the Jews by Diane Winston and the Jewish Labor Movement by Jerry Habush.

Sanders, Bernie. *Our Revolution: A Future to Believe In.* New York: Thomas Dunne Books, 2016.

Wakefield, Dan. *New York in the Fifties.* Boston and New York: Houghton Mifflin–Seymour Lawrence, 1992. The '50s were neither as dull nor as plastic as people thought, and in many ways, to understand the '60s (civil rights, democratic socialism, the hippies), you have to understand the '50s (sit-ins, the atom bomb, McCarthyism, the Beats). Wakefield knew everybody from C. Wright Mills to Marion Magid.

Wellstone, Paul. *The Conscience of a Liberal: Reclaiming the Compassionate Agenda.* New York: Random House, 2000. The late U.S. senator from Minnesota had a tremendous impact on such senators as Amy Klobuchar, Elizabeth Warren and Bernie Sanders. See the excellent biography by Antonia Felix, *Elizabeth Warren: Her Fight, Her Work, Her Life,* Naperville, Ill.: Sourcebooks, 2018.

Wistrich, Robert S. *Revolutionary Jews from Marx to Trotsky.* New York: Barnes & Noble, 1976. Written by one of the finest British historians, who died much too soon (his later works dealt with anti-Semitism), this book is the best single-volume analysis of radical Jews from Marx to Trotsky. (Especially see pp. 1-22 on the Jewish attraction to socialism and other radical thought.)

I. Early Writings

The Negro, the New Left, and the Hippy

This was my very first article ever, crude as it was, right smack in the middle of my being drafted for the Vietnam War, and just as I was about to enter Northwestern University. It appeared in an anti-Vietnam War newsletter called *The Milwaukee Organizer*, Vol. 1, No. 2, August-September 1967, which was the literary organ of the Milwaukee Organizing Committee. The years 1966-1968 were radical years; America was being torn apart by the riots after Martin Luther King Jr. was assassinated; there were massive anti-war protests; and various groups were forming—Black Panthers, SDS, the Yippies, and the countercultural Hippies (I spelled it "Hippys"). Even our language was changing. This was the first and only time I would use the word "negro" in an essay. A year later, as you will see in my next essay, I used the word "Blackman"; and the term was later transmuted to "Afro-American" and then "African-American," but I like the word "Blackman" or "Blackwoman." You can also see the influence of sociological thinking and how we typologized things into categories—Blacks, Leftists, Hippies. These were the basic splits of the "movement"; racially into Black and white and sociologically into political activists and Hippie "drop-outs."

* * *

The hippies, a relatively new social movement with deep roots in the Beat generation of the early 1950s, have recently been publicized in the mass media. In many ways, they may even have been nurtured and fed by such media. In the past year, these "psychedelic proletariats" have grown full-blown onto the covers of *Time*, *Life*, *Ramparts*, and *The New Republic*. They have influenced the music, the nouveau art, the morals, and the image of American youth, their parents, and the entire "establishment" that supports them.

Unlike typical movements of the past, however, the hippies are recruited from the staid middle-class income groups of America. There is a symbiotic relationship here whereby these classes are profoundly influenced by and conversely are influencing the hippies and their followers. The Madison Avenue junior executive who "turns on" with marijuana; the Rock Island housewife who "digs" the psychic rock music of the Jefferson Airplane; the thousands of high school and college studies who begin or end their parties with a euphoric trip on LSD, DMT, STP, Amphetamines, or other hallucinogenic or psychedelic drugs. The membership of this movement is unknown; the hardcore centers of Los Angeles, San Francisco, and New York are the New Meccas—these cities have always been in the mainstream and continue to be the local points of the Avant-Garde—not only for the hippies, but for the politically activist groups as well.

With love, the hippies have dominated the "scene." They have been blamed for every ailment—from the smell of alewife fish in Lake Michigan to the declining birthrate in the U.S. They are the new scapegoat for the establishment—the police, the politician, and the "turned off" parent. These latter three elements, to paraphrase C. Wright Mills, have become the unholy alliance that wields the power in our society.

Though nurtured from the same soil, the hippies and the New Left have confronted themselves against the unholy alliance mentioned above. This confrontation has had a deep and lasting effect on the New Left. (Though the term "New Left," like all concepts, is both vague and all-inclusive, it will be used in this essay to include and define any and all activist movements whose ideology is geared to a *radical change* in the policy of the status quo. Included under this rubric would be the anti-war in Vietnam organizations, the civil rights movements, the W.E.B. Du Bois clubs, and so forth.) The entire New Left, with all its inherent interlocking membership and multifaceted ideologies, its diversity and even delusiveness, is threatened by Dr. Timothy Leary's simple statement: "Tune in, turn on, and drop out."

Leary's "declaration of independence" is attractive, and what is far more important, is attracting the potential leaders, members, and followers of the New Left. There is protest, and there is PROTEST. Though both the hippies and the New Left are alienated (again using the hackneyed expression) and dissatisfied with the present state of realty—their major differences in philosophy lie not only in the type or degree of protest, but that, in many ways, they are polar opposites. The hippy is basically a conservative creature, politically speaking. His philosophical swan-song sounds like this: "Don't try and change the world, change yourself. The effort of marching and protesting is futile and useless. It is far better to reach inward and explore than outward and explode."

The irony of such a thesis is that it is reminiscent of the wailing of the bereaved mother in suburbia: "Be a *mensch* (a man)! Don't go around changing others."

This, then, is the threat from the hippies. Political and social "dropouts" are the result. And what is worse is that a similar shade of apathy results which in numerous ways is difficult to differentiate from the mass apathy that confronts the efforts of all New Left groups. Is it possible to "tune in" (to the realities as well as the eternities of the world); "turn on" (yes, even with dugs); and not "drop out"? There is strong evidence that states that it is possible. What the hippies have offered to us all is what we pray and fight for every day—love, peace, natural beauty. We want it politically; the hippies—psychedelically. Can there ever be a convergence of the two philosophies? It's doubtful, because the basic tenets of activism are disparaged by the hippies. The singing of "Yellow Submarine" by the Berkeley leftists at a San Francisco love-in has led to no reconciliation of the two groups at all.

This polar separation of hippy and leftist, however, may spring from other reasons—potentially more threatening than any conflict in philosophy. The white liberal and the white leftist are being pushed or are "dropping out" and leaving the fight. Why? Is it because the minority groups, i.e., the Negroes, are taking the cause into their own hands? Is the exodus to psychedeliaville generated by frustration and fear, of the disillusionment and disappointment of the many New Left groups' inability to get the ear over, to get the bomb banned, to get the Negroes freed? In fact, the fomenters of social change, the most ardent voices over Vietnam and other issues, let alone civil rights, comes not from the white liberal, but from the black man in SNCC[1] or CORE.[2] There are few Negro hippies, needless to say, and

---

1   The Student Nonviolent Coordinating Committee, which developed in 1960 as a result of the student-led sit-ins at segregated lunch counters in Greensboro, North Carolina, and Nashville, Tennessee, to help challenge the social segregation and political exclusion of African-Americans.

2   The Congress of Racial Equality, founded in 1942 "to bring about equality for all people regardless of race, creed, sex, age, disability, sexual orientation, religion or ethnic background."

the reason for this is quite simple: when the negroes will begin to "drop out" as Leary propounds, they will cease to survive. White middle-class youth can rush to Haight-Ashbury to join Ginsburg and Leary to find love and beauty because they have the time, money and freedom to do so. The Negro cannot forget the fight—he lives within it; and must battle for all that the New Left strives for every moment of his life. He is the epitome of the political animal, to paraphrase Plato.

There may be one further reason for the white youth's flight to join the hippies. Is it because violence is so much a part of the American way of life, as Rap Brown, SNCC chairman, maintains, that drives the white youths in droves to seek flowers and peace in San Francisco? Is the hippie cozy in his euphoric utopia because he is the proverbial dreamer seeking the eternal, or is he just afraid of the bloodshed and strife that will ensue, and that will bring the issue of the Negro's rights to the forefront and drop it on the front steps of the United States like a lit Molotov cocktail? Just as their parents have rushed to move to the suburbs, leaving the inner city to the Negro, so the hippy runs to his suburb of the mind and leaves the problems of the world for the "straight" people to solve.

The recent rioting in Milwaukee, Newark, Detroit, and tens of other cities throughout America is just the beginning. This new "theater of war," as *Newsweek* put it, will plague America for years. Who can afford to "drop out" now—the Negro? The New Left? The Hippy?

The New Left, the Blackman, and Israel

This essay was never published. It is original to this anthology. Again, I am using sociological typologies and categories, but this essay goes a bit deeper than the previous one. I am learning to write. It was also my first essay to confront the growing anti-Zionism of the Black and White Left. This essay was the ideological basis for my founding the Jewish Radical Student Movement at Northwestern University and is as relevant today as it was in 1967 when I first wrote it. Notice that the terminology for Blacks was radically changed in just a few years from "Negro" to "Blackman."

* * *

Even our "friends" are not likely to forgive that we were victorious—
we have suddenly stripped them of the chance to pity us or even
help us.

— Elie Wiesel, *Commentary*, October 1967

The Six-Day War caught the New Left and its multifaceted followers unawares. The neat system of cataloguing aggressors as those stemming from the West (or its "pawns"); and the defenseless victims as its poor hapless colonies, was no longer relevant. Those Leftists who view the situation in the Middle East as no different from South Africa, Vietnam, Venezuela or Detroit ignore the frustratingly complex political, social and economic elements underlying each of these separate arenas of revolution.

Many saw the Six-Day War in simplistic terms as a clash between Arab socialism on one hand and Israel neo-colonialism on the other. This neat formula crumbles under the impact of semantic observation. To call "neocolonialisms" as Western-induced and all "Liberation Fronts" as Communist-inspired is ironically (for the New Left) to dismiss the *raison d'être* of the self-determinative powers and aspirations of any Third-World country.

For example, now that Egypt is controlled militaristically and dependent economically on Russia, does this then make *her* a colony of Russia? Has not Russia stepped in (as has been her goal since Catherine the Great) to replace the United States and England before her as the increasingly dominant force in the Arab states, and soon the Levant? Will Russia "liberate" these countries just at the moment when England, France and presumably the United States have reduced their influence within the area?

Russia's dream of transforming the Mediterranean into a "Russian Sea" is well on the way to becoming a reality. As the revolutionaries in the New Left are well aware, whenever there is a vacuum of power—it will soon be filled by either the highest bidder or strongest trump card. The British are leaving Aden; the United States has lost its bases in Libya, the French are no threat in any area. Furthermore, all the Western powers are held in low esteem by the leadership of the Arab people. The entrance was open, ready-made, for Russian intervention, and Russia, aware of her "revolutionary destiny," has consolidated her position. Where are the self-determination powers of the Arab States now? Just as the New Left wants to see a Vietnam free from China as well as the United States, so too it must free from China as well as the United States, so too it must logically see that the Arab States should be free of manipulative control by Russia, as well as from the United States. There is the underlying assumption here, then, that whatever a Third-World country determines as its political and economic destiny is her choice, and her choice alone. But a New Left consensus on this point is a utopian idea.

This splintering of opinions of the New Left was observable at the conference on new politics held in Chicago, three months after the Six-Day War. The conference showed that the New Left, too diverse in its outlook, could only be welded into a unilateral force (on paper) only through the Black Man of the SNCC…*who is united*. But in order to accomplish this goal, it was to commit three acts:

a. Compromise emotionally and ideologically to the Black Caucus group (i.e., the statement on Israel—"Condemn the imperialistic Zionist War; this condemnation does not imply anti-Semitism").

b. Forsake democratic processes, presumably because democratic processes are too slow for revolution ("…regrouping all committees giving 50 per cent representation to black people," even though whites outnumbered blacks 5 to 1).

c. Expose the weakness of the New Left as to its grassroots support and its concomitant trust.

These three acts may have "destroyed" a convention, but they have clarified the role of both the New Left and the Black man in America, both for themselves and for each other. For this reason, the convention was a "success." For Zionists, a measure of success may also be accrued to the ledger. The emotional pro-Israel outburst by many New Leftists of the Jewish faith, both during the war and during the convention, can only be seen as gratifying to those within the Jewish community. To the Jewish establishment, this enclave of Jewish youth seemed unreachable to the call of Israel's survival. This opinion was refuted by the irreversible emotionalism of many Jewish Leftists during the war. The model attitude seemed to be that Israel must survive, we are joyful that it survived and sustained, but don't frighten us any more—we have too many important tasks to accomplish right her in the Diaspora. Of course, many will also add that Israel must return the conquered territory. But the central point is that the Middle East Crisis is not in the New Left "bag." This may shock or dismay Zionists here in America, but it is an obvious fact that the Six-Day War is slowly becoming history, and to the New Left it is now *old* history. The consequence of this outlook was shown after the war and even after SNCC's anti-Zionistic Semitic pronouncements in its newsletter culminating in the Conference for New Politics. The New Left, as well as the establishment Jewish Community, reacted with emotion. This is understandable, but what was missing was a dialogue with SNCC—a confrontation with the statements and an inspection of the reason for such an attack on Israel and the Jews.

Alarmists begin to see SNCC's accusations as the harbinger of a *dramatic* increase in anti-Semitism. Such concern may be without basis. The confusion occurs over interpreting anti-white for anti-Semitic sentiments. Anti-Semitism is *not* rooted in the Black's history, but in the white man's

history. To view the *Jewish* slumlord or storekeeper as "whitey" personified is too easily done by many Blacks. And yet quite as easy is to bring
in timeworn anti-Semitic epithets in order to "make it acceptable" to the
non-Jewish majority. But the tactics will not work here in America because
of a differential political power and status structure. Jews are *part of the
establishment*, and the non-Jew and the Jew are both white and are both
united against any violence. The Blackman may need a scapegoat; yet there
is none to be found. An alternative solution, that of controlling one's own
political, social and economic destiny (the true meaning of "Black Power"),
is more beneficial and more lasting to both Black man and white man
alike. However, overt and unfounded anti-Semitism will be *confronted and
uprooted*. The "New Jew," with new respect and pride, will not allow another
Kristallnacht.[3]

---

3   Also known as the Night of Broken Glass or the November Pogrom(s), *Kristallnacht*
    was a pogrom against Jews executed by the *Sturmabteilung* paramilitary forces as well as
    civilians throughout Nazi Germany on November 9-10, 1938.

Zionism, Racism, and the United Nations: Toward the Prostitution of Language

This essay was never published and appears for the first time. It is a continuation of the previous essay; however, it was presented as a paper at a luncheon roundtable at the American Sociological Association in August 1976 in New York City while I was a lecturer in sociology at Pine Manor College in Chestnut Hill, Massachusetts. It was written in reaction to the infamous resolution of the General Assembly of the United Nations which, by a vote of 72 to 35 with 32 abstentions, voted to condemn Zionism and Israel by determining that "Zionism is a form of racism and racial discrimination." I have also added two replies: one by Morris U. Schappes from the pro-Israel but non-Zionist *Jewish Currents*, and one by Yosef Tekoah of the Student Mobilization for Israel.

* * *

Abstract

On November 10, 1975, the General Assembly of the United Nations voted 72 to 35, with 32 abstentions, to condemn Zionism by determining that "Zionism is a form of racism and racial discrimination," to use the exact words of the resolution. This paper will define racism, Zionism, and the prostitution of language that has led to such a comparison. A series of questions will be posed in order to understand the implication of these charges. A short but incisive bibliography is also included for the benefit of the reader.

The Background

In the 1960s, quite a few words were abused—"revolution," "culture," "racism," "I.Q.," "sexism," "genocide"—abused to the point that they have become almost meaningless in some contexts, abused to the point that many teachers, myself included, were often intellectually intimidated and even physically threatened by some minority group members (Blacks, women, Jews, gay people, "Third World" revolutionaries), abused to the point that a subject itself became literally "taboo" unless one took the "proper" political and academic perspectives. What often occurred is what Dennis Wrong calls the "banalization and trivialization of a subject and its exploitation for partisan purposes."

Along with banalization and trivialization, I would like to use the word "prostitution of language" for low political means: blackmail with words. For on November 10, 1975, the General Assembly of the United Nations voted 72 to 35, with 32 abstentions, to condemn Zionism by determining that "Zionism is a form of racism and racial discrimination," to use the UN's exact words. This resolution was the end result of a series of anti-Israel measures beginning with Resolution 3151 G (XXVIII) of December 14, 1973, condemning the "unholy alliance between South African racism and zionism [sic]."[4] At the World Conference of the International Women's Year, held in Mexico City from June 19 to July 2, 1975, a resolution was passed that stated that "international cooperation and peace require the achievement of national liberation and independence, the elimination of colonialism and neo-colonialism, foreign occupation, zionism [sic], apartheid, and racial discrimination in all its forms as well as the recognition of the dignity of peoples and their right to self-determination."

At an assembly of heads of state and government leaders of the Organization of African Unity at its 12th ordinary session, held in Kampala from July 28 to August 1, 1975, a resolution was supported that stated "that the racist regime in occupied Palestine and racist regimes in Zimbabwe and South Africa have a common imperialist origin, forming a while and

---

4   The United Nations has the habit of using a small-case "z" when referring to Zionism. Zionism, like Marxism or Judaism, should be written with a capital Z.

having the same racist structure and being organically linked in their policy aimed at repression of the dignity and integrity of the human being."

And finally, the Conference of Ministers for Foreign Affairs of non-aligned (Third World) countries, held in Lima, Peru, from August 25-30, 1975, severely condemned Zionism as a threat to world peace and security and called upon all countries to oppose this racist and imperialist ideology. All these resolutions and conferences set the stage for the culmination event in November 1975.

It seems that Israel is the only country in the world whose legitimacy is seriously questioned, and it is ironic that it is the United Nations who has seen fit to condemn Israel's right to exist when, in fact, a quarter of a century ago, it was this very same United Nations that voted on and recognized Israeli independence. Over the threat of oil and some mythical "Third World" solidarity, the United Nations has truly prostituted itself by claiming that Zionism is a form of racism.

What is Racism?

According to Webster's Third New International Dictionary, racism is defined as "the assumption that...traits and capacities are determined by biological race and that races differ decisively from one another." It further involves "a belief in the inherent superiority of a particular race and its right to domination over others."

What is Colonialism?

According to The Dictionary of the Social Sciences, colonialism was used to denote the "system of government as generally applied to colonial possessions." The term now refers to a "state of inferiority or of servitude experienced by a community, a country, or a nation which is dominated politically and/or economically and/or culturally by another and more developed community or nation; applied especially when the dominant nation is European or North American, and the less-developed, a non-European people." Neo-colonialism means, among other things, the domination of a less-developed "third world" country or people by a European/North American nation but by utilizing another newly developing nation as the colonizer, i.e., the U.S. using Israel to dominate the Middle East or the Palestinians in particular.

What is Imperialism?

According to the above dictionary, imperialism is now considered an outdated, discredited word and a term of abuse. If a Communist says that Britain and the U.S.A. are practicing imperialism, he means that, as monopoly capitalist countries, they are fulfilling their nature by subduing foreign countries to their control. This is probably the most influential use of the word, going back to V.I. Lenin's book *Imperialism, the Highest Stage of Capitalism* (1916). However, the most recent use of the term is to apply the word very generally to the control of any one state by another, i.e., Russian control of East European countries is "Russian imperialism," and Chinese control of Tibet is "Chinese imperialism." It is a propaganda word and can be used by any side to defame the other.

What is Zionism?

Zionism is the national liberation movement of the Jews. Soviet Foreign Minister Andrei Gromyko in 1948 used the same term to describe the establishment of the State of Israel.

Zionism was the normal response of oppressed groups within the milieu of European nationalism wherein it sprang, but, as Arthur Hertzberg notes, Zionism cannot be typed, and therefore easily explained, as a "normal" kind of national *risorgimento*. It has unique qualities.

Zionism is one of the crucial facts of Jewish life in the modern age.

Zionism, according to Theodore Herzl, sought to secure for the Jewish people a publicly recognized, legally secured home in Palestine.

Zionism sought to build and liberate the land, not oppress its inhabitants. Many came as socialist revolutionaries, not as neo-colonialist capitalists.

Zionism consists of two parts: the spiritual return to *Tzion*, redemption in Zion, and the political return of Jews to their homeland.

Zionism arose as a response to anti-Semitism. Zionism, externally, is the enemy of anti-Semitism and other racisms, while internally Zionism is the enemy of assimilation.

Zionism comes in many packages; there are socialist Zionists and capitalist Zionists; religious Zionists and secular Zionists; "hawkish" Zionists and "dovish" Zionists.

Zionism is not only the physical center and homeland for the Jews; it is the spiritual and cultural center as well. World Jewry can choose to see it as any type of center it wishes to, but most Jews do see Israel as some form of center, as do Christians and Moslems, in their own spiritual ways.

Zionism may be over, but Israel exists, and Israel remains as the culmination of Zionism…for the time being…the future of Zionism is twofold—spiritual, as the coming of the messiah will foretell, and real, as the land to build a political and cultural utopia. Though both may fail to materialize, should we cease our labors?

Some Questions for Discussion:

1. Is Israel imperialistic?
2. Is it really colonialist? Expansionist?
3. Is there *institutionalized* racism against Jews? Against non-Moslem minorities like Christians and Druze? Against the Palestinians? Against other Arabs?
4. What about the Palestinians? Does Israel owe, morally and politically, the Palestinians anything? Should there be established a Palestinian state on the West Bank and Gaza?
5. Will the Arabs ever recognize a Jewish state in Israel? If not, what should Israel do?
6. What should be the role of the United States and United States Jewry *vis-à-vis* Israel?
7. Should America leave the U.N.? Should Israel?
8. Is there a future for Zionism, since Israel is now a reality?
9. Are Israel and Judaism synonymous? Anti-Zionism and anti-Semitism?
10. Why won't the world leave the Jews alone? Is there some historical conspiracy to eliminate Jews, first in Europe, now in Israel?

Paper presented at the Luncheon Roundtable discussions, American Sociological Association, August 1976, New York City. No quotation without permission of the author.

References

Chertoff, Mordecai (ed.). *Zionism: A Basic Reader.* New York: Herzl Press, 1975.

Dershowitz, Alan M. "Should America Leave the U.N.?" *Moment*, Vol. 1, No. 6, January 1976, pp. 78-80. (Also see the special section on Zionism in the same issue, pp. 37-44.)

Gould, Julius, and William L. Kolb (eds.). *The Dictionary of the Social Sciences.* New York: The Free Press and UNESCO, 1964.

Halpern, Ben. *The Idea of the Jewish State* (rev. ed.). Cambridge, Mass.: Harvard University Press, 1969.

Hertzberg, Arthur (ed.). *The Zionist Idea: An Historical Analysis and Reader.* New York: Atheneum, 1969.

Howe, Irving, and Carl Gershman (eds.). *Israel, the Arabs, and the Middle East.* New York: Quadrangle Books, 1972. (Also available in paperback from Bantam Books.)

Laqueur, Walter. *A History of Zionism.* New York: Holt, Rinehart and Winston, 1972.

Selzer, Michael. *Zionism Reconsidered.* New York: Macmillan, 1970.

Yosef Tekoah

Zionism: Liberation Movement of the Jewish People

Student Mobilization for Israel, 1970.

* * *

Zionism is the love of Zion. Zionism is the Jewish people's liberation movement, the quest for freedom, for equality with other nations. Yet in an organization in which liberation movements are hailed and supported, the Jewish people's struggle to restore its independence and sovereignty is maligned and slandered in an endless spate of malice and venom.

In his drive to annihilate the Jewish people, Hitler began by distorting the image of the Jew, by rewriting Jewish history, by fabricating some of the most odious historic and racial theories. The Arab Governments, in their campaign to complete Hitler's crimes against the Jewish people and destroy the Jewish State, have adopted the same method of falsifying Jewish history, and in particular the meaning of the Zionist movement and the significance of its ideals.

What is Zionism?

When the Jews, exiled from their land in the seventh century before the Christian era, sat by the rivers of Babylon and wept, but also prayed and sought ways to go home, that was Zionism.

When in a mass revolt against their exile they returned and rebuilt the Temple and re-established their State, that was Zionism.

When they were the last people in the entire Mediterranean basin to resist the forces of the Roman Empire and to struggle for independence, that was Zionism.

When for centuries after the Roman conquest they refused to surrender and rebelled again and again against the invaders, that was Zionism.

When, uprooted from their land by the conquerors and dispersed by them all over the world, they continued to dream and to strive to return to Israel, that was Zionism.

When, during the long succession of foreign invaders, they tried repeatedly to regain sovereignty at least in part of their homeland, that was Zionism.

When they volunteered from Palestine and from all over the world to establish Jewish armies that fought on the side of the Allies in the First World War and helped to end Ottoman subjugation, that was Zionism.

When they formed the Jewish Brigade in the Second World War to fight Hitler, while Arab leaders supported him, that was Zionism.

When Jews went to gas chambers with the name of Jerusalem on their lips, that was Zionism.

When, in the forests of Russia and the Ukraine and other parts of East Europe, Jewish partisans battled the Germans and sang of the land where palms are growing, that was Zionism.

When Jews fought British colonialism while the Arabs of Palestine and the neighboring Arab States were being helped by it, that was Zionism.

Zionism is one of the world's oldest anti-imperialist movements. It aims at securing for the Jewish people the rights possessed by other nations. It harbors malice towards none. It seeks co-operation and understanding with the Arab peoples and with their national movements.

Zionism is as sacred to the Jewish people as the national liberation movements are to the nations of Africa and Asia. Even if the Arab States are locked today in conflict with the Jewish national liberation movement, they must not stoop in their attitude towards it to the fanaticism and barbarism of the Nazis. If there is to be hope for peace in the Middle East, there must be between Israel and the Arab States mutual respect for each other's sacred national values—not distortion and abuse.

Zionism was not born in the Jewish ghettoes of Europe, but on the battlefield against imperialism in ancient Israel. It is not an outmoded nationalistic revival but an unparalleled epic of centuries of resistance to force and bondage. Those who attack it attack the fundamental principles and provisions of the United Nations Charter.

Morris U. Schappes

Zionism is Not Racism: An Editorial

Jewish Currents, December 1975, p. 3. Published by permission of *Jewish Currents*.

* * *

We are pro-Israel non-Zionist. We disagree with such Zionist principles as the centrality of Israel, the in-gathering of the exiles and the view that anti-Semitism is inherent in non-Jews and therefor eternal. We believe in Israel's right to exist and need to survive as a Jewish state, but criticize those Israeli policies that we think hinder the cause of Israel's security and cast a shadow on her democracy.

And we denounce as false and dangerous to peace the U.N. Resolution that "determined" that "Zionism is a form of racism and racial discrimination." Coincidentally but symbolically, the General Assembly passed that resolution Nov. 10, the date of *Kristallnacht* in 1938. Of this resolution we declare: its form is anti-Zionist, its content is anti-Semitic, its aim is the destruction of the Jewish State of Israel. For if Zionism were indeed "racist," the "racist" State of Israel presumably would have no right to exist.

The context of the Resolution reveals its anti-Semitic, anti-Israel intent and effect. On November 13, 1974, Arafat[5] in that UN Assembly proposed

---

5   Yasser Arafat, an Arab nationalist and Palestinian political leader, was Chairman of the Palestine Liberation Organization (PLO) from 1969 to 2004, President of the Palestinian National Authority (PNA) from 1994 to 2004, and a founding member of the Fatah political party, which he led from 1959 to 2004.

the dismantling of the Jewish state. On October 1, 1975, Idi Amin[6] called for the destruction of Israel and denounced "Zionist control" of the USA. On October 17, 1975, the UN Third Committee passed the proposition, introduced the day Amin spoke. On November 10, the resolution passed in the General Assembly by only 72 of 142 UN members voting for it, 35 opposing, 32 abstaining, and three, including Romania, absenting themselves from this ideological lynching bee. This bare majority of *one* included all Arab States, all Communist-led states (except Romania), and a few African states.

Confronted with a world-wide storm of disapproval by non-Jews ranging from the National Council of Negro Women to the Communist Party of Italy, some supporters of the Resolution aver that it is not aimed even at Zionism, much less at Jews and Judaism, but only at Israel's policy in the Mideast. But denunciation of Israel has not, forsooth, been sparing in the UN. The Arab extremists needed more: in a context in which racism is in words universally condemned, it was found necessary to affix the stamp of racism to Israel and to the overwhelming majority of Jews the world over who support its right to exist. One may of course show that not all Jews are Zionists, and of course Zionism is not a synonym for Judaism. But in reality every Jew, religious or secular, is now presumed by the Resolution to be in the position of having to deny he is a Zionist to prove he is not a racist! If you were a Jew in Moscow, how would you feel if you read in the homogenized Soviet Press, as in *Moskovskaya Pravda* Nov. 13, that the "overwhelming majority of the peoples of the world" condemns "Zionism as a form of racism"?

But since the Resolution is aimed at Israel's existence, the best counter-attack is to step up the impetus to peace generated by the Egyptian-Israeli Sinai Agreement. This can best be done at Geneva. It is now up to the USA and USSR to create the conditions necessary for all parties concerned, Israel, Palestinian Arabs and bordering Arab states, to convene in Geneva.

---

6   Idi Amin, called the "Butcher of Uganda" for his cruel despotism, was President of Uganda from 1971 to 1979.

Talking Police Blues

From *The Insurgent Sociologist*, newsletter of the Union of Radical Sociologists (URS) and the Sociology Liberation Movement (SLM) in the Department of Sociology at Douglass College (part of Rutgers University), New Brunswick, NJ, Vol. 1, No. 4, April 1971, pp. 6-7. This article was rejected for publication by *The American Sociologist*.

* * *

This essay, published in *The Insurgent Sociologist* in April 1971, Vol. 1, No. 4, pp. 6-7, was based on the first course ever taught on the police and society. I taught it in the spring of 1970 at De Paul University in Chicago long with a Black policeman, Edward "Buzz" Palmer. It was right after the so-called "police riot" at the 1968 Democratic Convention, the Chicago Conspiracy Trial where several of my friends were on trial, and the Martin Luther King Jr. and Robert F. Kennedy assassinations. This is what we would call "action pedagogy" at its best with gang members, police officers, Black Panthers, Puerto Rican Young Lords, all coming to class to speak, even Daniel Walker, director of the much-criticized Walker Report on that convention. I think I caught the flavor of the turbulent times. It was a fantastic experience.

The spring quarter of 1970 was a tumultuous one, both for the nation, and the city of Chicago. The police played a prominent role. Chicago was still reeling from the 1968 National Convention and the Walker report that followed, which reported that the police overreacted and touched off a police riot. The Chicago Conspiracy Trial and its almost daily demonstrations drew to a climax as the course was about to begin. "Shoot-outs" between police and Blacks were a weekly occurrence. Two leaders of the

Black Panther Party, Fred Hampton and Mark Clark, were assassinated by police. Harassment of Blacks occurred daily. October 1969 marked the Weathermen's "Days of Rage." It was in such an atmosphere that the course "The Police State" was introduced at De Paul.

There was a good deal of administration support for the course. The only overt fear was that the course title was biased and misleading—there is no police state in America so why label it as such, went the reasoning. The latent fear, however, was that the course might "stir things up" in the spring and cause some form of "confrontation." It did not. Kent State took care of that. The course did provoke and excite, but that was only one of its intentions. The other was to examine a neglected area of study—the policeman and his role.

IT WAS DECIDED that the course would be team-taught by a sociology instructor (the author) and a Black policeman—Mr. Edward "Buzz" Palmer. Mr. Palmer had given a successful lecture on the police earlier in the year and was qualified as a writer (he is presently writing a book on the Black policeman), an active member of Chicago's Black community, and a policeman (he was co-founder of the Afro-American Patrolmen's League of the Chicago Police Department). A reading list and syllabus were drawn up, the course was publicized, and finally was introduced with a budget that included guest lecturers. The lectures-discussions were broken down three ways: Mr. Palmer discussed such topics as the Black police within the police structure; how the white and Black communities view the Black policeman; the development of social consciousness among Black policemen; the Black community as a "colony" and a police state; and the cross-tensions that abound between forces bent on change and forces determined to maintain order. The perspective was that of the Black community bringing about a long overdue representation of the Black man's role in this area. This brought scattered criticism from the class (there were three or four police cadets taking the course). Some thought there was too much emphasis on Black problems and that the policeman (actually the "white" policeman) was being slighted. The Black students, including leaders of the Black Student Union, who flocked to the course were delighted. So too were the majority of white students. Most agreed that it was nearly impossible to discuss the police, and moreover, the police state, and *not* take into account non-white minority groups. This difference of opinion was pedagogically exciting—debate was stormy, some students broke down in tears over certain issues—especially over the definition of a police state or over personal accounts of police brutality.

The author, being white and sociologically oriented, took a different tack during his presentation. He lectured "around" Mr. Palmer's perspective and that of the guest speakers; the historical role of the police force; the role of police and courts in civil disturbances; police and violence; the history of racial and student rebellion; and the role of social science in defining police organizations and the police state. The basic question concerned the police state, or a police city. What are the parameters of a police state? Does it exist in American cities? Thus, the title of the course, which was purposely chosen by the instructors, turned out to be neither biased nor flamboyant, but went to the root of the problem and led to a spin-off of dilemmas and inconsistencies confronting the student as well as society.

THE THIRD PART OF THE PRESENTATIONS was the series of guest lecturers, some of who came for nominal fees. These lecturers were either friends of the instructors or speakers suggested by the De Paul administration. To avoid bias, lecturers were chosen who represented many points of view: liberal, radical, and conservative; that of the oppressed and of the police. They included Daniel Walker, former president of the Chicago Crime Commission and director of the much-criticized Walker Report on the 1968 Democratic Convention; members of the Young Lords (a Puerto Rican political group, but mistakenly considered a gang by most Chicagoans); an ACLU[7] lawyer, Michael Katz; Thomas Mitchell, an assistant director of the Adlai Stevenson Institute at the University of Chicago; Richard Rubenstein, an advisory member of the Presidential Commission on Violence; Richard Newhouse, a Black state senator from Illinois; and Lt. John J. Cody of the Chicago Police Department. The presentations attracted much publicity, for political as well as academic reasons, and De Paul students swelled the class of seventy students to over 200. Some speakers were so controversial that deans of the school attended, as well as a coterie of police and reporters who trailed in on occasion. It was "action" sociology at its best, as exciting for teachers as students.

What are some of the conclusions that can be drawn from all this? First, a few myths have to be shattered. One is that a course on the police, in order to be effective, must be value-free. Not only is this nearly impossible, it is unfair to one's students. Objectivity is defined by some professors as presenting everyone's opinion except your own. Further, many

---

7   The American Civil Liberties Union, a nonprofit organization founded in 1920 "to defend and preserve the individual rights and liberties guaranteed to every person in this country by the Constitution and laws of the United States."

teachers hide their beliefs behind the apron of academic objectivity. How could one be neutral when presented with the question one Black student posed: "Isn't it true that there is a kind of genocide taking place against the Black community?" The author asked the class what it defined as "genocide," and this led to a discussion of the police and their role in the community. If the professor "objectively" has discussed the issue, and then wishes to present *his* own views, there is a neat way out of the dilemma: just step back from the microphone (the symbol of authority) and state that what will follow will be the personal opinion of the professor. The lectern is a powerful tool in education. Yet to some, education is seen as propaganda, and possibly it is propaganda. Some forms of education impart knowledge; others are a move to action. The first is considered impartial and objective; the second, biased, subjective, and simply "propaganda." Guest lecturers were brought in and were told to present "all sides of the picture," a neat pedagogic trick which takes the professor off the hook. Yet the course on police proved presenting "all viewpoints" does not eliminate the changes that a teacher will be charged with bias. When the course was over, some 20 out of 70 students (28%) felt the course "slandered" the police and took the Black man's side. There is an old Yiddish saying, *Gornisht helfen*, nothing helps; you're damned if you do and damned if you don't.

MYTH NUMBER TWO IS that a course on the police should not be taught because there's too little known about them. It is true that there is inadequate literature on the police (aside from Earle Stanley Gardner or Mickey Spillane novels). But it does exist. There is a conspiracy of secrecy among policemen, but ironically some of the best literature is being written by ex-policemen. For example, see Herbert T. Klein, *The Police: A Cop's View of Law Enforcement* (1968) and Arthur Neiderhoffer, *Behind the Shield: The Police in Urban Society* (1969). There are the politically emasculated yet academically sound reports of the national and local commissions on violence or riots. There are the works of James Q. Wilson of Harvard, and the list, of course, is continually growing. As for the role of the Black policeman, there is only one book besides Mr. Palmer's as yet unpublished work—Nicholas Alex, *Black in Blue: A Study of the Negro Policeman* (1969), and it is a poor one at that.

One footnote to this is that the Ford Foundation has initiated a $30 million Police Development Fund. The agency will finance innovative police programs throughout the country. Some of this money should spin-off more research and investigation of the police. *The first tool of any police state is secrecy, and the role of academicians is to take the blinders off and promulgate information about the police.*

THE THIRD AND LAST MYTH is that a police course should not be taught because it is too controversial. There is no denying the police are controversial and provoke fear, anger, and sympathy. Yet dismissing such a course on these grounds merely delays detonation. The combustibility of police pitted against the counterculture is already present. To ignore or dismiss it is to opt for the status-quo. Thus, to do nothing, academically or politically, is to do something.

Furthermore, the definition of what is objective is transmutable to the definition of what is considered controversial. To be objective is to state the facts, the truth, if you will. It is not necessary to tell lies and prefabrications in order to provoke; ordinary truth will do very well. For example, here are a few research findings from student papers:

"BOTH THE DOCTOR and the cops are involved in the execution of split-second decisions over life and death, yet the policeman receives 200 hours of training (at police academies) while the doctor receives over 10,000 hours. Furthermore, beauticians receive 1,200 hours, and embalmers over 5,000 hours of instruction."

"Of the 350,000 men and women involved in municipal, county and state law enforcement agencies, a mere one-fourth are screened to rule out such conditions as racism, sadism, and pain under stress. In Portland, Oregon, when such psychological tests were instituted, over 25 percent of the recruits were dropped due to emotional unfitness."

"ONLY ONE POLICE FORCE (in Multromala, Oregon) requires a college degree. Only 20 out of some 40,000 state and local units in the United States require some college credits. The rest require a high-school degree or less."

These are relatively minor accusations, yet they were sharply denied or rationalized by police cadets in class when brought up for discussion. The greatest source of controversy was whether there existed a police state (or city). There are the beginnings of a police city if the following occurs:

1. **LEGITIMATE EXPRESSION** of public opinion is stifled by parade and permit difficulties. For example, the difficulties encountered by peace groups at the Democratic National Convention in August 1968.

2. Citizen complaints against the police are investigated by the police themselves. Rarely are the complaints treated as well founded and more rarely is discipline administered.

3. **PUBLIC RALLIES** when slowed are harassed and the participants clubbed and scattered. An example is the police attack on a peace rally in Chicago held on April 27, 1968.

4. The police sometimes kill those they come to protect. Not long ago neighbors in a Chicago area heard screams from an apartment. They called the police. To enter, the police shot off the front-door lock, killing a nineteen-year-old mother of two.

5. Police infiltrate private organizations to spy on their activities. The spies may act as agents of provocateurs.

6. Blacks anywhere, and especially Blacks in white neighborhoods, are harassed.

7. Midnight raids occur frequently to both Black groups and teenagers. The proposed "no knock" bill will aid in these raids.

THERE ARE OTHER EXAMPLES, and as protest, even peaceful protest, increases, there will even be more intimations of a police city. As Willard Lassers of the Illinois branch of the ACLU says, "The advent of a police city is not marked by a revolution, or even overt change in law. Rather, in the name of impartial law enforcement, the police enforce their own prejudices." On the other hand, one has the view of the police. Klein, in his book, is quoted: "As long as this law (the Fourth Amendment to the Constitution) is in effect in the United States, this nation cannot have a police state. It is the greatest guarantee against petty and/or vicious harassment by government officials that the citizen can have."

What has all this to do with teaching a course on the police? First, the question of values and value-judgments becomes acute for the social scientists when he enters a discussion of the police. This is the essential dilemma of the social scientist's role as academician and citizen. For example, during the quarter that the course was taught, five Chicago policemen were killed, at least a dozen police officers were killed across the country, more than 100 were wounded, and thousands of dollars of damage had been done to police stations, patrol cars, and other police property. How can the academic present a completely detached series of lectures on such a sensitive issue? In my own opinion, he cannot and should not, but let me present the possible alternatives:

1. One approach is to take the side of the police and defend the action from a "functionalist" position, i.e., the police are necessary to protect the status-quo. They simply enforce the law; they do not make the law. Furthermore, they are dealing with hoodlums, criminals, revolutionists, or what have you, and must use force to maintain law and order.

2. The second is to take the side of the oppressed, whether it be Blacks, white radicals, or hippies. The position here is that Blacks, for example, have the right to defend themselves against police oppression; police, in many cases, use brutality (beatings, intimidation) against Blacks, and furthermore, police have neither respect for Black people nor an understanding of black lifestyles. In short, police are "pigs."

3. The third approach is to take neither side, to blandly ignore any or all accusations and counter-accusations, and to present as detached and therefore "objective" a position as possible.

4. The fourth approach is to transcend the immediate and obvious conflict between Blacks and police by raising the level of discussion to include a systematic perspective of the entire society. In this case, the lone patrolman is seen as a man caught in the middle (but not by the Black who is brutalized). Furthermore, shooting policemen will not change this system. What is necessary then is for the academic to point out the oppressive nature of police along with their relationship to the judicial system, the political machinery, the federal police force (FBI, Secret Service), and the prisons.

FROM THIS PERSPECTIVE, one can see that mere reform is not enough. What is necessary is a radical social transformation of all these institutions. It is this last approach that the academic should use in the classroom, in his research, and in the "outside" world. It is this last approach that is ultimately the most productive. It does not avoid value-judgments; but simply puts them "up-front."

Shortly after the course was over, I lost my job at De Paul, and Edward "Buzz" Palmer, the Black policeman who team-taught the course with me, was kicked off the Chicago police force.

J. Porter, April 1971

Student Protest and the Technocratic Society: The Case of ROTC

This is a selection from my sociology Ph.D. dissertation, *Student Protest and the Technocratic Society: The Case of ROTC*, Northwestern University, June 1971. It was published in 1973 by Adams Press of Chicago. Again, it is some of the best writing I have ever done to describe our technocratic society and is as relevant in the twenty-first century as it was in the late 1960s and early 1970s when I wrote it. I took a big chance on this topic. In many schools, it would have been considered too "political" and not "objective" enough; but the times had changed and I had great professors who recognized my "genius" even if they questioned my style. I was also lucky that we had many well-known radicals in the department including James Turner, a Black leader; Steve Buff, and Lee Weiner, one of the Chicago Eight, who would go on trial soon. Plus, I had teachers who were sympathetic to the study of protest: Bernie Beck, Howie Becker, Janet Abu-Lughod, Jack Sawyer, and Richard Schwartz. It still reads well even today.

* * *

Preface

Students are really frightening. The following story should suffice. During my first year in graduate school in order to make some extra money, I taught "Sunday school" on Saturday at a synagogue in Evanston, Illinois.

One spring, I thought to try something innovative, and I asked the class to write a poem about God and nature and the religious experience. I thought it would be a nice idea since *my* teachers had once made *me* do it, and I thought I'd attempt the same thing. Well, the students (all of them sweet young nine- and ten-year-olds) were busy scribbling away, when one tiny little girl in granny glasses and a mini-skirt sidled up and asked, "Mr. Porter, do you want this poem to be in the style of Japanese Haiku with a 3-5-3 cadence and deal with *satori*, or what?"

I nearly fell off my chair. I thought to myself: *Doesn't anybody write about the robins and the trees and God in simple all-American rhyming couplets? Yes, the student is changing, and he is frightening, and since I am, while writing this, still a student, then I too must be frightening...to someone. Revenge is an evolutionary process.*

This story may symbolize in some small way what is occurring on campuses, and since that little girl will be in college one day, what is occurring today will accelerate in the future. The student arrives on campus, after having dined on 20,000 hours of TV and parental freedom, and finds an institution where he feels constrained, where teachers are afraid to lose the freedom to teach in the ways they've traditionally been taught, and where administrators are afraid to share their power with students.

Most students plunk down their $4,000 to get a room and board, and accept it all, albeit grudgingly. They say: "What can we do?," "You can't beat the system," "Anyway, education is a privilege, not a right," and then commence to toil away four, five or more years for good grades, a degree, a job, and a "good" wife or husband.

That cycle lasted for a long time (and still continues), but some students somehow and in some ways decided to announce to the world what Herbert Marcuse calls The Great Refusal. They simply said—no! That small word stands like a rock with all of its devastating and delegitimizing force. Maybe Black people taught them the word; maybe the European or Latin American student; maybe ironically their own parents showed them the way. Whoever it was, when the word was finally given, the world was never the same again. Some say it started at Berkeley, refined at Columbia, honed at the 1968 Democratic Convention, sharpened at Cornell and San Francisco State College, and climaxed at Kent State University and at Jackson State University. These are all landmarks; who is next and what forms the protest will take is anyone's guess, but one thing is sure: the Great Refusal will continue far into this century.

The purpose of this study is to examine one portion of this Great Refusal—the history of protest, particularly that protest directed against the military presence of the Reserve Officers Training Corps Program, ROTC, at a prestigious, private Big-Ten school, Northwestern University. It will outline the course of that protest and its impact on faculty, administrators, and students. It will describe the various factions of student "subcultures"—the radical, liberal, and conservative. It will trace the history of ROTC protest from the very first "guerrilla theater" action in the spring of 1969 to the events surrounding the Kent State killings in the spring of 1970. It will examine the ideological pros and cons of ROTC, and finally, it will go beyond the rhetoric to examine why ROTC was considered a symbol of the entire technocratic society.

In short, protest, both symbolic and direct protest, must be seen not simply as a hit-or-miss attempt to rectify minor disillusions, nor as a clash between spoiled and pampered children and their authoritarian father-figures, nor as a short-lived description of the status-quo, but as an ongoing, tenacious, even revolutionary quest for legitimization. To delegitimize the most dehumanizing and debasing aspects of the technocracy and to legitimate in their place new and creative alternative lifestyles is the ultimate aim of student-Black-hip protest.

The entire issue of student protest somehow does not fit neatly into a sociological slot. It is not quite within the sociology of education, though protest occurs within educational institutions, nor does it fit well within the realm of collective behavior, even though it manifests certain qualities that might. It would be more productive to place it within the arena of political sociology, since, in essence, student protest, like all of this past decade's protest, has two aims: the redistributions of power and/or wealth, and the alteration of consciousness. Thus, it is best seen as a direct political struggle for power and influence on one hand, and the introduction of a higher, transcendental form of reason on the other. It is a new consciousness that, according to Charles Reich in *The Greening of America*, will change politics and, ultimately, the structure of society, by first changing the culture and the quality of individual lives.

It is by this "transcendental vision" that I have been guided. I do not claim to be objective in the narrow sense of that word, but I have attempted to back up nearly all my statements with facts, reason, and other scholar's data. Seymour Martin Lipset has said that in the case of student protest, it is almost impossible to separate one's role as scholar and citizen. Let me add that it is also difficult to separate, at times, the role of political pamphleteer and political sociologist. This book walks that narrow line.

Finally, it must be reiterated that the events described in this study are only minute catalysts. What is labeled an "apocalypse" at one point in time is merely a flash across the skies when seen from a distant historical perspective. By combining sociology, journalism, and history, I hope to examine that particular social "flash" known as student protest.

Introduction: The Transformed University

This country was founded by heretics. Its universities were founded by heretics. The "heresy" now found on our campuses had its precedents 350 years ago, and we've come around first circle. Protestant dissenters from England and Holland, many alumni of Oxford or Cambridge before being branded dissenters, were among those who landed at Plymouth Rock in the fall of 1620. By 1800, there were nine college institutions: Harvard (founded in 1636), Yale, Brown, Dartmouth, Pennsylvania, Princeton, Columbia, Rutgers, and William and Mary. They were mainly preparatory schools for the clergy; mathematics, speculative natural philosophy, Hebrew, Latin, Greek, and the classics were the "pith and marrow" of the curriculum. They combined the traditions of learning of ancient Greece, Rome, and Israel with the Christian Church with the demands and freedoms of the new world. The college of that time was a cloister for an intellectual and social elite, an aristocracy for the colonies.[8]

The university of today, however, is derived mainly from developments that arose immediately following the Civil War. The populist movement, the westward movement, the swirling rush of democratizing forces set in motion by the sudden changes induced by the War Between the States led to the rise of the university as we know it today. The community of scholars extolled by Cardinal Newman with its "pure" pursuit of knowledge was soon to be a nostalgic memory. Imitating the German model with its emphasis on graduate training, scientific research, and professional schools, a new form of education arose. Land-grant colleges were built by the Morrill Act of 1862; the first Ph.D. was awarded in 1861 by Yale; Northwestern University was founded in 1851 and awarded its first Ph.D. in 1896. Johns

---

8   For a more complete historical analysis of the university, see Stewart (1962) and Rudolph (1962).

Hopkins was the prime example of the new graduate school universities. In the 1890s, the University of Chicago was founded, and it, along with Stanford, Columbia, and others, followed the "German model." National professional societies and journals were founded and knowledge was subdivided by departmental categories (i.e., history, sociology, physics, etc.), and the department emerged as the basic unit of academic administration. By World War I, two dozen major universities had emerged. An "academic revolution," as Jencks and Reisman (1968) have called it, was completed at this time, or at least the first round of it was.

If the first transformation of the American university occurred in the last quarter of the nineteenth century and dealt mainly with the professionalization of academia, the second transformation occurred after World War II, where the symbiotic relationship between the federal government and the university first bloomed. This "love affair" has intensified and continued up until this day.

Though there were efforts to restore the primacy of intimate "liberal education" with a stress on undergraduate training (mainly by Robert Hutchins at the University of Chicago), the mold, however, was set; the multiversity, the "closed corporation" as James Ridgeway calls it, became a reality. To aid the war effort, the collective minds of scientists and college administrators were needed. The "bomb" was developed under a tennis court at the University of Chicago. The innocence of academia was over; the newly emerged research-oriented, government-subsidized, IBM card-controlled multiversity was here to stay. Since World War II, the "knowledge explosion" has grown to enormous heights. About $2 billion was spent on scientific research and development in the United States in 1945. Today, the figure has risen to over $15 billion. Federal expenditure for research has multiplied 200 times in the past twenty-five years from $74 million in 1940 to $15 billion in 1965.[9] The post-war baby boom sent thousands of eager students into the colleges of the land; the building boom constructed hundreds of new classrooms, dormitories and laboratories to house these students; the G.I. Bill and other federal incentives induced even more young people to seek college degrees. The armies of meritocracy were on the march. In 1900, only ten percent of college-age youth went on to college; now nearly sixty percent attend. If in 1900, there were nearly a quarter

---

9   These figures are drawn from secondary sources discussed in Raymond Mack, *Transforming America: Patterns of Social Change* (New York: Random House, 1967), p. 12.

million students, by 1950 there were 2 ½ million, and today that figure has more than doubled to over six million students enrolled in the over 2,500 colleges and universities of the United States.

These educational institutions were caught by surprise. It is important to note that the Berkeley revolt of 1964 came exactly eighteen years after the "baby-boom" of 1945-1946. The stage was set for the third transformation of the American university. This new stage resounded from the small Catholic institutions of the Midwest to the Negro colleges of the South; from the sophisticated Ivy League schools of the East to the sun-drenched "surfboard" colleges of the West. What had happened was that, in its rush to build and expand in order to accommodate the huge numbers of students wanting to get in, the university was forced to change. In their rush to build bigger and bigger universities, there arose indifference to the needs of students, and bureaucratic rules replaced human contact.

Along with the crush of over-population, there arose in the sixties other movements and events: the draft, the War in Vietnam, the Black protest movement, ecological problems, and the entire series of counter-cultures that opposed the meanest aspects of the growing technocracy. All these issues were, of course, developing over a period of years; it happened that, in the '60s and now the '70s, they "bloomed."

It soon became clear that these forces of revolt and change developed dialectically in opposition to a growing phenomenon: the Corporate State. As Charles Reich has put it:

> Our present system has gone beyond anything that could be properly called the creation of capitalism or imperialism or a power elite. That, at least, would be a human shape. Of course a power elite does exist and is made rich by the system, but the elite are no longer in control, they are now merely taking advantage of forces that have a life of their own. Nor is our system a purely technological society, although technology has increasingly supplied the basis for our choices and superseded other values. What we have is technology, organization, and administration out of control, running for their own sake, but at the same time subject to manipulation and profiteering by the power interests of our society for their own non-human needs.[10]

---

10   Reich, Charles A., *The Greening of America* (New York: Random House, 1970), pp. 88-89.

In this Corporate State, the universities, or at least the largest and/or most prestigious of them, find themselves "deputized," that is, linked into the military-industrial complex that lies at the foundation of the technocratic society. The government hires "private" firms to build national defense systems, to supply the space program, to construct the interstate highway system, to do research, and to train its military personnel (ROTC). We call these "private" firms by various names—corporations, research and development institutes, foundations, "think tanks," or universities; they are no longer separate and autonomous units, but are tied in directly to the Corporate State.

It is not that this situation is inherently cause for protest, but the very institution that many students (and faculty) felt was an autonomous and moral institution—the university—was ensconced within this Corporate State and contributed to those aspects of the relationship that were most abhorrent to these students: the WAR, military training, chemical-biological warfare research, etc. Thus the university itself becomes "part of the problem."

The focus of this book manifestly is student protest—particularly protest over the presence of NROTC, Naval Reserve Officers Training Corps, on the university campus. Yet the latent, and ultimately the most important, issue is not NROTC, nor the other campus issues, nor the radical's symbols, nor the "suicidal" acts of protest and confrontation—it is the *technocratic society* itself. The issues of NROTC or the war or oppression at home are only the most manifest symbols of the technostructure of post-industrial nations.

The issue of technocracy transcends the parochial and often narrow viewpoint of capitalism or communism; of liberal, conservative, radical, or revolutionary politics; of any left, right, or centrist ideology. The issue of technocracy allows us to transcend such viewpoints, to see the historical and transnational effects, and to go beyond the restraints of the present. To view student protest as a response to technocratic pressures raises our horizons by merging the individual, his society, and his historical setting. Social scientists have too often concentrated on the psychological and the parental reasons for student protest, and have avoided intensively analyzing, or even mentioning, the technocratic. Yet it is both the psychological *and* the technocratic that cause protest, revolt, and ultimately revolution. To avoid understanding the impact of the technocracy is to view student protest in a piecemeal fashion—with little comprehension of the historical and macro-societal forces at work. One then misses the forest because of the trees.

Robert K. Merton, in his introduction to Jacques Ellul's excellent analysis of the technical civilization, *The Technological Society* (translated from the French: *La Technique: L'enjeu du Siècle*), has stated:

> By "technique," [one] means far more than machine technology. Technique refers to any complex of standardized means of attaining a predetermined result... Politics in turn becomes an arena for contention among rival techniques. The technician sees the nation quite differently from the political man: to the technician, the nation is nothing more than another sphere in which to apply the instruments he has developed. To him, the state is not the expression of the will of the people nor a divine creation nor a creature of class conflict. It is an enterprise providing services that must be made to function *efficiently.*[11]

It is the capacity to utilize techniques efficiently, to harness manpower effectively, and to employ deliberate and rationalized means which eventually become ends in themselves, thus replacing the very ends for which they were originally designed that is the *raison d'être* of technocracy. The era of expertise and of "know-how" is upon us, displacing the spontaneous, the inspirational, and the natural.

It should not then come as a shock that an entire series of countercultures emerged during the 1960s to provide alternatives to the dehumanization caused by the technocracy. Whether one calls them hippies, or yippies, or revolutionists, or Black militants (the very terms are coined by the right arm of the technocratic state, the mass media), all are responses to the very same ethos: the technological and organizational imperative. I will, in this study, recount the activities of one of these "groups"—the radical left—but the very same technocratic repressiveness that the "left" fights against is also the one that the hippies, yippies, Blacks, and all other cultural and political insurgents fight against.

The "enemy" is not only powerful; he is devious. He is able not only to stifle, but to co-opt. He not only dehumanizes, but he "cools-out" his antagonists. The "new authoritarianism" (as Herbert Marcuse calls it) seems to

---

11 Merton, Robert K., "Introduction," in Jacques Ellul, *The Technological Society,* John Wilkinson, trans. (New York: Random House, 1964), pp. vi-vii, original emphasis.

be able to anabolize every form of discontent into its system. The technocracy is able to co-opt its dissidents, generate submissiveness, and weaken the rationality of protest. Such "repressive desublimation" (another Marcusian term) can undermine any discontent. Theodore Roszak gives the finest example, the sexual:

> To liberate sexuality would be to create a society in which *technocratic discipline would be impossible.* But to thwart sexuality outright would create a widespread, explosive resentment that required constant policing; and besides, this would associate the technocracy with various puritanical traditions that enlightened men cannot but regard as superstitious. The strategy chosen, therefore, is not harsh repression, but rather the *Playboy* version of total permissiveness... Yes, there is permissiveness in the technocratic society; but it is only for the swingers and the big spenders. It is the reward that goes to reliable, politically safe henchmen of the status-quo. Before our would-be playboy can be an assembly-line seducer, he must be a *loyal employee.*[12]

It is important only that the social machine, whether it be the corporation or the university, continue to roll onward and upward. All protest, no matter how irritating or embarrassing, will be tolerated only so long as the vital machinery is left untouched. The dean of students at Northwestern University refers to his job as a "crisis manager." He is correct. His duty is to see that crises are mediated and cooled-out, so that the machine can function with a minimum of disruption. The cry of "business as usual" during the Cambodia-Kent State strikes across the land in May 1970 was not necessary: the technocratic imperative is so powerful that by force of habit and design, universities would have returned to their pre-strike function anyway.

The reason that protest is seen both as a minor irritant and a major sore is that technocrats and their intellectual counterpart, the *academocrats*,[13] see such protest as essentially a temporary blockage of the technocratic dam, but know in the recesses of their mind that if such minor irritants are not

---

12 Roszak, Theodore, *The Making of a Counter Culture: Reflections on the Technocratic Society and its Youthful Opposition* (New York: Doubleday [Anchor Books], 1969), pp. 14-15, emphasis added.

13 This term, which the author has newly coined, exemplifies the role of the educator and educator-administrator who has "sold his soul" to the technocracy.

dealt with effectively *today*, tomorrow they will swell and bring ever more complications. Furthermore, the technocrats are aware, albeit uncertainly, that the protest is *not* aimed only at an issue here or there, but that one's very lifestyle is also threatened, and moreover, the very function, role, and efficiency of the technocratic society itself is at stake! Again, Roszak says:

> We call it "education," the "life of the mind," "the pursuit of truth." But it is a matter of machine-tooling the young to the needs of our various baroque bureaucracies: corporate, governmental, military, trade union, educational.[14]

Since the radical critique of these institutions touches at a vital nerve center, the technocratic society is ready to do battle in order to protect itself. The purpose of this study is to articulate the history and sociology of this confrontation between a technocratic institution and the forces that oppose it. Suffice it say that this third transformation, the student revolt of the 1960s (and soon into the 1970s), is more than the transformation of only the academic institution: all the nooks and crannies of our society are its target. If academia has lost its "soul" and its "heart," so then have most societal institutions, and they all must be redefined. If the first transformation of the universities dealt mainly with pedagogic instruction, and the second transformation dealt mainly with national involvement, the third transformation deals mostly with moral principles. It is the search for a more human "community," a struggle for participation in the formulation of those rules and regulations that control one's life, a desire for "relevance" in all areas, a seeking of contact and compassion from teachers and office workers, an honest reappraisal of the university's involvement with non-intellectual (i.e., military) pursuits, an end to the myopic and deadening posture of academia, and a return to creativity, spontaneity, and love. If these demands seem naïve and romantic, the response to them has nevertheless led to confrontations of fire and blood. Let us now begin to examine the setting for one of these "confrontations."

— November 1972

---

14 Roszak, *op. cit.*, p. 16.

References

Ellul, Jacques. *The Technological Society.* John Wilkinson, trans. New York: Random House, 1964.

Jencks, Christopher, and David Reisman. *The Academic Revolution.* New York: Doubleday, 1968.

Mack, Raymond W. *Transforming America: Patterns of Social Change.* New York: Random House, 1967.

Reich, Charles A. *The Greening of America.* New York: Random House, 1970.

Roszak, Theodore. *The Making of a Counter Culture: Reflections on the Technocratic Society and its Youthful Opposition.* New York: Doubleday (Anchor Books), 1969.

Rudolph, Frederick. *The American College and University: A History.* New York: Alfred A. Knopf, 1962.

Stewart, Campbell. "The Place of Higher Education in a Changing Society." In Levitt Sanford (ed.), *The American College.* New York: John Wiley, 1962, pp. 894-939.

II. Jewish Radicals: Theory

The Jewish Rebel

The following essay appeared in the June 1973 issue of *Jewish Spectator*, pp. 15-17.

* * *

A fish will be the last to discover water.

— Edmund Carpenter

The synthesis of universalism and Judaism burns in my mind. How does one bridge the gap? When I first began to ponder the question, I thought I was alone, that my generation was alone in trying to come to grips with this problem. Eventually with further reading and discussion with friends, my ahistorical perspective gave way to new insights: Jews have always struggled with the question of universalism versus particularism. I was really part of a long tradition.

Though the roots of Jewish radical universalism go back to the prophetic vision of the Bible and to the Talmud, the real dialogue began in the modern era, with nineteenth-century *Haskalah*—"Enlightenment," when European Jews left the ghetto and entered the non-Jewish world. The struggle between allegiance to one's people and community and cosmopolitan ideals only comes into play when there are options.

The response to these options set the stage for the confrontation with secularism and intellectualism.

Other questions trouble me: Who is a Rebel? Why are the Jew and the Rebel often seen as one and the same? Why and how does one become a Rebel?

I see the Jew and the Rebel as classical outsiders: Max Weber's "pariah people" or Georg Simmel's "the stranger." Everett Stonequist and Robert Park used the term "the marginal man." They can be either men or women who, according to Veblen,[1] are doubly alienated—cut of first from their people, traditions, and community, and secondly, from the male society.

The Jewish rebels who transcended Judaism to mysticism and radical politics sought a secular form of "revolutionary Messianism." They considered Judaism too constrictive, but they transformed their alienation into an asset by contributing vastly to Western thought.

The essence of this process is distilled in a story by the Marxist scholar, Isaac Deutscher, in his book *The Non-Jewish Jew* (1968):

> I remember that when as a child I read the *Mirash* (the Biblical commentary), I came across a story and a description of a scene which gripped my imagination. It was the story of Rabbi Meir, the great saint and sage, the pillar of Mosaic orthodoxy, and co-author of the *Mishnah* (codified Jewish law), who took lessons from a heretic, Elisha ben Abuyah, called *Akher* (The Stranger). Once on a Sabbath, Rabbi Meir was with his teacher, and as usual they became engaged in a deep argument.
>
> The heretic was riding a donkey, and Rabbi Meir, as he could not ride on a Sabbath, walked by his side and listened so intently to the words of wisdom falling from the heretical lips that he failed to notice that he and his teacher had reached the ritual boundary which Jews were not allowed to cross on a Sabbath.
>
> The great heretic turned to his orthodox pupil and said: "Look, we have reached the boundary—we must part now; you must not accompany me any further—go back!" Rabbi Meir went back to the Jewish community, while the heretic rode on—beyond the boundaries of Jewry...
>
> The Jewish heretic who transcends Jewry belongs to a Jewish tradition. You may, if you like, see *Akher* as a prototype of those great revolutionaries of modern thought: Spinoza, Heine, Marx, Rosa Luxemburg, Trotsky, and Freud... They all found Jewry too

---

1   Thorstein Veblen (1857-1929), American economist and sociologist known for his critiques of capitalism and for-profit production and for conceiving the sociological school of institutional economics.

narrow, too archaic... They all looked for ideals and fulfillment beyond it...

I recognize this alienation in my own life. It particularly struck me when I read books by Frantz Fanon, especially one of his lesser-known works, *Peau Noire, Masques Blancs (Black Skin, White Masks)*, and also the works of Albert Memmi, *Portrait of a Jew, The Liberation of the Jew, The colonizer and the Colonized*, and *Dominated Man*. Both authors gave me the impetus to rediscover my identity.

Only when I was able to discard the shackles of graduate school training and academic "objectivity" could I begin to liberate myself. I then began to understand what Memmi wrote in his preface to the 1965 edition of *The Colonizer and the Colonized*:

> ...I undertook this inventory of conditions of colonized people in order to understand myself and to identify my place in the society of other men.

The very definition of the word *galut*, diaspora, implies that the Jew lives in two cultures. This "cultural schizophrenia" has always existed. For me this has meant creativity as well as anxiety. To be a marginal man is not healthy—it breeds neurosis, yet from this neurosis a rich creativity can emerge.

Looking at it another way, I have often been curious about the reasons for the Jews' disproportionate contribution to western civilization. Why and how did they contribute so much? The question is hard to answer, but let me try.

The Jewish Rebel appears in two forms. First, there is the *Rebel from within*: Moses, Moses Maimonides, Baal Shem Tov, Franz Rosenzweig, Martin Buber, Abraham Joshua Heschel, Gershom Scholem, Theodore Herzl, Mordecai Kaplan, David Ben-Gurion, and other activists, poets, mystics, communards, and ideologists of liberation movements. Not usually thought of as "rebels," they are innovators from within, who, as Alan Mintz puts it, engage in a process of reverse assimilation, i.e., the host culture is Judaized, and employed for the enrichment of Jewish expression. This Jewish Rebel makes it possible for Judaism to revitalize itself.

Secondly, there is the Jewish *Rebel from without*, the Jews who have found Judaism too confining and too narrow. They search for new paths outside the confines of their religion and their ghetto people. Their lives are filled by secular substitutes for a faith that is restrictive, yet has the ingenious ability to spread out and create new heretical seed-beds.

Judaism's greatness is that it possesses both compassion and pity for the heretic. It has the kind of ambivalence that exists in us all. It is the tightrope between universalism and particularism. Hillel's saying confuses me even more. I am enticed by the universalistic concerns around me ("If I am only for myself, what am I?"); but I am enjoined to protect and partake in the celebration of my own people ("If I am not for myself, what am I?"). The answer is not an easy one.

In discussing the Rebel from within and from without, I am not saying that it is a strict dichotomy. There is an overlap. To call Freud, Bob Dylan, or Jerry Rubin a (let's be careful with this word) self-hating, assimilated Jew is much too simple. All three had a Jewish education, Jewish friends, and a Jewish home. All three went to Hebrew school and read the Bible. All three were Bar Mitzvahed. All three were sympathetic to Zionism (at least for a while, in Rubin's case). Dylan is reported to have been to Israel, as has Rubin; Dylan has studied with a Hasidic rebbe; he has even reported to have met and donated money to Rabbi Meir Kahane and the Jewish Defense League. Freud respected Theodor Herzl and sent him a copy of one of his works with a personal dedication. His son was a member of *Kadimah*, a Zionist organization; and Freud himself was an honorary member of it, as well as of the Vienna B'nai B'rith. All three had deep roots in Judaism, yet became alienated.

This process of Jewish rebellion is explained by what I call *multiple alienation*—alienation from general society due to anti-Semitism, alienation from one's religion, alienation from one's family, and finally, alienation from one's own self. From this alienation emerges the marginal person, as well as the creative impulse.

The Jew is the eternal outsider, the eternal witness. He stands back from society and can see its new potentials. The fish will never discover water. The fisherman will. But the outsider takes risks: alienation, "cultural schizophrenia," and marginality. The Jew's uniqueness can lead to Sweden and the Nobel Prize as well as to Auschwitz and the gas chamber.

Obviously we define ourselves before others define us. We may not have power over *their* definition of us, but we do have power over ourselves. And this *is* being done today: Judaism *is* being redefined in new and provocative ways.

My generation will have to "rewrite" Jewish history: replace what was omitted, emphasize what was brushed over, recall what was forgotten. We need a "usable past," a past that has the power to shape creatively our destiny and stir our emotions. We must do the job that our teachers have not done.

It is a search for authenticity—authentic heroes, authentic teachers, and authentic models—in a world that has left many of us without models and no blueprint for the future. We must rediscover our own and ourselves.

June 1973

The Jewishness of Karl Marx

From *The Jewish Radical*, Vol. 2, No. 11, 1986, pp. 1-6. First appeared in a collection of my articles entitled *The Jew as Outsider* (Spencer Press, 2014).

* * *

Karl Marx was born in 1818 in the small, predominantly Catholic city of Trier in the Rhineland, Germany. His father, Heinrich (Hershel), was the son of Marx Levi (Mordechai ben Samuel Halevi), who was the rabbi of Trier. The name Marx itself derives from an abbreviated form of Mordechai, later changed to Markus. Marx's grandfather Mordechai was the descendant of a long line of rabbinical scholars, and his grandmother Eva Lwow had an equally illustrious ancestry. Thus, from both sides of his family tree, Marx had distinguished rabbis.

Marx's father, Heinrich, was a knowledgeable, industrious lawyer in the high court of Trier, but given the anti-Semitism of the times, he was forced to convert to Lutheranism (in 1817) in order to practice his legal profession. In 1824, when his children were of school age, Heinrich Marx had them all baptized into the Lutheran religion.

Thus, at the age of six, Karl Marx became a Christian without having any say in the matter at all. His mother (née Henrietta Pressburg) delayed her conversion until 1825 when her father, Isaac Pressburg, rabbi in Nujmegen, Holland, died. The reason for the delay was obvious: her parents were against such conversion. Perhaps, too, she ha a greater love of her religion. Only with great reluctance did she finally convert.

Robert Wistrich, in *Revolutionary Jews from Marx to Trotsky*, points out that, though Marx completely rejected his background, it did not mean that it exercised no influence on his revolutionary career. As Wistrich says:

His intransigent hostility to Judaism should not blind one to the role which insecurity about his origins played in shaping the intellectual and moral character of his outlook… Although Marx was to give his name to a secular, universalist ideology, as hostile to Christianity as it was to Judaism, he never freed himself from subjective prejudices which reflected the oldest anti-Semitic stereotypes of European Christian society.

Wistrich feels that Marx came by his anti-Semitic feelings quiet easily: he was raised as a Lutheran in Lutheran schools, and he could not avoid seeing Jews and the "Jewish problem" through the distorted lens of the Christian Judeophobia of his era. Often, as we will see, he continued to describe Jews and Judaism, not in a tolerant way, but in the emotional and often belligerent stereotypes of the day, that is, the Jew as international banker; the Jew as "money-grubber"; the Jew as "Capitalist"; all the while forgetting or ignoring that most Jews in the world were poor, impoverished ghetto or *shtetl* dwellers.

Marxism and Judaism

By its very definition, orthodox Marxism is opposed to religion and nationality. Marxism is international, materialistic, and the very negation of religion. The optimism of Marxist theory is based on the idea that mankind can solve its problems without divine assistance because of man's essentially rational nature. Religion is seen by Marx as the "opium of the people" because it drugs and clouds the vision of the masses with irrational, mystical thoughts, thus delaying the making of political revolution. Marx identified Jews and Judaism with capitalism, and Judaism he saw as anti-materialistic, chauvinistic, reactionary, and resigned to the scrapheap of history when the revolution of the proletariat was accomplished.

According to Marx, the elimination of capitalism will emancipate Jews along with the rest of the world that has been victimized by capitalism. The abolition of both capitalism and, thereby, Judaism will therefore liberate the Jews from their religion. Under communism, the Jews will no longer have to live as Jews. Their real nature will be rejected, and Jews should actively facilitate this process by rejecting their Judaism and taking part in the rebellion against capitalism. Furthermore, Jewish nationalism (Zionism) is a bourgeois concept and diverts the attention of the Jewish workers away from revolutionary action. Later Marxists saw Zionism and its instrument, the state of Israel, as archaic vestiges of capitalism in the form of neo-colonialism and imperialism. An important point to stress is that Marx's view of the Jews (and by extension as applied to Israel), written over one hundred years ago, has influenced the attitudes of many Marxists today.

Robert Wistrich feels that the term "self-hatred" should be applied to Karl Marx and several other Jewish radical thinkers (i.e., Ferdinand Lassalle, Rosa Luxemburg, and Julius Martov). Wistrich emphasizes that Marx, the assimilated descendant of a distinguished line of rabbis, felt embarrassed and ambivalent about his Jewish "roots" and, furthermore, lashed out against Jews and Judaism in vulgar anti-Semitic stereotypes. Being of Jewish parentage and never being allowed to forget that he was in fact a Jew, Marx turned upon not only the Christian society but against Jews themselves, attempting in the process to transcend both Christianity and Judaism with the ideology of revolutionary socialism. Since Marx was, according to Wistrich, an anti-Semitic Jew, he feels that the label of a self-hating Jew is applicable to Karl Marx.

Some writers, such as W.H. Friedland and Tamara Deutscher, have disagreed with Wistrich. Friedland, in the *American Journal of Sociology* in May of 1978, feels that Marx, Lassalle, Luxemburg *et al.* did not hate themselves. He will concede that many Jewish radicals had "reservations" about Jews and about their own Jewish antecedents, but he feels that the term "self-hatred" is essentially a psychological process, and Jews who assimilate or who are anti- or non-Zionist are not necessarily people who hate themselves. Friedland feels that the term "self-hatred" as applied to Marx is "incorrect"; an example of "name-calling"; and ultimately "inadequate and unsatisfactory."

He maintains that Marx and other radicals of Jewish background rejected Judaism not out of self-hatred but because they felt that Judaism and Jewishness as a philosophy of life was too limiting a background. He sees assimilation as a rejection of the social group that one has come out of rather than as hatred of self. What Friedland may have overlooked is that it could be *both* reasons rather than either one. And does not rejection of one's group include disgust with the behavior of that group?

Deutscher, in *Olam* of Winter-Spring 1977, takes exception with the self-hatred theory, because she feels that Marx was not concerned with the religion of the Jews but with the "exceptional" role that Jews played in feudal and early capitalist development where they represented the oncoming money economy in societies in transition from natural economy. Marx felt that Christian society had been "Judaized." According to Deutscher, he did not mean to apply anti-Semitic connotations to this fact, but only meant that money has become a world power, and as Christian society became more capitalist, it became more "Judaized." What both Marx and Deutscher forgot is that the bulk of the Jewish masses were not involved in banking or money-lending but were poor tradesmen. Because of the prominence of a few Jewish banking houses (most notably the Rothschilds), Marx and other radicals accepted the prevailing anti-Semitic stereotype of the "money-hoarding Jew."

Despite the protestations of Friedland and Deutscher, there are other authorities who disagree with their formulations and do in fact feel that Marx's ideological system does contain some anti-Semitic elements:

> Some socialists, including Marx himself, used the symbol of Jewish capitalism (of the Jews as merchants and "Shylocks") in their propaganda. Without going into the whole question of Marx's curious relationship with Judaism—it is certainly not a simple one—there can be little doubt Marx's belief system included some components which must be describe as anti-Semitism.
>
> — S.M. Lipset

> Judaism for Marx was a totally negative phenomenon, something to be got rid of as quickly and as radically as possible. As far as he personally was concerned, his Jewish origin must have appeared an unfortunate accident of birth and a matter of considerable embarrassment. But this was by no means an original or specially "Marxist" attitude. Many of his anti-socialist contemporaries reacted in exactly the same way. They were first and foremost citizens of the world and only secondarily German, Austrian, or Russian nationals.
>
> — Walter Laqueur

However, Karl Marx often stepped beyond this line from internationalist sentiments to anti-Semitic statements, and it is here where I stress that self-hatred may not be too strong a term to describe aspects of Marx's personality. Edmund Silberner, in *Historica Judaica*, April, 1949, states:

> In his correspondence with Engels, Marx used a variety of expressions to designate Jews. In some instances, the proper names are preceded or followed by the word "Jew," "English Jew,"

French Jew," etc. In other cases, *der Jud* ("Yid"), *der verfluchte Jude* ("the damned Jew"), or *Jud Suss* fulfill the same function… A very rich vocabulary is displayed by Marx in his comments on Ferdinand Lassalle… He…designates Lassalle as "the Jewish nigger," about whom he tells a very witty story. Lassalle's head and hair, says Marx, perfectly indicate that "he is descended from the Negroes who joined Moses on the exodus from Egypt (unless his mother or grandmother on the father's side were crossed with a nigger). This union of Jew and German on a Negro base must create a singular product. The importunity of the fellow is also nigger-like."

Marx makes his most concise statement on the Jews in his 1843 essay *Zur Judenfrage* ("On the Jewish Question"), which is really a review of two articles by the German philosopher Bruno Bauer, the leader of the Young Hegelian movement. Marx's reply originally appeared in the *Deutsch-franzosische Jahrbucher* in Paris in 1844 when he was twenty-six years old. (The entire essay has been reprinted many times in the collected works of Marx and Engels.) Marx dealt with the Jewish problem in depth in only two writings—his 1843 essay mentioned above, and in an extension of that essay in his first book with Engels, *The Holy Family* (1845). We will quote only the most controversial section of *Zur Judenfrage:*

Let us consider the actual, secular Jew, not the *Sabbath Jew* as does Bauer, but the *everyday Jew*. Let us look for the secret of the Jew not in his religion, but let us look for the secret of religion in the actual Jew.

What is the secular basis of Judaism? *Practical* need, *self-interest*.

What is the worldly cult of the Jew? *Huckstering* (*Schacher*).

What is his worldly god? Money.

What actually was the foundation, in and of itself, of the Jewish religion? Practical need, egoism…

Money is the jealous god of Israel before whom no other god may exist. Money degrades all the gods of mankind—and converts them into a commodity…

The god of the Jews has been secularized and has become the god of the world. The bill of exchange is the real god of the Jew. His god is only an illusory bill of exchange…

What is contained abstractly in the Jewish religion—contempt for theory, for art, for history, for man as an end in himself—is the *actual conscious* standpoint, the virtue of the money-man…

The *chimerical* nationality of the Jew is the nationality of the merchant…

And the last sentence of *Zur Judenfrage* reads:

The social emancipation of the Jew is the *emancipation of society from Judaism*. [All emphasized words are by Marx himself.]

It is this section from Marx's *Zur Judenfrage* that has been the cause of most of the controversy through the years. Julius Carlebach has in fact written a 466-page book with nearly ninety-five pages of notes and an annotated bibliography of ninety-one books and articles that deal with Marx's essays on, or associations with, Jews. These items are in six languages and span viewpoints both for and against Marx. It is a wonderment that Marx's short essays, which the scholar Isaiah Berlin called "dull and shallow," could provoke such a number of responses. If Marx were simply an anti-Semite like Hitler (as suggested by Dagobert Runes), why all the debate? Why? Because Marx was not a simple man. In his life, he showed signs that he was also philo-Semitic. Furthermore, the many responses to his essay have been colored by the writer's own personal ideology (whether for or against communism), his desire to see or avoid seeing certain aspects of Marx's life, or his own personal agenda (an "axe to grind"). Marx has this power to churn up intellectuals 150 years later.

On the balance sheet, one should mention the apologetical arguments in favor of Karl Marx. First, he did speak out in favor of Jewish emancipation, and the *Rheinische Zeitung*, a Cologne paper that Marx edited form 1842 until its suppression in March, 1843, was one of the strongest supporters of such emancipation as one aspect of the struggle against the clerical monarchy. It was because of the paper's strong support of Jewish rights that the leading Jews of Cologne, early in 1843, turned to Karl Marx to draw up a petition for Jewish rights to be submitted to the government. Furthermore, it should be noted that Marx wrote a moving passage about the wretched condition of the Jews of Jerusalem in the April 15, 1854 issue of the *New York Tribune*. He also exchanged letters with the Jewish historian Heinrich Graetz (1817-1891), and Graetz wrote back in warm personal terms. Finally, Marx should be excused, because he wrote those fateful essays at a young age before his mature thinking had been published. He had not yet developed his theory of the class struggle, and his views of Jews were based entirely on a preoccupation with money and were influenced by the non-class perspective of Ludwig Feuerbach. He would shortly discard such views.

These are most of the arguments, but there are a few others that should be mentioned. One has to do with the translation or mistranslation of certain phrases in *Zur Judenfrage*. Marx meant that the "social emancipation of the Jew (*des Juden*) is the emancipation of society from Judaism (*Judentum*)." Some translators (for example, Runes) changed the wording of "Judaism" and say "Jews" or "Jewry." This then would make it sound genocidal, that is, "...the emancipation of society from Jews." This would be false and misleading. Marx did not wish to rid the world of Jews but the Jews of their Judaism. In essence, the outcome, however, would be the same. By eliminating Judaism, the cultural and religious source blood of the Jews, one would assimilate Jews. If one destroys a culture and a religion, one ultimately destroys a nation. Still, we must be precise in what Marx wrote and avoid mistranslations.

Furthermore, some apologists such as Ruchwarger maintain that Marx's attitudes toward Jews were no different from other liberals of his time, and that his views should be placed in the context of Germany of the 1840s, not America of the 1980s. Even those who were in favor of Jewish emancipation for German Jews held such anti-Semitic stereotypes. Ruchwarger even goes so far as to say that many early Zionists held similar positions, for example, Pinsker, Syrkin, Ber Borochov, A.D. Gordon, and Hayim Greenberg. He quotes Draper that "to be a good Zionist one must first be somewhat of an anti-Semite," meaning that one must hate the "unclean" commerciality and speculation of Jewish businessmen and bankers in order to be a good socialist Zionist!

Yet, despite the many sophisticated and (almost) persuasive apologetics for Marx, I remain unconvinced. Marx was, in my estimation, an anti-Semite, and, despite his brilliance, he accepted the most vulgar stereotypes of his time. He did nothing to refute such views in his later, more mature works, and even Engels was embarrassed by Marx's anti-Semitic outbursts.

Was Marx blind to or ignorant of the Jewish situation? Was the Jewish question really insignificant within his overall philosophy? Was it disgust for his own identity as a Jew and with Jews in general? Was his "hysterical hatred of the Jews" (Feuer) based on a reaction to his mother? Even when he favored Jewish emancipation, was he simply (and cynically) using Jews as part of his attack against the clerical monarchy and the bourgeoisie? Or, should we not agree that the violently anti-Semitic tone of Marx's essays influenced untold generations of communists and, in Berlin's succinct phrase, became "one of the most neurotic and revolting aspects of his masterful but vulgar personality"?

Thus, aside from his personal anti-Semitic remarks regarding Lassalle and other Jews, we see that anti-Semitic stereotypes of a negative kind crept into Marx's philosophy-ideology as well. Saul Padover has noted the following: As a student of religion, Marx should have known that Jews did not worship Mammon but an all-pervasive deity, and that their rabbis were often profoundly mystical and otherworldly people with a dedication to saving souls rather than saving money. They worshipped a monotheistic God, not money. Furthermore, as a historian, Marx should have known that the founders and early practitioners of Judaism were not men obsessed with trade and money but with their deity. And that later, when Jews in Christian Europe were involved in money affairs, it was out of desperate necessity and not out of inner faith, because most other means of livelihood (farming, the military, etc.) were closed to them. Furthermore, Marx's concept of the "capitalist Jew" held true for some Jews in Western Europe (Germany, France, England, and Holland) and not for the majority of world Jewry who lived in small towns or urban ghettos in Czarist Russia and in Poland.

If Marx and later Marxists would have been more aware of anti-Semitism and of the Jewish proletariat in Eastern Europe, they might have sympathized with their plight and written in a different manner about Jews and their economic situation. Edmund Silberner takes the view that Karl Marx was not only anti-Semitic, but that he was one of the major contributors to the anti-Semitic "tradition" in modern socialism. He writes:

> Already half a century ago, Thomas G. Masaryk drew attention to what he plainly called "the anti-Semitism of Marx." More sympathetic commentators preferred not to use such a blunt term, and spoke of "an anti-Jewish prejudice" of the master. Still

others, *without adducing evidence*, however, assert that "one cannot say that Marx was an anti-Semite," "that nothing is more erroneous" than to consider him as such, because he treated the Jewish problem "entirely without prejudice," and that after all he did not really have "such a bad opinion" of the Jews as his harsh attacks would suggest. Finally, there are those for whom the whole problem seemingly does not exist, and who pass over it in complete silence… It would obviously be futile to argue with those whose wishful thinking is stronger than verifiable facts. If the pronouncements of Marx are not chosen at random, but are examined as a whole…Marx not only can but *must* be regarded as an outspoken anti-Semite…

Basically the same contempt for the Jews, though couched in a different language, is to be found in the writings of Karl Kautsky, Victor Adler, Franz Mehring, Otto Bauer, and others. Their cumulative impact, added to that of the master, must have been a considerable one… Hundreds of thousands, if not millions, of his adepts read *Zur Judenfrage* with the same zeal and ardor as they read the *Communist Manifesto*. Those who accepted his views were much more numerous than those who ventured to formulate objections or qualifications. Thus, willingly or not, Karl Marx contributed powerfully to provoke or to strengthen anti-Jewish prejudice among his Christian followers, and to estrange from their own people a good number of his Jewish admirers. He thus unquestionably holds one of the key positions in what may, or rather must, be designated by a new but appropriate term as the *anti-Semitic tradition of modern Socialism.* [Original emphasis]

Conclusions

While Karl Marx has had his apologists over the years, and while many have attempted to ignore, overlook, or whitewash his personal feelings, it can definitely be concluded that he did hold anti-Semitic attitudes. Some might say that one should not engage in "psychohistory," that is, one should ignore a man's personal life when one discusses his contribution to science, art, or politics, that it is at best interesting but irrelevant. Others might conclude that Marx's animosity towards individual Jews should not be confused with his attitudes toward Jews as a whole. Still other might say that one cannot become an "Anti-Defamation League of the past" and apply the same standards of today to Karl Marx's historical life and times.

While I will agree that Marx was a very complex man and that his attitude toward Jews and Judaism was likewise complex (see, for example, the works of Kurt Lewin on the subject of Jewish self-hatred), I remain unconvinced. Through Marx's writings, his own words, and through the interpretations of important scholars in the field, I have attempted to show that a form of self-hatred toward his people and his Jewish identity did in fact occur. Contrary to Friedland, Karl Marx went beyond simply having "reservations" about Jews and his Jewish antecedents. He went beyond indifference and minor annoyance about his Jewish past. He had a real and palpable disgust for Jews!

Though he was born a Jew and came from a long line of rabbis, some of his writings show a deep embarrassment and antipathy toward that Jewish identity. Many respected authorities (Silberner, Padover, Lipset, Laqueur, Bloom) have all come to the same conclusion—that Karl Marx's belief system had strong anti-Semitic components, and his view of the "Jew as Capitalist" has been echoing in anti-Semitic literature from both right-wing and left-wing anti-Semites. Such anti-Semitism, coming from a man like Karl Marx, can be considered a form of self-hatred regarding one's Jewish identity, an identity that Marx attempted to expunge during his entire life.

Marx's attitude toward the Jews was influenced by Bruno Bauer, but Marx went even further than Bauer by elaborating on Bauer's assertion that the Jews must overcome their religious parochialism (their Judaism) as a precondition for political and social emancipation. Marx went one step further and emphasized that the *religious* base of the Jews was essentially *secular*. To him, the natural role of *Judentum* (a German word, difficult to translate, that means not only Judaism but also commerce, hucksterism, or mercantilism), was its secular "money-hustling." In order to be truly liberated, the Jews must give up their huckstering and their reliance upon the "Jewish god of money."

Interestingly, Marx wanted to liberate the Jews not simply from Judaism but from what he saw as a Judaized form of Christianity. He felt that Jews should return to a more primal form of Christianity, a Christianity of sharing, doing good, living for others—in short, a form of primitive communism. Then, in such an atmosphere of a "dissolved" communitarian Christianity and a disappearing Judaism could European Jews truly be emancipated. This is what he meant when he wrote that the emancipation of the Jews is the emancipation of society from *Judentum*.

Implications

This essay has not been an exercise in "red-baiting," nor is it meant in any way to diminish Marx's enormous influence on Western civilization. I have simply attempted to point out a serious dilemma in Marxian philosophy regarding religion in general and Judaism in particular. While there have been numerous attempts both within the Jewish world (Labor Zionism, Bundism, the Jewish student movement of the 1960s) and within the non-Jewish (the Catholic left, the New Left) to modify orthodox Marxism on the question of religion and Judaism/Zionism and to find some middle road or compromise, the dilemma continues to exist. The situation of the Jews in the Soviet Union and in Israel and the leftist and Third World position on Zionism bears witness to Marx's legacy. The issue has *not* been resolved.

1981

Self-Hatred and Self-Esteem

From *Jewish Spectator*, Fall 1985, pp. 51-53.

* * *

THE TERM "self-hatred" is one of several concepts in sociology that remains controversial and ill-defined. Self-hatred, especially Jewish self-hatred, is not a new phenomenon; it was observed during the emancipation of minorities in Europe in the eighteenth and nineteenth centuries. The issue was raised by Otto Weininger in his 1903 book *Geschlecht und Character* [Sex and Character] and by Theodor Lessing in his 1930 book *Der Judische Selbsthass* [Jewish Self-Hate]. A number of novels and short stories have also dealt with various aspects of this theme, including the stories of Arthur Schnitzler, written at the turn of the century; Ludwig Lewisohn's *The Island Within*, published in 1928; and the works of contemporary writers such as Philip Roth's *Portnoy's Complaint*, Herman Wouk's *Marjorie Morningstar*, and Myron Kaufman's *Remember Me to God*.

The concept of self-hatred was first defined and analyzed *sociologically* in 1941 by the social psychologist Kurt Lewin, but since then very little research has been done to clarify the term. Lewin described Jewish self-hatred as follows:

> Jewish self-hatred is both a group phenomenon and an individual phenomenon...the self-hatred of a Jew may be directed against the Jews as a group, against a particular fraction of the Jews, against his own family, or against himself. It may be directed against Jewish institutions, Jewish mannerisms, Jewish language, or Jewish ideals... There is an almost endless variety of forms

which Jewish self-hatred may take... Most of them, and the most dangerous forms, are a kind of indirect, under-cover self-hatred. If I should count the instances where I have encountered open and straightforward contempt among Jews, I could name but a few... In most cases, expressions of hatred of the Jew against his fellow Jew or against himself as a Jew are more subtle. This hatred is so blended with other motives that it is difficult to decide in any one particular case whether or not self-hatred is involved.

The classic definition of self-hatred is disgust with aspects of one's identity or one's past. Self-hatred seems, however, to be the most extreme of many forms of self-denial. The concept has been applied to many minority groups; not only to Jews but also to Blacks, Chinese, women, and homosexuals, among others. It must be applied carefully because it can be misused. "Self-hatred" is a highly charged term, and because it falls into the cracks between sociology and psychology, social scientists have tended to shy away from using it or applying it too widely.

The following propositions pertain to self-hatred and self-denial.

Hypothesis 1: I propose that self-hatred should be regarded as a subcategory of *self-denial*; that self-denial be seen as the general concept, and self-hatred as the most extreme form of self-denial. Self-hatred is still a powerful and useful concept in understanding the dilemma of ethnic, racial, and religious identification, but it is really only one form of self-denial, and not the major one.

Hypothesis 2: Not only can minorities experience self-denial and self-hatred, but self-denial can exist to some degree within almost every human being. Everyone has some traits or aspects that are considered negative, abhorrent, or undesirable by others or by oneself. The individual may view these traits, whether ascribed or acquired, as something to deny, play down, or cover up. They can include weight, education or lack of education, facial features, ancestry, race, religion, or nationality. Almost any individual trait can be the basis for self-denial or self-hatred.

Hypothesis 3: Self-denial is simply the attempt to deny or cover up a trait that is seen as negative. When one begins to denigrate and hate that particular feature both in oneself and in others who share that feature, then self-denial becomes self-hatred. Self-hatred is the most extreme form of individual response to a "negative" trait.

Hypothesis 4: Although self-hatred is sometimes a psychopathological phenomenon growing out of a neurotic or abnormal personality, in the great majority of cases it occurs among people of normal mental health. This brings the concept of self-hatred out of the realm of psychology and into the area of sociology and social psychology.

Hypothesis 5: Self-denial can pertain to various aspects of personality, physiognomy, and lifestyle (see, for example, the book *Stigma* by Erving Goffman), but it has been applied most commonly in the area of ethnic relations. In the process of acculturation, the host culture encourages all immigrant groups to accentuate certain qualities and to suppress or remove others. These may include speech patterns, language, "old-fashioned" customs, religious values, or political beliefs. In fact, one price of liberation and emancipation is to deny or suppress one's past religious, ethnic, sexual or other kind of identity. This was especially true in the nineteenth and early to middle twentieth centuries, but today's minority groups, to their credit, want to be accepted as they are.

Hypothesis 6: Self-denial should be seen as a series of categories ranging from very extreme to very mild forms. We can identify the following types of self-denial.

a. *Extreme self-hatred:* Examples of extreme self-denial or self-hatred are individuals of Jewish or part-Jewish ancestry who join the Nazi Party. Leading examples are the American Frank Collins, who leads the Chicago Nazi party, or the late Daniel Burros, the young man of Jewish background who rose to leadership in the Ku Klux Klan and the American Nazi Party, and who committed suicide when his secret was discovered. Both men saw something weak and despicable in their previous identity and wished not only to rid themselves of it but to eliminate all others (i.e., Jews) who shared that identity. Vander Zanden provides other examples of this type in describing American Blacks and Japanese who are disgusted by others of their own race and who wish to deny their own roots.

b. *Mild self-hatred:* This category includes minor forms of self-denial such as "passing," conversion, or assimilation, but without the extreme and sometimes pathological acts of type (a).

c. *Indifference:* One can feel indifferent to one's identity or one's past, neither hating it nor loving it. More activist members of the minority, however, may see this kind of indifference as a form of denial or assimilation. It may be likened to "fiddling while Rome burns," especially if the minority group is currently under persecution. Thus indifference can be considered a form of "copping out" from the struggle for liberation.

d.   *Ambivalence:* Human beings, being complex creatures, may sometimes manifest two attitudes that seem on the surface to be mutually exclusive: they may reject part of their identity but still have fond feelings for it. That is, complete self-denial is as rare as complete self-hatred or complete self-acceptance. Conversion, assimilation, self-denial, or "passing" do not necessarily mean that the individual feels totally negative about all aspects of his or her previous religious, ethnic, or sexual identity. The former homosexual who is now living as a heterosexual may have pleasant memories of his earlier life. The Black who has "passed" may feel the same way. Ambivalence is especially prevalent if self-denial brings a reward: if, by denying aspects of the self, one gains wider access to society or attains a higher socioeconomic status. In such cases, one must deny in order to be socially mobile. In the nineteenth century, for example, Jews had to convert to Christianity in order to practice law or medicine or to enter universities or "high society." Karl Marx's father had to convert to practice law—in short, out of sheer economic necessity—but he retained an affection for Judaism and his Jewish ancestry for the rest of his life. Although some aspects of self-denial can always be found in conversion, some types of intermarriage, and assimilation, it need not be an extreme form of self-hatred.

e.   *Acceptance of self with minor self-denial:* This is a most common form of self-denial: one basically accepts one's identity and past but may not be totally happy with all aspects of it. In this case one changes some aspects, rejects others, feels ambivalent or indifferent toward still others. If one is unhappy about one's weight or hair, one gains (or loses) weight or hair; if one is unhappy about one's sexuality, one can change it, deny it, or suppress it; if one is uncomfortable about one's racial or religious identity, one can accept some parts of it and reject other parts. Individuals vary in what they will accept and what they will deny or change, and it is impossible to predict the variations. Certain traits are easier to suppress than others, and the general society may not allow one to forget some traits. A Jew may convert or attempt to "pass," for example, but others will not allow him to forget that he is still a Jew despite his new religion or appearance.

Self-hatred is often indirect and accompanied by ambivalent feelings of superiority and chauvinism. As long as those of higher status define a minority as inferior in some way, and as long as discrimination and prejudicial attitudes within the higher-status group prevent an individual from escaping minority status, the minority person is caught in a dilemma. This dilemma generates various responses, such as self-denial in various forms, including self-hatred. Self-denial may include feelings of unworthiness and negative attitudes towards one's ancestry. In the case of Jews it may lead to the "anti-Semitic Jew" or the "non-Jewish Jew."

It must be added that self-denial and self-hatred are only one set of responses to minority status. Others include militancy and exaggerated chauvinism on the part of the minority, accommodation, or isolation. A fourth possibility is a secessionist movement, such as Zionism or the Black Muslim movement, which wishes to find a homeland for the minority so that it will no longer be forced to live in an oppressive or prejudiced society. In this way a "new man or woman" can emerge, who will not suffer from self-denial or self-hatred.

SECESSIONISM often goes hand in hand with minority militancy or activism because in order to conceive of a new homeland, one must first have sufficient pride in one's minority ancestry and traditions. Thus, Jewish or Black activism stresses Jewish or Black pride. Most Zionists, for example, are proud and actively involved Jews. A second theory posits that secessionism may reduce prejudice against minorities. This has not happened, but early Zionist thinkers felt that the return of the Jewish people to the land of Israel would significantly reduce anti-Semitism.

In any case, minority militancy and activism are "enemies" of minority self-hatred. They are the antidote for self-hatred because they demand that the minority member feel pride for his or her identity. Activism and militancy fight prejudice rather than attempting to acquiesce, ignore, or accommodate it. They are powerful tools in counteracting self-hatred.

A more sophisticated form of denial is to reject the particularism of the minority and embrace a more universalistic philosophy or ideology. For Jews, this has meant the rejection of Judaism as too limiting and constricting and the acceptance, for example, of socialism.

The concept of self-hatred must be handled with care because it can be used as an *ad hominem* oversimplification. The term was used first by Kurt Lewin, not in a pejorative but in a scientific way.

"Self-hatred" should not be used as the generic term for *all* forms of assimilation or rejection of previous socialization and identity. A better and less confusing generic term would be *self-denial*. This concept would embrace a range of responses including ambivalence, indifference, rejection mixed with affection, and mild to extreme self-hatred.

The reluctance on the part of sociologists to use the term "self-hatred" is based on two factors: the provocative and oversimplified connotation of the term and the confusion over whether self-hatred describes a psychological state of mind or a sociological reaction to minority status. Because it can slide into the realm of psychological reductionism, sociologists have made only limited use of "self-hatred" since Kurt Lewin first wrote about it. The term is still useful, however, when applied correctly and with precision. Self-hatred can be defined as the extreme rejection of a previous or present identity or aspects of that identity, and the development of an extreme form of denial or denigration of that identity.

Regarding minority groups, those groups that have suffered persecution or discrimination are likely to include members who exhibit some for of self-denial, including self-hatred. This self-denial may manifest itself in various ways: embarrassment and avoidance of fellow group members; stereotyping of fellow members; a desire to assimilate into the host society; or a desire to transcend both the minority and majority culture by constructing an entirely new identity that goes beyond both.

In the last example, the person will reject both the minority and the majority group and will not attempt to assimilate into the higher-status group. Instead, he or she will attempt to build a new society that transcends categorization of people into ethnic, religious, racial, or sexual compartments. This kind of person is exemplified best by the political revolutionaries, who wish to classify people according to economic status and not by race, religion, sex, or ethnicity. Such people can manifest self-hatred, but they transcend even that with their desire to go beyond simple hatred of their past identities and to build a new society in which such "old-fashioned" categories as religion or race are no longer necessary. Because of this more complex response some sociologists (and others) have rejected the notion of self-hatred when applied to political revolutionaries.

Self-denial and self-hatred have been common among Jews, but the Jews have succeeded in replacing these feelings with self-esteem. Certainly Zionism and the establishment of the State of Israel were (and still are) factors in limiting and reducing Jewish self-hatred. Now that the process is under way, we would do well to examine other means within the Jewish community for increasing self-esteem; these might include education, counseling, and positive Jewish programming.

Fall 1985

Can a Sociologist be a Revolutionist?

This essay has never been published before; it was written probably around 1969 while I was a sociology graduate student at Northwestern and heavily influenced by the radical movements of the times. We were all struggling with the time-honored question: can one be a scholar and an activist at the same time? Can one do good scholarly work while at the same time being a radical or a revolutionary, or is the university a place only for *objective* scholarship? And, is scholarship ever totally "objective"? These debates resonate today and for all time.

* * *

What is a rebel? A man who says no, but whose refusal does not imply a renunciation. He is also a man who says yes, from the moment he makes his first gesture of rebellion.
— Albert Camus, 1956:13

Introduction

The title of this paper is not an academic exercise. It has been restated before in many formats and in many ways, though I seriously doubt whether it has been allowed to be debated in the "establishment" journals of the social sciences to a degree commensurate to its importance.

The rise of radical sociology is not new—see the "social agitator" works of E.A. Ross, Robert Lynd, and C. Wright Mills. Today it is a response to the radical times we live in. One can find many definitions for revolution, but one can use Webster's just as well: "Revolution is a state of rapid social change, with or without violence, leading to a dispersal or reversal of power and a new political consciousness and/or life style."

That this word may cause dismay to many social scientists is due to the milieu they find themselves in. America has lost its charisma; its history of revolution has been relegated to a storybook tale of some men who masquerade as Indians; its history of violence and hate has been subdued or repressed.

Those of us who have begun to ask "new questions" have been forced to relearn our history and our sociology in order to find a more "useable past." I am reminded of a quote by Henry Steele Commager: "We should not forget that our tradition is one of protest and revolt, and it is stultifying to celebrate the rebels of the past while we silence the rebels of the present."

A generation of sociologists has been born who seek not only a "useable past" but a model for the future—a model to rid ourselves of racism, poverty, political repression, and imperialist wars. It is a search for a utopian model in an age of technocratic expertise and "overkill."

The Question at Hand

The question at hand is whether a sociologist can also be a revolutionist? Allow me to state my thesis now and discuss its rationale shortly. I believe it is extremely difficult, if not impossible, to be a revolutionist and a sociologist. The question is a difficult one, since it assumes at its foundation a commonalty of meaning, a common definition for both the words "revolutionist" and "sociologist." And since there are nearly as many definitions for these words as there are sociologists and revolutionists, then one can easily see the pitfalls of this discussion. We will never agree on terms.

Words are only words, but Sartre and others have said we are defined and we define others by our acts. It is in action, in what we do, that we come to grips with not only the ramifications of the present discussion, but also the meaning of our own existential lifestyles. I'd rather judge a man or woman by what they *do* than by what they *say*. And I define the revolutionist and the sociologist by his or her acts. There is no question that the revolutionist is first off considered a man of action, and secondly, a man of words; the sociologist is the reverse. For the sociologist, words, both written and verbal, lay the foundation for his *Weltanschauung* (world outlook); words comes first, acts come later if at all. Here we already see a split, a bifurcation, between the two worlds.

How one defines the words "revolutionist" and "sociologist" will lead directly to how one answers the question. By "revolutionist," I mean anyone who proclaims what Herbert Marcuse called "the Great Refusal" and is ready, willing and able to give his energies, and even his life, for an ideolog-ical, religious, economic or political cause. Unless one is willing to give up his life for the cause, one can never call oneself a revolutionist—a radical, yes; but not a revolutionist—never.

Some will say that this is a very narrow or even naïve or romantic notion of what a revolutionist is. That may very well be true, yet I want to "save" the word "revolutionist" for this special case. I fear that the word is too easily applied, too easily misused, and too easily clichéd.

In America, especially in this vast technocratic McLuhanist society, when we see a "revolution in soap" or a "new revolutionary pair of nylons," we can see how first the word, and then the individual, is co-opted by the mechanical fingers of the mass media. I want a new, non-co-optable definition.

Now for the definition of a sociologist. Somehow, defining a sociol-ogist is more difficult for me. I can define a sociologist simply in occupa-tional terms and then cop-out nicely from the argument. But I'll make it tougher on myself—and define "sociologist" in a more disciplined, more intellectual manner. My definition will probably not satisfy everyone, but here goes:

"A sociologist is a man or woman who seeks truth, seeks to understand, empathize, and explain the profundities and complexities of society and its components within a historical, theoretical, and methodological discipline called sociology."

One can do this within the confines of a university or in one's own home. One's lifestyle and mode of inquiry may be radical, liberal, conserv-ative, or reactionary, either as a citizen or as a scholar but almost never as a revolutionist *qua* sociologist.

Well, one could say, "I agree with your definition. I attempt to under-stand and empathize with the society, yet I still define myself as a revolu-tionist—so I can be both—and I am willing even to give up my life."

"For sociology?" I will ask.

"No, of course not," he will answer. "For the oppressed, for the colo-nized, for the Blacks, for my own commitment to freedom and truth."

Yet in answering in this way, his allegiance is no longer to sociology but to a higher ideal. This form of intellectual ambivalence, this split personal-ity, is common among many radicals or left-liberal sociologists. They will never find peace of mind (will any of us?) if this ambivalence persists. It is the plight of all intellectuals, not just of sociologists.

We sociologists should not become martyrs. We must make a choice—to be a full-time revolutionist or a full-time sociologist. What shall it be? Che Guevara was not a revolutionist sitting behind a desk—he went to Bolivia. A sociologist cannot be a revolutionist by dealing with chi-squares or distributing questionnaires, or even by giving radicalizing speeches and/or lectures to his class—or even by speaking at SDS[2] rallies and scurrying back to his desk. It won't work that way.

Yet many will live this dual life and by doing so will fail ultimately as revolutionists. There are sociologists, their patron saints being C. Wright Mills or maybe Herbert Marcuse, who attempt an amalgamation. They are the radical sociologists. They have brought, and will continue to bring, innovations into the sociological discipline; they will expand what Mills called the "sociological imagination"; they will make sociology more relevant, more active, and more vibrant; they may even transform sociology.

They will not, however, transform society; they will not attack the seats of power; they will not overturn the economic and political structure; they will not release Blacks and other oppressed groups from bondage; in short, they will win the battle and lose the war. They will shake up the discipline of sociology but not the technocratic structures of today. Maybe a Marx could have done it, but how many Marx's are there in history?

But the argument will fall on deaf ears to some sociologists. There are radical sociologists at places like Northwestern, Rutgers, UC–Santa Barbara, McGill, the University of Oregon, who are fine sociologists, but they are not revolutionists as long as they hold onto their jobs and tenure.

There is, however, a strong argument for being both a sociologist and a revolutionist, namely that it is the role of the sociologists to learn, understand and describe the objective conditions of the society such that the masses will acquire revolutionary consciousness and thereby bring about the revolution. This is the traditional Marxian role of the intellectuals—to act as a guide for the masses over the revolutionary terrain, to forecast and predict the conditions manifested in the society in order to facilitate and accelerate the revolution.

A good argument, but it suffers from two shortcomings. One, sociologists, like all social scientists, are poor prophets; they are still struggling to define the present conditions to themselves, let alone to the masses and

---

2   Students for a Democratic Society, a national student activist organization in the United States from 1960 to 1970. A main representation of the New Left, it was conceived as a broad exercise in "participatory democracy."

let alone to predict the future. Furthermore, the American intellectual has distrust and a fear of the working class, of the masses. Two, the sociologist is constrained by his own discipline—to seek answers slowly and methodically. This disciplined approach impedes action, though it may absolve mistakes due to faulty planning.

Thus, because the consciousness of the revolutionist is so different from the sociologist, because his tactics are so different, and because his lifestyle is so different, I see no compromise and thus no solution to the dilemma. To merge the two will perforce change one or the other, and it is sociology that will change. It will in the process be so transformed that it will no longer be sociology—but an intellectual appendage to the revolution.

The process of being a sociologist and then becoming a revolutionist is painful but interesting to observe. C. Wright Mills may have come closest, and may even have succeeded, but he no longer would have been a sociologist! In fact, toward the end of his life, he was a pamphleteer, not a sociologist. This is fine—pamphleteers are needed. Mills knew this and understood his own transformation. It is a pity he is not alive today. I would have liked to have gone to him for an answer to these questions (Mills died at age 45 in 1962, seven years before this essay—author's note).

The question is not new. Max Weber grappled with it when he wrote "Science as a Vocation" and "Politics as a Vocation" (see Gerth & Mills, 1960). Durkheim[3] also exhibited the strain of this conflict, and so have all thinking and active sociologists. The question will continue to be asked by radical sociologists like myself and by my peers. And as the "revolution" approaches, we will still be asking the question. In fact, we will be asking before, during and after the revolution. For, like the revolutionists, we sociologists also seek the truth and the ultimate answers to our own existence.

1969

---

3   Émile Durkheim (1858-1917), a French sociologist who formally established the academic discipline of sociology as one of the main founders of modern social science besides W. E. B. Du Bois, Karl Marx and Max Weber.

III. Jewish Radicals: History

Morris U. Schappes:
Jewish Radical Historian—
An Interview

Morris U. Schappes, born in the Ukraine on May 3, 1907, was 85 years old when I taped this interview with him in his Manhattan apartment on a hot, muggy afternoon, July 14, 1992. The apartment itself is a miniature library, a scholar's library of immense strength and utility. Ever since the early 1970s, Morris has been an inspiration and a mentor to me. He published my very first article, "Jewish Student Activism," in *Jewish Currents* in May 1970 and reprinted it also as a pamphlet. His integrity and perseverance have been a steadying influence on me and many other radical Jews and Jewish radicals of my generation for a quarter century—longer, of course, for others. In *Jewish Currents*, May 1997, p. 5-7, 32-33. Reprinted by permission of *Jewish Currents*.

* * *

JNP: How did you become a radical Jew / Jewish radical?

MUS: You have to give me a timeframe, Jack. How did I become a radical? Well, it's a long story. As you know, I was born in Kamenetz-Pololsk, Ukraine, in 1907 and was brought to America in July, 1914, by my parents, who came to the USA by way of Argentina and Brazil. I was educated in the New York public school system, graduate from City College in 1928 and was promptly appointed to a minimal teaching post in the English Department of that college, where I taught until 1941. In 1930 I obtained an M.A. degree from Columbia University, but discontinued my doctoral work in 1934 for reasons I will soon explain.

JNP: You were fired from City College in 1941?

MUS: Yes, there was a purge of Communists on campus, and I and some 40 others were fired, forced to resign, or not reappointed. I later went to prison for 13½ months in upstate New York for refusing to become an informer, but we are getting off-track. That is another story that I have told in the pages of *Jewish Currents*, a journal I have edited since 1958 in New York. But I'd like to get back to your original question, Jack.

JNP: On how you became a radical?

MUS: Yes, but the answer takes a bit of time to unfold. During my first two years of teaching at City College, I was a graduate student at Columbia, doing my M.A. thesis on an obscure English literary critic and poet named William Ernest Henley (1849-1903).

JNP: Never heard of him.

MUS: Yes, most people haven't, but perhaps you've heard of a poem called "Invictus," and its line, "My head is bloody but unbowed."

JNP: Yes, that line I've heard.

MUS: Well, it was by Henley. I bring it up only to show you that at the beginning I was not concerned with Jewish matters at all, and I was not even a historian. I taught English literature and composition. I wanted to be a teacher. I won all three English Department prizes at City College. But I was also an immigrant boy. I spoke Yiddish, Spanish and a little Portuguese. I had been a brilliant student in elementary school (P.S. 64 on Ave. B and 10th St. on the Lower East Side), and so I was skipped into upper grades. They didn't have special classes for the gifted then as they do now. They just skipped you ahead a grade. I came from the Yiddish-speaking Lower East Side. I still remember the Jacob Schiff milk stations in the adjoining Tompkins Square Park. You didn't have bottled milk then; the grocer dipped a dipper into a big can and poured it into the container you brought. You paid a few pennies, and that's what you drank.

JNP: You came from a poor family?

MUS: Yes, I came from poverty, but I was very bright. That's important to understand. I dressed in knickers, a clean-cut kid, and all the rest. It was a different era. Because I was bright, a sympathetic teacher arranged that I be sent to Townsend Harris Hall High School, a special prep school for City College. In 1920 I entered this high school for gifted kids who were expected to complete the four-year high school curriculum in three years.

The "culture shock" was enormous, going from the poor Yiddish-speaking Lower East Side to what was then an upper-class, German-Jewish neighborhood on the Upper West Side, and because of this "shock" I began to stammer. I had been a *fluent* public speaker at P.S. 64; in selling World War I 25-cent war-saving stamps, I was making two-minute public speeches on street corners. We Lower East Side kids dressed differently; we had different manners, etc. It's no wonder it was all a "shock." As a result, it took me four years to finish instead of three!

I was literally thrown into the melting pot. I was a product...no, a victim...of the compulsory assimilation prevailing in the educational system of the 1920s, forcing us to stop being Jewish and melt into "Americans." I can still remember the teachers in the City College Education Department warning me about retaining any Yiddish "inflection" (not even a Yiddish accent) if I ever wanted to be a public school teacher. This attitude to Yiddish drove a wedge between me and my parents. Here's an example:

Sometimes on weekends my parents took a long subway ride way out to Brooklyn to visit my cousin. My mother read Yiddish but my father was illiterate, so my mother read the newspaper to him quietly as we rode. But I would have nothing to do with them. I tried to sit as far away as possible on the train so as not to be seen with parents reading a Yiddish newspaper! The desire to be a teacher taught me to fear my own roots, my own family's language and traditions.

JNP: And this was your "Americanization" process, a separation from your roots?

MUS: Yes, and mind you, I was still no radical. Just to show you: I won a City College English Department prize for an essay extolling the virtues of Mussolini and fascism, noting how he made the trains run on time and other nonsense. So, how did I evolve into a radical?

My first contact with protest against our social system came when, as a Lower East Side boy, I saw my father come home with the strike committee of his shop for a meeting one afternoon. My father, a wood-turner, was a union member and had become an anarchist in Argentina.

My next contact with social activism came when, at a City College dance in 1927, I met the Hunter College student who, in 1930, became my wife for 62 years (she died April 9, 1992). But let me pick this up later in our interview.

Then came the influence of some of the City College students. When the economic crisis of 1929 hit this country and unemployment was staggering, many high school graduates, unable to get any jobs, applied to the then totally tuition-free municipal colleges, City, Hunter and Brooklyn College. The student body expanded. In fact, one reason why I was appointed in 1928 to teach as a humble Fellow in the City College English Department was that new, poorly paid, untenured teachers were needed to meet the new influx of students.

Among the Jewish students, there were many who had parents who were trade unionists, and some were socialists and communists. On campus also there was the Young Communist League (YCL) and the Young People's Socialist League (YPSL). In fact, in 1932 the socialist candidate Norman Thomas got the biggest vote at City College during the mock student elections. These students definitely had an effect on their teachers. So my students were an influence on me.

I also remember a number of Black clubs: the Frederick Douglass Society and the Meroë Society (Meroë was an ancient African kingdom). My first experience in Black-Jewish relations (in which I have in a sense specialized ever since) came from that time in the early 1930s at City College.

JNP: Were there other influences?

MUS: Yes. The rise of Hitlerism and the growth of anti-Semitic organizations in the 1930s both in Europe and here in the USA helped radicalize me. So did the Bund: not the European Socialist Yiddish Bund but the German Hitlerite Bund. So did Father Charles E. Coughlin in the Midwest, with his Union for Social Justice and his anti-Semitic newspaper, *Social Justice*. Remember him? There was also the Christian Front, another right-wing group, with a strong base in Brooklyn. They all made City College a target of abuse—it was seen as a nest of "Jewish commies."

Christian Frontists attacked Jews with beards right here in Brooklyn. Do you know where Yorkville is? You were just there, near the UN Building and the Anti-Defamation League Building, between 55th and 90th Street on the East Side. Many German-Americans lived there. These hate groups, the Christian Front, the German Bund, appealed to them, and Jews were physically attacked in Yorkville.

I became aware of all this. I started reading the papers, the left-wing papers, including the *Daily Worker*. I studied Marx's economic and historical writings. This radicalized me.

JNP: And your schooling?

MUS: After getting my 1930 M.A. at Columbia, I continued my doctoral studies at Columbia and began work on a dissertation on Emily Dickinson (1830-1886). I got in touch with the Dickinson family. They liked me and I got access to all her papers. Dickinson, as you know, wrote her poems in off-rhymes, but I discovered that her family was unhappy with that and changed her lines so that, if possible, they rhymed! In a paper in *American Literature*, a learned journal, I listed how the family had corrupted her rhymes.

After that, the family practically "excommunicated" me and barred me from access to her papers on which the family still owned the copyright. This exercise of capitalist property rights in the field of poetry itself outraged me, and confirmed my studies of Marxism. I dropped all my Ph.D. work at Columbia and to this day I have never gotten my Ph.D.

JNP: And now, back to your wife, or I should say, future wife and her influence.

MUS: Yes. My wife's name was Sonya Laffer. Her mother, Celia Laffer, had been an active member of the Jewish Bund in Latvia, an underground revolutionary movement. When I began to visit Sonya at her home in the Bronx, where her parents made a poor living by running a little fishing-tackle store in which most of the business was in selling worms to fishermen, I was fascinated by her mother's accounts of the Bund activities and socialist ideology.

Celia Laffer was a very unusual woman. She read Tolstoy, Dostoyevsky, and Plekhanov in Yiddish translation! She told me fantastic stories about her work in the Bund underground. One story I remember was about her hiding radical pamphlets in her corset in order to smuggle them to another city in Latvia where the Bund was active. She was searched by police but they never looked into her corset. So, Sonya, my future wife, was brought up in that kind of atmosphere, and her mother had an impact on me. When I courted Sonya, I was received very cordially by her mother. Mrs. Laffer not only had an impact on my radicalization but also in my Jewish-ization, so to speak, contributing to my Jewish consciousness. She had read the great Yiddish writers and talked to me about them.

Also, Sonya went to a Bronx Yiddish *shule* (school) run by a socially conscious secular Yiddish group. After we got married in 1930, we joined the IWO (International Workers Order), which provided medical services and a life insurance policy for $1,000, which was a lot of money in those days.

Early in the 1930s, when I was teaching at City College, I was invited to teach at the *mittelshul* (Jewish high school) run by the education department of the IWO. There, on Friday evenings, I met kids who had Yiddish-speaking radical parents. I taught them English literature based on the courses I taught at the college.

The IWO also had a women's division, which was interested in Emma Lazarus (1849-1887), the Jewish poet whose famous sonnet, "The New Colossus," is on a plaque in the base of the Statue of Liberty. She was kind of a hero to them. She wrote about Jewish immigrants—the "huddled masses yearning to breathe free"—and defended them.

This women's division, which later became the Emma Lazarus Federation of Jewish Women's Clubs, asked me to prepare a book of her poetry and prose, which I did in the winter of 1944, completing it just before I had to go to prison. Incidentally, the book has gone through five editions up to 1982 [and is still in print in 1997—M.U.S.].

JNP: So literature was the bridge?

MUS: Yes, poetry was the bridge from Jewish radicalism to a radically committed Jew with an expending awareness of Jewish culture and literature. I turned from Emily Dickinson to Emma Lazarus. Of course, my serving 13½ months in prison put an end to any possibility of an academic career for over 30 years, when I was invited to teach at Queens College, 1972-1976.

The next stage in this radicalization process and "Jewish-ization" (a cultural/ethnic process, not a religious one) came when, in preparing my work on Emma Lazarus, I had to do research in American Jewish history of that period. I learned that no historian with a Marxist approach had written anything extensive in American Jewish history. The result was *A Documentary History of the Jews in the United States, 1654-1875*, published in 1950, which soon won for me a respected place in American Jewish historiography. My book, *The Jews in the United States: A Pictorial History, 1654 to the Present*, was published in 1958.

I came up with fresh new material and perspectives that other American Jewish historians had understated, such as the history of workers, the labor movement and of women, Blacks and other minorities. All of this was intertwined, the merging of my Jewish/Yiddish background with my radical Marxian ideology.

May 1997

Yizhak Ahren and Jack Nusan Porter

Martin Buber and the American Jewish Counterculture

In *Judaism: A Quarterly Magazine*, 115, Vol. 29, No. 3, Summer 1980, pp. 332-339. Reprinted by permission of co-author Yitzhak Ahren.

* * *

I

Every society has its heroes and its intimate enemies. Such relationships are especially evident in a so-called counterculture whose members feud with a certain "Establishment" and its visible representatives, and who strive to identify alternatives, strike out in new directions, and propagate new options. In the 1960s, the New Left celebrated Ho Chi Minh and Che Guevara, and the books of Wilhelm Reich, Paul Goodman and Herbert Marcuse became required reading in leftist subcultures and on college campuses. American hippies made Thoreau their patron saint and Hermann Hesse's works experienced a revival.

Certain books served as the basis for communal experiments—an attempt to turn a literary work into actuality. The best-known examples are the Walden Two communes, modeled after a novel by psychologist B.F. Skinner, and the Harrad West experiment, patterned after a novel by Robert Rimmer. Sometimes the counterculture revives traditions which, at first glance, strike one as strange. For several groups in the American counterculture, the *I Ching*, the ancient Chinese "Book of Transformations," assumed an importance that should not be underestimate. Klaus Mehnert reports about one commune that decided, on the basis of the *I Ching* oracle, to transfer itself completely from Vermont to New Mexico.

The Jewish counterculture, which came into being in America and Europe after the 1967 Six-Day War, has its "gurus" and "rebbes" as well. This counterculture had two aspects: a political one and a spiritual-cultural one. Martin Buber (1878-1965) had a great influence on the American Jewish counterculture movement and was instrumental in bringing the two halves; that is, finding a means of politicizing theology and theologizing politics. We will investigate what use of misuse the counterculture made of Buber's writings and what can be pursued with those writings in the future.

II

A new culture, a new religio-political movement of renewal, like the Jewish student movement, is a diverse and multi-varied area of activity that is not easy to describe. Where shall one begin? What divisions are meaningful? One must realize that it is problematic to expect unambiguous situations and precise definitions. Rather, we observe constant transformations, and we must acknowledge that things are far more complex than an outsider may at first imagine. Only when one is ready to work with paradoxical categories like conflict, ambivalence, and transitions of this type will one understand why Buber's work became so important to the American Jewish counterculture.

Anyone familiar with the literature of the Jewish counterculture will have no difficulty in documenting Buber's influence, for he is quoted rather frequently, and often in decisive places. The first anthology from this new movement has, as an epigraph, a passage from Buber's *Hasidism and Modern Man*. Mark Goldes chose a Buber statement as a motto for his Seder haggadah and dedicated this liturgical work "to the living memory of Martin Buber." Evidently Buber is not only a recognized authority whom the members of the Jewish counterculture like to cite as support, but they find in his writings excellent formulations of what they really want to express. Here is a good example: When, in the fall of 1974, the editors of the highly regarded periodical, *Response*, presented their individual plans, one editor contented herself with a quotation from Buber! Furthermore, Buber's name need not always be mentioned; e.g., a Los Angeles poet, Mark

Hurvitz, arranged a Buber anecdote about the Baal Shem Tov (the founder of Hasidism) in the form of a Star of David and juxtaposed a few additions, thus turning it into a riddle, but did not deem it necessary to state his source. Even if no direct reference is made to the master, there sometimes is no disregarding the fact that the authors of certain writings still are in their "buberty," if one can be pardoned that expression. The polemical poem, "This Is the Bus to Auschwitz" written by members of a group called Jews for Urban Justice, invokes Buber's ideals (prophets, Hasidic communities, kibbutzim). It was prompted by the inauguration of an "Establishment" institution (a synagogue and J.C.C.[1]), and the aggressive verses, to be sure, are a very American "translation" whose tone would probably have shocked Buber. As was to be expected, preoccupation with Buber's work has also led to criticism of him.

Which writings of Buber have attracted the attention of the American Jewish student movement? If we follow his own arrangement of his collected writings, we can proceed from four units: Hasidism, I-Thou philosophy, Bible and Zionism/Israel/Judaism. This handy arrangement should not blind us to the inner connection of the various areas; only if one is aware of the structure of the complete work does one notice "gaps." To give an immediate answer to the question, we can say that young Americans have taken cognizance of and "worked on" all *four* units of Buber's work.

III

Buber's most popular work is, undoubtedly, his *Tales of the Hasidim.* In some circles these anecdotes are regarded as Torah; they are read aloud during the Sabbath meal and, side-by-side with the writings of Erich Fromm and A.J. Heschel, they are even included in English-language religious services. Waskow's justification for including these writings in the liturgy is remarkable; he points to a precedent: "Services in our liturgy treated Buber, Fromm, and Heschel as seriously as our forefathers' liturgy treated Maimonides in *Yigdal.*" Let us mention parenthetically that this comparison is quite strange. Martin Buber did not participate in synagogue services as a matter of principle, yet the Jews for Urban Justice in Washington include him in their services. They want to "learn" something from the master, but they do not want to copy his lifestyle.

---

1   Jewish Cultural Center.

The renowned Hebrew writer, S.J. Agnon, remarked several decades ago that Buber's writings on Hasidism helped many Jews who had strayed from Judaism to rediscover the religion of their forefathers. Evidently, the Hasidic anecdotes make access possible to the world of a specifically Jewish tradition. While reading these stories, an outsider makes discoveries; he gains insight into new connections, comprehends the meaning of certain symbols or customs, and finds himself force to revise his own prejudices about Hasidism and religious life. Occasionally, the reader will come to terms with a hitherto disregarded aspect of Judaism. Arthur I. Waskow's autobiographical and confessional work, *The Bush Is Burning! Radical Judaism Faces the Pharaohs of the Modern Superstate*, contains, among other things, a detailed description of a transformation which took place in 1968-69 and which the author reduces to this formula: "From Jewish Radical to Radical Jew." Many events and encounters led to this metamorphosis, and tales about Hasidic masters also play a certain role. Let us note here that Buber's anecdotes can act as such a catalyst.

A further possibility for entering the world of the Jewish faith that Martin Buber has created may be seen in his translation of the Bible into German. The intention of this new translation, which attempts to preserve the original character of the Hebrew language, has not always been understood. For example, an article on Buber's 100th birthday contained this objection: "Why [is there] such a senseless obscuring of the Bible's contents?" Many years ago, Ernst Simon formulate the answer to this question as follows: "It is a matter of estranging the Bible in order to make it accessible again, now that it has been freed from the 'taint of familiarity' (Buber) and can once again arouse primal attention." At the celebration of Buber's completion of the Bible, Gershom Scholem said that the main intent of the enterprise may have been an invitation to the reader to go and study Hebrew! This meant that Buber wanted to guide his readers back to the original text. "Study Hebrew" means, of course, more than simply learning the language.

Buber's invitation to the Bible was also proclaimed by the American Jewish counterculture. Here we must refer to Everett Fox's writings in *Response* magazine. Fox not only wrote essays about Buber's and Franz Rosenzweig's method of translation, but also tried his hand at the difficult art of Bible translation himself. He rendered the Book of Genesis into English, based on the Buber-Rosenzweig German version. Fox also translated additional texts—the Book of Jonah, Psalm 137, and the first two chapters of the Book of Job. In the religious communities of the Jewish student movement (e.g., the Boston group, Havurat Shalom), Fox's work is greatly appreciated.

To Scholem's worried question as to the medium in which Buber's translation would be effective, we can give an answer which Scholem certainly did not expect, and which certainly could not have been foreseen in 1961. It is true that most of the children of those who have escaped the Holocaust cannot read German, but English-speaking young people now have a chance at least to become acquainted with the Bible in the way that Buber saw it and had taught others to see it.

In the Jewish counterculture, religion and politics often coalesce. Its members study not only Buber's writings on religion but, also, his socio-philosophical and political analyses. The newsletter of a group in Washington included this notice:

> Weekly seminar on Marxism, Anarchism, and Judaism. Bring a copy of Buber's *Paths in Utopia* and Marcuse's *Essay on Liberation;* we will read aloud from them as in Talmud study, stopping to discuss and raise questions whenever we wish.

Buber's basic attitude toward controversial issues in the Zionist movement is generally known in student circles and it is safe to say that his position is regarded as correct and relevant by many activists of the younger generation, though not by all.

It is not hard to guess why Buber's conflict with the prevailing Zionist ideology is so greatly admired. He wanted to work within the Zionist Organization, but, at the same time, he wished to effect basic change in its position on important questions. The "New Jews" of the 1960s saw themselves in a similar position. They fought on campus against the increasingly anti-Israel attitude of the New Left by presenting Zionism as a liberation movement which every progressive-minded person had to support; therefore, they received financial support for various projects from established Zionist sources. But these Zionist activists did not conceal their critical attitude toward the Zionist "Establishment" in both America and Israel. The World Union of Jewish Students (WUJS) which, after 1968, tried to bring about changes in major Zionist policies, finally had to fight for its own independent existence and had trouble surviving the 27th Zionist Congress (1972). In internal Zionist debates, Buber represented the "loyal opposition," and that is what the representatives of the Jewish counterculture want to do.

IV

Let us now turn to another area of Buber's impact. In 1963, Eugen Rosenstock-Huessy wrote:

> Buber's philosophy of I and Thou has not been absorbed, but it is respectfully quoted, though in strangely constricted form. Everyone knows the title of the book and everyone bows solemnly when it is mentioned, but that is all. For this reverence costs nothing, and everyone busily continues to treat his fellow human beings as objects of his study.

In the American counterculture, the words "I and Thou" are often referred to and, invariably, problems of norms of behavior are involved. Reminiscing about his period in the Boston Havurat Shalom, Joseph Reimer writes:

> We believed—following Buber—that the test of a religious community is the extent to which its members overcome the impersonality of "I—It" relationships and are open to one another as "Thou's." I think we overestimate the extent to which intimacies could be shared among a whole community. It was hard, though, to admit this to ourselves.

Arthur Waskow has also tried to demonstrate that even complex problems of modern society can be dealt with, with the aid of Buber's basic words.

The word-pair "I—Thou" frequently crops us in discussions about Jewish religious law (*halakhah*). In this context, the reference to Buber's philosophy serves as a defense against the demand that the codified *halakhah* be recognized as a binding norm and that the law be fulfilled as far as possible. Michael G. Berenbaum has pointed out that the debate about Jewish law which took place between Rosenzweig and Buber in the 1920s is being revived in the American Jewish counterculture fifty years later. He writes: "I contend that the values which inform the Havurah movement are Buberian." This statement contains some truth, but, in the counterculture, one can also find women and men who have followed in Rosenzweig's path and are fulfilling the commandments of the Torah today. However, if one speaks of the program of a "new *halakhah*" (and it is significant that the news bulletin of the Havurah movement is called *Kesher: A Havurot and New Halacha Newsletter*), antinomian tendencies are bound to be noticed. Buber said about his view of the law that it was not an a-nomism and

certainly not a nomism either. This in-between definition is also characteristic of those who construct a "New *Halakhah*."

V

If one wishes to summarize the above analyses, the first surprising thing
one notices is that Buber's works are placed in the service of conflicting
tendencies. On the one hand, they facilitate access to the world of Judaism;
on the other, they supply the justification for a detachment from the traditional forms of Jewish religion. Two questions suggest themselves: How
can this paradoxical effect be made more comprehensible, and how can one
imagine the construction (the "blueprint") of the American Jewish counterculture which makes possible such an extension of Buber's work?

Buber's teachings have been characterized as a philosophy of *religious
anarchism* by pupils and interpreters like Gershom Scholem and Baruch
Kurzweil, writing independently of each other. The formulation—religious
anarchism—can help us understand the strange history of its reception. In
simplified form, one can say that a synthesis of different lifestyles and philosophies of life is effected, and Buber spoke of this as a "mixture." Both
those who shift their original, politically oriented anarchism to the religious sphere (thus changing it), and those who break open their religious
attitudes towards anarchism find themselves in the position of a religious
anarchist. In this realm, various types of development are conceivable. In
each case, however, Buber propagandizes for the other side, and this can
lead not only to a metamorphosis, but to a reinforcement of the attitude
that is brought along.

To see in the American Jewish counterculture a movement marching
in closed ranks towards a certain direction would be to overlook its special
qualities. It would be better to compare it to a revolving stage; the individuals and the groups "revolve" for a while, getting to know new things and
trying them on for size. In this situation one can always observe processes
running in the other direction. Ralph Simon has noted that members of
the same Jewish community or school of thought have taken diametrically
opposed paths. When the periodical, *Response*, questioned the "veterans" of the Jewish student movement about changes in their views, many
answers made it clear that the counterculture had enabled them to try out a
new lifestyle and to abandon earlier positions. The detailed replies of those
questioned showed that there is no such thing as a *typical* direction; it is

always a matter of a concrete point of departure and the special circumstances surrounding it.

Paradoxical mixture, revolving stage, experimental communities: these are the catchwords that we need in order to understand Martin Buber's influence on the "New Jews." In short, we cannot imagine the Jewish counterculture in America without Buber's work.

While Buber is thought of as a utopian socialist and an exemplary figure in "infantile socialism" by many contemporary Marxists (and is, therefore, rejected), Jewish socialists and Jewish activists who are committed to Jewish survival needed a powerful figure to rival Marx and Marcuse. They found one in Buber, who combined an active spiritual approach to social and political problems with a spiritually active and progressive nuance. This made him a conservative among the radicals but a radical among the Jewishly committed. In that sense, he saved Jewish "souls" from the clutches of atheistic Marxism. Such Jewish radicals were then able to "return home" to Judaism, albeit now as radical Jews. It is an often overlooked legacy that "Reb" Martin Buber saved Jews even though many Jewish traditionalists may not have liked the political and religious direction that he and they took.

Yizhak Ahren works as a psychologist at the Institut für Psychologie, Universität Köln, Cologne, Germany. Jack Nusan Porter is presenting visiting lecturer at the University of Lowell.

Summer 1980

IV. Jewish Radicals:
Praxis/Action

Jewish Student Activism

From *Jewish Currents*, Vol. 24, No. 5, May 1970, pp. 28-34. One of my most influential and widely quoted and distributed essays. It was made into a booklet by Morris U. Schappes for *Jewish Currents*. Reprinted by permission of *Jewish Currents*.

* * *

Jewish students, like other students, are disenchanted with the world as they find it; and they blame their parents for its condition. Ideological generation splits are no new thing to Judaism; the second generation of American immigrants broke with their parents, if not physically, certainly in values and lifestyles. Many left Judaism entirely, many in all-but-nominal ways. Not until this first American-born generation had children did they begin to raise questions about their Jewish identity.

This is the group that has succeeded economically, has been the mainstay of liberal politics, and whose children are now reevaluating traditional Jewish values to fit into the modern scene.

The Jewish community is small, and Jewish parents are concerned about and influenced by their children. Jewish students are a larger proportion of students than the Jews are of the population; therefore, what goes on among the small group of radical students described below will have greater repercussions than their number would indicate.

All action has been speeded up during this past decade. Social upheaval has occurred at an unprecedented level. In fact, it is both fascinating and frightening to note what changes can take place in simply one year. For example, in the winter 1969 issue of *Judaism*, two articulate Jewish intellectuals,

Milton Himmelfarb and Prof. Leonard Fein, both wrote articles despairing of the role and identity of Jewish students and disparaging the role and duties of the Jewish "establishment." They were right on target as to the failings of the latter, but as for the former, neither of them foresaw the changes that were to take place among Jewish college students. As a graduate student myself at an "elite" Midwestern university, I have seen a transformation take place.

Fein, however, did delineate the dilemmas confronting Jewish identity and he is correct—there are serious conflicts between being a Jew and being an intellectual; between being a Jew and being a student; between being a Jew and being a pants manufacturer's son; and, yes, between being a Jew and being a radical.

Fein, furthermore, is correct in his view that the Jewish "establishment" is patronizing and self-serving in its dealings with Jewish young people. It is true, as he stated, that:

> …we have tended not to take the kinds of problems that students have very seriously… We have tried to convert the student to a Judaism organize in forms which have little to do with his position and with his understanding. Neither defense nor fund-raising are the sorts of things to inspire a student…

These statements point out the serious gap in communication and education between our generations. How does one bridge the gap? Unfortunately, both Fein and Himmelfarb offer very few concrete solutions. Himmelfarb, for example, feels that increased proselytism and intermarriage will turn the trick. This, as he says, will be "furiously controversial" and will "shake up" both synagogue and community center. Himmelfarb is, sadly, off base and, moreover, he badly misgauges the temper of the present Jewish youth culture. As for Fein, he is more cautious in his proposals, and I respect him for this, but he, too, like many social scientists, is a poor prophet. However, Fein did put his finger on an important topic—the need for "Jewish identity projects," serious introspection into the Jewish student psyche. One needs fewer symposia, and more innovative, imaginative and, yes, *radical* programs.

The gist of my argument is simply that both Fein, Himmelfarb and nearly every other Jewish commentator failed to predict the militant mood of many of today's Jewish college students, especially among a growing radical vanguard that will directly influence modern Jewish institutions. Only "repression," which is unlikely among libertarian Jews, or apathy, which is a distinct possibility, on the part of the over-40 (I upped the age) generation will "kill" this movement. I am even optimistic enough to predict that the movement will succeed despite these obstacles and disabilities.

What really happened this past year—1969? Stated simply, the following occurred: What the parents forgot, the children wanted to remember! If the second generation was interested in "making it," financially and socially, and wanted their Judaism reduced to a sparseness that would be parallel to their lifestyle, the third generation (and even fourth) wants to reconstitute Judaism with vigor and pride. This has occurred not only because Judaism is "in" today, even campy; no, it goes even deeper. There is a sincere desire on the students' part not to only re-educate themselves, but to go two steps further—to re-educate their elders and to re-educate the gentile. In doing so, they hope to transform the Jewish community.

The rise of such activism stems directly out of the swirl of social movements that envelop our society. The Jew is a product of his age and reflects its madness, its idealism and its love of freedom.

The following are posited as "theories" as to why Jewish activism arose in the latter half of this decade:

a. The spread of racial and ethnic chauvinism
b. The Israeli-Arab Six-Day War and its influence
c. The impact of the New Left and general student unrest
d. Anti-Zionist and anti-Semitic postures in the New Left
e. The abhorrence of middle-class, middle-brow Jewishness (not Judaism, if the distinction can be understood)

Let's take these issues one by one.

Racial pride and ethnic pride, whether it be among blacks, Indians, Mexicans or Puerto Ricans, have influenced and laid the foundation for Jewish "nationalism," Jewish pride and the cries of Jewish "power." The rise of the Jewish Student Movement at Northwestern University (one of the first), the Jewish Liberation Project in New York, the Jewish Radical Union in Berkeley, and similar groups at UCLA, CCNY, University of Chicago, University of Illinois, and Columbia, among others, is a manifestation of today's "new" radical Jew. Other radical and/or socialist organizations that should be included are Habonim, Students for Israel, Havurah, the Jews for Urban Justice, and the representatives of the University Service department of the Jewish Agency. Even the names of their journals and newspapers give notice of their ideals: *The Jewish Radical, Jewish Liberation Journal, Flame, Other Stand, Ha-Orah (The Light), Jewish Urban Guerrilla, Response, Echo* and the *Jewish Peace Fellowship Newsletter.*

The list is extensive and growing; it is what sociologists can rightly label a *movement.* It has already had an exhilarating effect upon the American Jewish community. Yet as I have emphasized, it has its roots in the drive for freedom among oppressed groups in this country and, particularly, in the new racial pride of black people. The reasoning goes as follows: when blacks began to look to their collective past, to their historical roots, and to their culture, they implicitly asked each American to seek and understand his own roots, his own culture and his own past. Afro-Americans directed white and brown people to do this so that the latter could better comprehend the black man's own search for manhood and dignity in "Babylon."

Therefore, one sees militant Indians "on the warpath"; Mexicans organizing behind Cesar Chavez; and Puerto Ricans organizing into radical groups. Whether these movements will lead to further divisiveness and hatred is not the point for now—what is essential is that it is happening to Jews. And some may ask—why not?

Such stirrings have brought fear and apprehension. Some have labeled it a "revolution"—yet it is a revolution of values, and dramatic return to the cultural pluralism that is essentially America. The "beef stew analogy" of Leonard Fein is apt here. We are all individual components composing a very "sloppy, messy, but tasty dish" called the U.S.A. The present Jewish radical is a product of this cultural pluralism.

The Israeli-Arab Six-Day War in June, 1967 shocked many people, and they were not all Arabs either. This war also awakened an entire generation to the possibility that Israel could be destroyed. One must remember that the present Jewish college student population (age 18-24) has *never* known what it was like *not* to have the presence of a Jewish State, and they had begun simply to take it for granted. To them, unlike their elders who had suffered through Auschwitz, Babi Yar and finally the creation of a Jewish homeland, Israel had "always" existed. They needed a jolt, and they received it in the early dawn of June 5, 1967.

Hundreds wished to emigrate, make *aliyah;* thousands attended rallies and donated money, and waited for Israel to survive. This "jolt" carried over into the school year in the fall of 1967 and into 1968. It was like tinder-wood waiting for a spark to touch it off into an acclamation of pro-Jewish and pro-Zionist sentiment. The Six-Day War then was a catalyst for the latent feelings of Jewish pride and identity that were bubbling beneath the surface. These feelings developed slowly, but were nurtured by the violence and tumult of the years between 1967-1970.

One parenthetical influence of Israel and its militancy: fear of violence among Diaspora Jews. For years the Jew was portrayed as a pathetic, frightened proprietor. While this is still relatively true, a significant portion of young Jews has conquered their fear of bloodshed, of the gun and the rock. One has only to mention that a *third* of the SDS Weathermen[1] arrested in their confrontation with police were *Jewish*, and of these there were a disproportionate number of Jewish *women*. The resort to violence is a manifestation of the violence climate in America, yet it is an acclamation of the gun-toting Jew represented by Warsaw Ghetto fighters and Israeli paratroopers. I am not so bold as to compare Jewish partisans to Jewish Weathermen, for the comparison is unfair to the memory of the former, yet this acquiescence to violence by the "new" Jew is obviously not a historical quirk. The Dayan image of cool unruffled force is a two-edged sword. It provokes both fear and adulation. For Jews these are ambivalent feelings, yet conquering the fear of violence is a healthy sign. Jewish radical groups arose to meet this challenge. What exactly happened between the years 1967 to now in 1970?

These years found America with more bloodshed, riot, rebellion, and revolt than any in this century. The cries of Black Power sprang up in 1967 when Stokely Carmichael crusaded in the South and the consequences of this movement surfaced at the August, 1967 Conference on New Politics in Chicago. This convention of leftist groups in America cleared the air between black and white radicals, and Jews at the conference had to make a painful decision and a more painful rerouting of their position. This event is a landmark in the history of U.S. radicalism. (See Jack Weinman's fine article in *Jewish Currents*, Dec., 1967.)

What occurred to Jews was the following: one, they were no longer welcome in the Black Power Movement. If they wished to do "something," they would *now* have to do it among their *own people* (i.e., among whites). Two, they knew that they would face (at least in the form of verbal abuse)

---

1   The Weather Underground Organization (WUO), or the Weathermen, a radical left militant organization founded on the Ann Arbor campus of the University of Michigan in 1969 as a faction of SDS, with the intent to create a revolutionary party to supplant "American imperialism."

anti-Zionist, anti-Israel and even anti-Semitic rhetoric from black and white radicals. What was to occur was common in the Jewish tradition: the struggle between the universalism of radical/socialist thought and the particularism of one's Judaism and concern for Jews. However, it is subtler. Radical Jews began to feel the "pinch" of their more liberal, more conservative, and more reactionary coreligionists, who had come under attack as avaricious ghetto slumlords and merchants by militant black and white radicals (including Jews).

Thus, many young Jewish activists were caught in a bind between one's professed ideals of freedom for all and one's concern for one's fellow Jews, especially those who were not "living up" to the noble and prophetic vision of Judaism. Student unrest, led mainly by SDS, had begun to increase rapidly during this period. There were arrests, marches, broken windows and busted heads. Students, many of them Jews, began to understand what it was like to be "niggers"—to feel oppression, fear and hatred.

White radicals began to relate to the new emerging black struggle, that of the Newark rebellion of 1967, Detroit in 1968, the killing of Martin Luther King, the exile of Black Panther leader Eldridge Cleaver, the jailing of other Black Panthers, the gun-toting of Cornell black students. The mood was increasingly militant. Jews felt that they too had to respond to this newly articulated violence. The goal was to develop a militancy that would appeal to young Jews as well as be a forum for Jewish radicals in their confrontation with the sterility of the Jewish "establishment" and the ignorance and/or naiveté of the black and the SDSer.

The irrationality of this era, at times, led radical groups to take stands and present ideological positions that are neither correct nor productive, i.e., the status of Israel as an imperialist nation. As the *Jewish Radical* stated in an editorial (Jan., 1969):

> ...One of the reasons that so many of us came together to start this paper was a growing concern with our radial communities' increasingly anti-Israel posture. As radicals we find this inappropriate, at best. We believe that the easy acceptance of empty metaphors and lack of desire to make meaningful distinctions between vague analogies concerning the Middle East does irreparable damage to the morality of the movement.

However, for the sake of revolutionary solidarity and Third World rhetoric, black and white radicals have taken anti-Israel and anti-Semitic stances.

Jewish student movements have arisen to meet this challenge, to correct and refute these ideologies, and to seek a *rapprochement* with such revolutionaries. Furthermore, when "real" anti-Semitism might raise its head, Jewish radical groups can easily mobilize into defense groups to neutralize such action. For the time being, Jewish radicals will take what is *good* from blacks and SDSers, but will reject what is *bad*, i.e., any invalid anti-Israel or anti-Jewish positions.

Unlike liberal Jews, radical Jews are not afraid of using militant tactics, nor will they "throw the baby out with the bath water." They will condemn Jewish slumlords, but will support Black Power demands of, let us say, more jobs, better housing, community control of schools, police, and political structures. They will denounce the New Left's biased account of Zionism, yet will seek a homeland for the Arab Palestinians. They will denounce the Jewish establishment, yet will work within the Jewish structure to change it.

SDS's *New Left Notes*, the Weathermen's *Fire*, the Black Muslims' *Muhammed Speaks*, the Black Panther paper, plus the house organs of Progressive Labor, the Young Socialist Alliance, Youth Against War and Fascism, and others—all contain biased and unbalanced accounts of Jews and Israel. These statements must be met vigorously with a more balanced picture. However, the goals and ideas of the Black Panther Party, SDS, or the Black Muslims, those goals that are within the prophetic vision of Judaism, must be supported by radical Jewish groups, and indeed they are, to the astonishment and trepidation of many Jewish liberals in Hadassah, B'nai B'rith and the Jewish Welfare Boards.

The final theory (or theoretical perspective) explaining why Jewish students are forming activist groups on campus is their distaste for their elders' lifestyles. Though there are many fine Jewish parents who attempt an imaginative and provocative left-liberal lifestyle, there are far too many of the type found in a Philip Roth novella, Brenda Patemkin's parents in *Goodbye, Columbus*. This is manifested as a revolt against the ostentatiousness of a Miami Beach or a Grossinger's; the traumatic vulgarity of a Jewish wedding or bar mitzvah; the single-minded pursuit of materialism of a parent that, in one generation, has moved from a Newark to a Scarsdale or from a Rogers Park to a Skokie.

The available alternatives for a young Jewish person coming out of this environment are few; to join a commune in Haight-Ashbury; to be in the streets with a rock in one's hand ready for the "pigs," or simply to get a degree, a wife, a job, a career, a split-level and a mahjong game, and move right back into that sterile suburb. However, an alternative to all of this is to become a Jewish radical. Happily, this is being done today.

These then are five theories that can explain the drive toward Jewish activism. There are others, but these are the major ones. However, what has passed is only intellectual exercise.

Let me conclude this article with what Jews call *tachlis*, which can be defined as the Protestant ethic of putting ideas into action. In short, what does a Jewish activist do? What does a Jewish activist movement do?

First, like all good radicals, one must first *talk*, and then talk some more. A dialogue with the Jewish community must begin, goals must be articulated, for this is a new phenomenon, a new movement. Let me speak then about the Jewish Student Movement in Chicago, since I know it best. Unlike many "establishment" Jewish groups, what such movements *idealize* and what they *do* are identical. The following are the goals of the JSM (in the form of our program):

1. *We first recognize that we have not been educated properly as Jews. Our lack of education has weakened our identity, and because action must be based on knowledge, we therefore must re-educate ourselves.*

2. *We will continue to work for humane, just, and right causes, and we will identify as Jews with other movements striving to improve society, because 4,000 years of prophetic tradition demand that we do.*

3. *We recognize and actively support the integral role that the State of Israel plays in the life of the Jewish people. In addition, we will not identify with or join with any groups that argue for the destruction of the State of Israel.*

4. *We feel that we can help ourselves and our Jewish brothers all over the world by building a strong, united American Jewish community.*

5. *We welcome the support of non-Jews in our struggle if they concur with our goals and means.*

6. *Similar movements are now arising on other campuses. We must establish and maintain close contact with them to achieve our common aims.*

These then are the goals of a typical Jewish activist group. It is similar to many such groups throughout the country. But what do we do? Sartre is correct: our actions determine our life.

Here is a recent sampling: a picketing of the French consulate in the winter of 1968 protesting de Gaulle's anti-Israel policies; a vigil and a protest on campus to mourn the hanging murder of nine Jews by the Iraqi government; a continuing local struggle over our university's consistent policy of scheduling school registration and orientation on Jewish holidays; this led to the first "Jewish sit-in" in the 1960s in the dean's office in the spring of 1969 over a Jewish issue, not an SDS one (the struggle continues since the administration has done nothing); and last, an involvement in the controversy in Chicago between exploitive Jewish contract-housing sellers/realtors and their black victims.

Our re-education process is undertaken by weekly seminars given by *our* members to *our* members. We educate ourselves. We have the task of destroying the myths upon which we have been brought up. We, like the blacks, need a new look at our history and image. Furthermore, armed with facts and vigor, we have sent student speakers to Jewish fraternities, sororities, temples, men's clubs, luncheons, and even mahjong socials, and we have left our audiences impressed.

A dialogue began. Such events are occurring elsewhere and are garnering a great deal of publicity. One need only see the coverage in *Newsweek* Dec. 8, 1969 for a description of the confrontation in Boston between Jewish activists and the leaders of the national welfare funds.

We are now preparing for an even more difficult decade, the 1970s, and Jewish radicalism must met the challenge. As we enter this new decade, we, the products of our age, must dare to struggle for a new self, a new manhood, a new Jew. We have joined with our Jewish brothers in movements elsewhere in a solidarity that will bring grace and strength to Jews in America.

Hippies may be "dead," yet people have become hip; SDS may be "dying," yet people have become radicalized; God may be "dead," yet people have faith; Judaism may be "dying," yet young Jews have begun to rejuvenate it, as young Jews have begun to vitalize secular Jewishness too.

May 1970

The Origins of the Jewish Student Movement: A Personal Reflection

From *genesis 2*, Vol. II, No. 5, February 1980, p. 19. No longer publishing.

* * *

*Recently, Rabbi Benjamin Kahn of the B'nai B'rith Hillel Foundations asked me to send him a tape dealing with the founding of the Jewish student movement in the Midwest and its connections with Hillel. Rabbi Kahn is writing a book on the history of Hillel foundations in the United States. Talking into that tape recorder brought back wonderful and exhilarating memories I'd like to share with **genesis 2** readers.*

Edy Rauch, in a March 1974 **genesis 2** review of the book *Jewish Radicalism* which I co-edited with Peter Dreier, noted correctly that no analysis of the Jewish student movement could leave aside the Six-Day War or the Struggle for Soviet Jewry as "potent influences on the developments of this period." Edy, a former editor of **genesis 2**, is correct. The key events that led to the establishment of Jewish student-radical-countercultural groups were Israel's victory in June of 1967 and the militancy surrounding the Soviet Jews. To my mind, the Six-Day War was even more crucial.

Soon after that war, I remember the Conference on New Politics in Chicago in August 1967. This conference hoped to form a coalition of labor union workers, blacks, radicals, students, and intellectuals into a third party with a presidential slate consisting of Martin Luther King and Benjamin Spock. But the blacks had other ideas. It was the time of Stokely Carmichael and the "Black Power" movement, and black people were turning away from their white comrades to form their own groups.

These radical blacks were not only anti-white; they were anti-liberal blacks or those they labeled "Uncle Toms," and Martin Luther King, while respected, was seen as moving too slowly and too nonviolently to suit his more radical compatriots. What divided the Conference on New Politics and, ultimately, the Movement (and that is why this conference is so crucial in understanding the history of the 1960s) was a series of demands that the black caucus presented to the delegates—demands for equality, freedom, equal representation on all committees, and other similar issues. It was really one issue that divided blacks and whites and blacks and Jews, and which ultimately led to the rise of the Jewish student movement—a resolution condemning Israel as an "imperialist tool" of American corporations. The conference had to accept all eighteen demands or else the black caucus would walk out.

I have never seen such anguished debate from trade unionists, academics, and others defending Israel. In the end, the eighteen-point program was accepted, but the blacks walked out of the conference anyway. This act and the consequences that followed told Jews in the civil rights and leftist groups that a painful decision had to be made.

Jews were no longer welcome in the black movement, and if they wished to do something, they would have to do it among their own people. Secondly, they knew they would face anti-Zionist, anti-Israel and even anti-Semitic abuse from black and white radicals. What was to occur was familiar from Jewish history, the failure of the universalism and radical/socialist thought to adequately address the particular needs of Jews and the Jewish community. This tension would continue for the rest of the decade, and was the great impetus for the rise of a particular *Jewish* student movement that would be active in the civil rights and later anti-war movement while it addressed itself to issues particularly sensitive to the Jewish people.

Every sub-movement in the greater Movement had its counterpart in the Jewish student movement. If the Movement was split between its countercultural/communalistic and political aspects, so too the Jewish student movement had its countercultural (*havurot*, new approaches in art, poetry, liturgy, and theology) and its political side (Soviet Jewry, Israel, the Jewish "establishment"). If later, there was a feminist movement, the Jewish students and adults had a Jewish feminist movement; if there was a gay movement, there was also a Jewish gay movement; if there was a radical theology in the Movement (the Berrigan brothers, for example), there was also a Jewish radical theology, e.g., Arthur Waskow, Everett Gendler, Arthur Green, and Zalman Schachter. This division between the countercultural/ theological and the radical/political was never neat and clean, and just as the Yippies and Abbie Hoffman and Jerry Rubin tried to bridge the gap, people like Arthur Waskow and the Jews for Urban Justice and *Farbrengen* succeeded in doing the same. No more dualities. Art, liturgy, culture, and politics were all one interwoven act of defiance.

The reaction of Jewish student to the actions of the blacks and their white radical supporters took a little time, but by the end of 1967 and early 1968, we began to move toward the formation of the Jewish Student Movement at Northwestern University. It was a heady time. We thought we were the very first group in the U.S., even the world, and were pleasantly surprised when we heard of other groups forming in Boston, New York, Los Angeles, and Berkeley.

The Jewish Student Movement (JSM) in Chicago was founded with the support of the local Hillel foundation at Northwestern University, which was led by Rabbi Boris Rackovsky. Since then, and especially during the establishment of *Breira* (which I consider the adult version of the Jewish student movement), the Hillels have been one of the staunchest support- ers of whatever is new and innovative among Jewish youth. Together with Rabbi Rackovsky and several graduate students—astronomy grad and Yiddishist Jeffrey Mallow, psychology grad Stanley Rosenbaum, under- graduate Byron Kohl, and a few others whose names I have forgotten, plus myself, we founded the JSM, dedicated to "humane, just and right causes." Our program stated that "we will identify as Jews with other movements striving to improve society, because 4,000 years of prophetic tradition demand that we do so." In the process, as Jeff Mallow so aptly put it, we found ourselves fighting Fatah and the Federation at the same time.

These ringing words propelled us into action. Words were (and are) not enough. Here is a sampling of our actions from 1968-1971: a picket- ing of the French consulate in the winter of 1968 protesting Charles de Gaulle's anti-Israel policies; a vigil and protest on campus to mourn the hanging of nine Jews by the Iraqi government; a local struggle over the university's consistent policy of scheduling school registration, orientation and final exams on Jewish holidays (this led to the first "Jewish sit-in" at

Northwestern in the dean's office in the spring of 1969); conferences on Israel, the PLO, and other Mid-East issues; and last, an involvement in Chicago between exploitive Jewish contract-housing Realtors and their black "victims." Thus we were involved in all aspects of the Movement, but from a Jewish perspective.

As the Jewish movement grew, such journals as *Response* (the oldest, founded in 1967 at Columbia University), *The Jewish Radical*, *Jewish Liberation Journal*, *Flame*, *Otherstand*, *Jewish Urban Guerrilla*, *Echo*, *Davks*, and, of course, **genesis 2**, emerged. "Classic" statements and essays were published, such as "To Uncle Tom and Other Jews" by M.J. Rosenberg, "The Oppression of America's Jews" by Aviva Cantor Zuckoff, and "To Share a Vision" by Hillel Levine. These articles and other comprised the anthology *Jewish Radicalism* (Grove Press) that Peter Dreier and I completed in 1970 or 1971 but which was finally published in 1973.

By then the heyday of the movement was over and editorials in **genesis 2** and other papers were saying that the campuses were cooling down in the wake of the killings at Kent State University and Jackson State College and the winding down of the war by the Nixon administration. Economic recession and energy shortages were also being felt as early as 1971.

While the Jewish student movement was less active in the mid-to-late 1970s, it was not dead; it had just institutionalized; that is, the various movements solidified around distinct groups and journals. The Jewish women's movement launched by NETWORK's first Jewish Women's Conference produced an important and lasting publication, *Lilith*; the Jewish gay movement had its "synagogues" and meeting places; the Soviet Jewry movement had its own organization; the first Conference on Alternatives in Jewish Education sponsored by NETWORK in 1973 grew into the nationwide Coalition for Alternatives in Jewish Education (CAJE), claiming over 1,500 teachers and educators in its membership by 1979.

While *Breira* is sadly missed, there are stirrings of another "congress" in the making called The Organizing Committee for a New Jewish Agenda initiated by Rabbi Gerry Serotta and others. I foresee activism around the corner, and it will be initiated not by the students of the '70s but by the veterans of the '60s. What is needed is only the proper chain of events and the proper leadership. The Jewish movement will live on, fed by the memories of past struggles.

As one looks back, one sees that the same problems continue to nag us but in new forms and with greater possibilities for solution: the PLO,

Soviet Jews, Jews in troubled lands, anti-Zionism vs. anti-Semitism, and so on. When one picks up an issue of *genesis 2* of 1980, one is reading about a 1980 dilemma.

About a year ago, at the Martin Buber Centennial Symposium at Harvard University, I told an Israeli from the Ministry of Education that Buber had an enormous influence on the Jewish student movement and that that movement in turn had a great impact on the American Jewish community. He turned to me and said: "What impact? What movement?" He had hardly heard of it, and as for any impact, he thought it was nil. How quickly memories fade! Or is it that knowledge simply is not passed on? We can't let that happen either to scholars or to our children.

Jack Nusan Porter was one of the founders of the Jewish student movement in the Midwest, co-editor of the movement anthology Jewish Radicalism, *an editorial board member of* **genesis 2** *in the mid-'70s, and author of many articles and reviews in the fields of sociology and contemporary Jewry.*

February 1980

M. Jay Rosenberg

The Press of Freedom:
To Uncle Tom and
Other Such Jews

In *The Village Voice*, February 13, 1969.

* * *

> I added this essay since it was the classic statement to the Left
> from the Jewish leftist writer
>
> — M. Jay Rosenberg.

It is becoming increasingly fashionable in certain left-wing Jewish circles
to put down everything Jewish. These Jewish leftists, still hung-up because
they were not born Protestant, find that they can glibly resort to anti-Jewish
stereotypes today without being referred to a good psychiatrist. It is now
quite acceptable for the Jew to attempt to ingratiate himself with the goyim
by condemning what he has always been ashamed of. It's a sad sight.

We are living in a time of exploding nationalisms. The blacks in
America are the first to abjure the idea of assimilation, to realize the inherent lie in the concept of melting-pot. Through black nationalism has development a new black pride and hence the ticket to liberation.

Today's young American Jew is a good bit slower. He desperately wants
assimilation; Jewishness embarrasses him. He finds the idea of Jewish
nationalism, Israel notwithstanding, laughable. The leftist Jewish student
is today's Uncle Tom. He scrapes along, demonstrating for a John Hatchett,

ashamed of his identity, and obsessed with it. He cannot accept the fact that he is seen as a Jew, that his destiny is that of the Jews, and that his only effectiveness is as a Jew. But he wants to be an "American," a leftist American, talking liberation and aspiring WASP. He is a ludicrous figure.

He joins black nationalist groups, not as a Jew but as a white man. His whiteness, his precious whiteness, is too valuable to him for it to be relegated to a secondary position. He does not understand that his relevance to the black struggle is as a Jew and a fellow victim of endless white exploitation. He can comprehend the black struggle but only in the context of his own. His involvement in these black nationalist organizations makes him a living lie. Blacks don't need his white leadership and they don't want it. The sad fact is that the Jewish Tom is an inevitable product of American civilization. But it is time that he realize that he, not today's black, is the invisible man; he, like yesterday's Negro, wanders in a no-man's land.

The Jew can be an ally of the black liberation movement, and he should be. But first he must find himself. He must realize that his own struggle for liberation is a continuing one, that he too has much to fear and also much of which to be proud. The miracle of Israel, a national liberation deferred for 2000 years, should be his inspiration. The Jew did it alone, as the black knows he must, and he did it with guns.

Therefore it is as a Jew that I must accept black nationalism. The black militants may or may not be the equivalent of the Irgun and Stern gang, but surely the parallel is there. The Jewish war of national liberation is different from that of the blacks or the Viet Cong only in that the Jews are closer to success, but what was won by Jewish fighters on the battlefields of Palestine will not be lost by Jewish moral cowards here in America. The black revolution also will succeed, but when it does the blacks will lose all their white "friends." They will be called "anti-progressive." They will be labeled the aggressors. If they win again and again, they will be called "oppressors." As he does now, the black will surely stand alone.

He can learn this much from the Jewish experience. When they slaughtered six million of us, the good people offered us sympathy, and nothing else. They uttered brotherly noises. It was when the fighting Jew arose from the blood and ashes of Europe that we began to lose our friends. The world began to accept our national existence but was prepared to mourn our imminent demise. Who can forget those "glorious" days before the Six-Day War? All over the world good people demonstrated for Israel. One can almost picture the left's reaction to the death of Israel: never-ending sympathy rallies, leftists wearing the Star of David on black armbands. Israel could have come to represent the fight for freedom, the struggle to exist. Her people, driven to the sea, could have been martyrs. It would have been beautiful. But Israel won the war and in so doing she lost her "friends." Because she survived, she shall be punished.

But that is not the issue; the absurdity of the left's anti-Israel position can be taken up on another day. The issue is one of Jewish pride. All those Jewish students who whisper the word "Jew" and lower their heads when a Philip Roth story is discussed in a literature course, the Mark Rudds who are prepared to die for the Vietnamese, the Biafrans, the Greeks, and the Czechs yet who reject Israel—these are our Uncle Toms (let's call them "Uncle Jakes") and our shame. The Jew must accept his identity, he's not just another white man. It's time he realizes he's a Jew, and he'd better accept it. Many Jews are quick to criticize blacks for being impolitic enough to call us Jews in public. But that is what we are. From Hillel Club to the New Left is a short jump. And the inevitable jump back, by the Jewish Tom, is even shorter. A man who cannot accept his own identity is a hypocrite and a liar when he pretends to accept someone else's.

Black nationalism and Jewish nationalism will exist concurrently. To accept one you must accept the other. The black is America's Jew; a common fight must be waged. And yet when some black spokesman tells us we are poisoning his children's minds, when he calls us "kikes," we must see him for what he is. Then he is just another goy using the Jew, the available and accepted victim, as scapegoat. We must then fight him as well. That's the way it must be. We shall scrape for no one.

And thus from this point on, I shall join no movement that does not accept and support my people's struggle. If I must choose between the Jewish cause and a "progressive" anti-Israel SDS, I shall choose the Jewish cause. If the barricades are erected, I will fight as a Jew. Not arbitrarily, not in support of the UFT,[2] but in support of myself. In the final analysis, Mark Rudd and Albert Shanker will be on the same side—that's the lesson of the last 30 years. It will be learned.

It has been written that after "the death camps, we retain but one supreme value: to exist." Masada will not fall again.

There is still time, but the burden of proof is not on the Jewish nationalist, it is on you. You who reject your identity and do not realize that it

---

2   United Federation of Teachers.

follows you wherever you go. You who are so trapped in your Long Island split-level childhood that you can't see straight. You who fight everything you are—and against the one element that gave you your goddam social consciousness: your Jewish social idealism. In the aftermath of the crematoriums, you are flippant. After Auschwitz, you are embarrassed. Thirty years after the Holocaust, you have learned nothing and forgotten everything. Ghetto Jew, you'd better do some fast thinking.

February 1969

V. Jewish Radicals on the Right: Meir Kahane and the JDL

Jewish Conservative Backlash

In *Commonweal*, October 13, 1972, pp. 33-37. It was no surprise that one of the most popular of the Democratic runners among Jews was Senator Jackson, a "hawk" in support of Israel and on law and order.

* * *

There is a growing conservatism among American Jews. At times I ask if it is really conservatism; e.g. an over-riding concern for the status quo and an equally strong defense of one's own class and/or ethnic interests, or is it simply muted liberalism? Is it a passing thing, a temporary isolationism from a circle of "enemies"—a temporary defense against attacks from within (radical Jewish youth, the Jewish Defense League), and from without (black anti-Semitism, general anti-Israel feelings), or is it a permanent turn inwards prompted by the economic and political recession; a return to ethnic self-interest, caused by the widespread *zeitgeist* of fear and disillusionment?

And when I ask this question of Jews, I am really asking this question of most Americans. Let me state my argument in the form of a dialectical process: if this conservatism of the elders is the thesis, and the activism of the young is the antithesis, then what is the synthesis?

There are no simple answers. I will describe this synthesis (or at least my view of it) later, but let me first paint a picture of this conservatism.

The most visible indication is the growing "Jewish vote" for Richard Nixon in the upcoming election. Nixon will receive at least 30 percent of the Jewish vote, maybe more; McGovern will probably lose New York State because of it, and possibly Illinois, Pennsylvania and New Jersey.

Political analysts tell us that the American public votes not so much *for* a candidate, but *against* his opponent. This seems to be the case here to some degree. The anti-McGovern sentiments among many, but not all, Jews are based on emotions, fantasies, intuitive feelings. These fantasies are often more important than cold reality. The fantasy, the rumors going round, is that McGovern is "soft" on Israel. Though there are no hard data to support this, nevertheless many Jews feel that he will not support Israel as staunchly as Nixon has.

Israel is the most sacred and most emotional of issues for Jews. They have seen Nixon *doing*—providing more jets and war material than any previous President; talking to Golda Meir about Israel's security; speaking to Russian leaders about the plight of the Soviet Jewry. With McGovern, many Jews have only vague promises; with Nixon they have seen concrete action. McGovern has his work cut out for him when he confronts Jewish voters.

The second major reason for the Jewish swing to Nixon is that many Jews believe the propaganda that McGovern is "socialist" and "radical." This has become an effective campaign weapon. Jews feel that McGovern will take from the middle-class (read: Jews) and give to the blacks, the Puerto Ricans and the young. The old zero-sum game: what they get, we lose.

But though the pro-Nixon vote is the apex of this conservative trend, there have been numerous other signs along the way over the past few years. Here are some examples, some trivial, most are significant. They all prophesied this shift.

— The Anti-Defamation League of B'nai B'rith recently turned over to the FBI their files on the Jewish Defense League. (It is a bitter irony that, twenty-five years after the Nazi Holocaust, Jews will act as informers on other Jews, no matter what their political or tactical differences.)

— On May 6, 1989, the Oakland chapter of B'nai B'rith bestowed on S.I. Hayakawa, conservative president of San Francisco State College, its "Man of the Year" award. "We honor men whose exemplary conduct manifests the true spirit of America in its finest hour," the lodge president said of the man who used National Guard troops and brutal police tactics to squash student protest.

— Philadelphia Police Chief Frank Rizzo was given the same award by a local chapter of the Histadrut Zionist Organization in November

1970. As a successful law-and-order candidate in the Democratic mayoral primary in April 1971, Rizzo received about three-quarters of the Jewish vote. In his successful campaign in November 1971 for mayor, Rizzo was elected with the overwhelming support of Jewish voters.

— In Los Angeles, Mayor Sam Yorty, the flamboyant reactionary, conjured up images of black militants' running city hall if black opponent Thomas Bradley overcame Yorty's reelection bid. Yorty's histrionics increased his Jewish support from 18 percent in the primary (against Bradley and several others) to 43 percent in the two-way run-off in 1969.

— During the New York City teachers' strike of 1968-69, Jewish spokesmen fanned the flames of racism, initiated by some anti-Semitic remarks by isolated blacks, and turned an essentially class and educational conflict into an ethnic and racial one. Alert Shanker, head of the predominantly Jewish Teachers' Union, talked of "Nazis" and "Gestapo tactics"; the New York Board of Rabbis created hysteria by preaching sermons about alleged arson of synagogues by blacks; and the Anti-Defamation League of B'nai B'rith issued a report which announced that "raw, undisguised anti-Semitism is at a crisis level" in New York.

The tensions produced by these events are still being felt within the Jewish community; black demands symbolically threaten many Jews—teachers, social workers and businessmen in the city, and professionals and intellectuals in the suburbs.

— The Anti-Defamation League last spring launched bitter attacks against a number of radical health groups such as the Medical Committee for Human Rights, Physicians for Social Responsibility, and the Student Health Organization.

A news story in the *New York Times* (January 24, 1971) summarizes the ADL's indictment: the Physicians for Social Responsibility, for example, had the nerve to concern itself with "peace issues as they relate to medicine and health—the use of chemical and biological warfare weapons." The Student Health Organization is suspect, since it has engaged in ghetto community projects funded by the Office of Economic Opportunity. And the Medical Committee for Human Rights is committed to "radical restructuring of the health industries through political action."

The reason for the indictment is simple: there are many doctors in positions of power who are threatened by the coming democratization of health care, and among these doctors are, of course, many Jews—prominent and influential in the Jewish establishment…and in the B'nai B'rith. Of course, what the ADL failed to notice, however, is that these radical medical groups *also* contain many Jews. In short, it seems that what's good for medical institutions is what's good for the *established* Jewish doctors and teachers, *not* the young ones, nor the poor in this society.

— Numerous young Jewish Hebrew teachers and rabbis have been fired or severely criticized after attempting innovative pedagogical techniques in their classrooms or synagogues.
— In the fall of 1970, major Jewish organizations boycotted the visit of Uri Avnery, outspoken opposition member of the Israeli parliament, to campuses. They urged local Jewish groups not to sponsor talks by Avnery, a popular figure among the Jewish and Israeli Left, who had been critical of Israel's handling of the Palestinian refugees.

A memorandum of the Anti-Defamation League of B'nai B'rith sent out on September 18, 1970, to its regional offices, specifically advised Jewish organizations "not to sponsor or co-sponsor his appearances and not engage in public debate with him." It went on to say that "As an opponent of the traditional concepts of Zionism and Judaism, Avnery may say things which will trouble and even embarrass the Jewish community."

— Each year various Jewish communities spend small fortunes to undertake population surveys of their members, usually for the purpose of philanthropy. Yet major Jewish organizations have consistently fought against inclusion of questions on religion on the U.S. Census, which could provide sophisticated—and free— up-to-date information about American Jews.

When the Jewish "Establishment" of interlocking philanthropic and social organizations launched the National Jewish Population Study (cost: $650,000), young Jewish activists in Berkeley, in their journal *The Jewish Radical*, condemned this as the "Jewish reluctance to be collectively suspicious." In other words, it pointed out a long-lasting fear among Jews that Christians would use figures on Jewish median income and education (both extremely high) against them. Young militant Jews see in this, however, the persistence of the Jewish "Establishment" to define Jews as a religious group (the early German Reform Jews in America called themselves "Americans of the Mosaic persuasion"), rather than as an ethnic group, to insure their assimilation into what Will Herberg termed the "triple melting pot" of Protestant, Catholic and Jew.

— When Jacques Toreyner, president of the Zionist Organization of America, adopted a hawkish position on Vietnam to win Administration support for Israel, the *Jewish Radical* called him "Nixon's hatchet man in the Jewish community," while the radical Zionist Jewish Liberation Project picketed the ZOA building in New York.

— Well-known Jewish professors and educators write for right-wing magazines. For example, in the 1971 issues of *Ideas* (Vol. 2, No. 4), a quarterly sponsored by the Jewish Society of America, the "Jewish wing" of the John Birch Society, there are the following articles: One, by Charles A. Weil, calls for Nixon aid to Israel exclusively on anti-Soviet grounds. Prof. Joseph Dunner of Yeshiva University, a Goldwater admirer, looks to corral more Jewish votes for Nixon in 1972. Rabbi Jakob J. Petuchowski, a theologian of Reform Judaism at Hebrew Union College, scores what he calls the "left turn" in American Reform Judaism. Rabbi Jacob Neusner, an Orthodox Jew and professor at Rutgers, is enthusiastic about Vice President Agnew and regards "the entrenched Liberal organizational structure of the Jewish community" as a barrier to winning Jews to Agnew, although his article is entitled "The Jews Move Right."

— On a different level, and more significantly, *Commentary* magazine, once the darling of American liberal journals, has gone reactionary. In a recent article in *Commonweal*, Peter Steinfels defines this reaction as a "cooling" of American intellectuals toward the predominant social movements of the past decade.

Recent issues of *Commentary*, the monthly publication of the American Jewish Committee, have suggested a parallel between New Leftists and German Communists who helped pave the way for Hitler; have argued that repression in America is a lot of nonsense and that militants bring it upon themselves anyway; have condemned or chided an entire succession of movements: Black Panthers, Women's Liberation, the counter-culture, innovative education, and the Jewish radical movement.

Yet, the editors and writers of *Commentary* reflect not only the thinking of some intellectuals, but also that Jewish pawnbroker in the ghettos of Bedford-Stuyvesant, New York.

Now, the question is what is one to make out of all of this? It seems there is now ample evidence, although I have no systematic data, of a *political shift within a significant majority of the American Jewish community.*

From the heyday of the Civil Rights movement with the names of Goodman and Schwerner ringing in our ears, there has been a perceptible shift among American Jews to a muted liberalism, bordering on conservative withdrawal. If this is true, and I believe it is, then the Jews should be watched because they are a barometer for other liberal groups in America. The effect of this political shift can be seen in two areas: the first, internal, within the Jewish community, and the second, external, within the national political structure. Internally, there has also developed a "mini-generation gap" between young post-Israel, post-Holocaust Jews and the older Jewish "Establishment." The political, cultural and ethnic estrangement of many young Jews is the result.

This estrangement was made manifest in a new movement that began after the 1967 Israeli-Arab Six-Day War. Caught between the anti-Zionist New Left and Black Panther Party, the lox-and-bagels campus Hillel "society," and the Jewish adult organizations, a new way, another stand, was necessary—an activist *and* Jewish one. Since 1967, over 100 such groups, such as the Jewish Liberation Project, the Radical Zionist Alliance, the Jews for Urban Justice and the Jewish Radical Union, have sprung up on and off campuses from Boston to Berkeley. The names of their journals and newspapers (nearly 40 of them, with a reading public of 150-200,000) give notice of their ideas; *The Jewish Radical, Response, Davka, the Voice of Micah, Otherstand* and the *Jewish Liberation Journal.*

Walking the "tightrope" between messianic universalism and Jewish ethnic particularism, these groups will have a direct confrontation with their elders over this political shift. These young Jews reject the diaspora mentality of caution and fear—fear of what the "goyim" (non-Jews) think; they reject the idea that ethnic survival must become an end in itself; they will not support Vietnam just because they think that Administration support for Israel may be undercut; they will not assimilate into the melting pot nor will they become, like the Jewish Defense League, their youthful reactionary counterpart, ethnically separated from the struggles of blacks, Puerto Ricans, Chicanos, or Indians. Out of the memories of their own oppression, history and identity, they feel they must identify with other people's oppression.

This internal schism should be noted, but the political shift of American Jews on a national level is of utmost importance to track. First, it seems that in local political campaigns, even in New York, there may no longer be a distinctly Democratic "Jewish vote." No politician can be sure, even on a national ticket, about such a vote. Appeals to the Jews' liberalism may be over; a Jewish "backlash" is the result.

Law and order, unqualified support for Israel (even if that means political arm-twisting over other issues), anti-busing, anti-open-admissions, and anti-integration—all those areas that were traditional "hard-hat" blue-collar issues are now of concern to Jewish voters. Political leaders and analysis will have to ponder these changes. Democrats who hope to capture the Jewish vote and the Jewish money will have to change their tune. It was no surprise that one of the most popular of the Democratic runners among Jews was Senator Henry Jackson—a "hawk" in support of Israel and a "hawk" on law and order.

This political shift, plus a blurring of differences between "Republican" and "Democratic" leaders, both nationally and locally, may see many Jews voting for the candidate that offers *them*, not others such as blacks, the best offer. They will swing either way politically, voting for the man, not the party. Yet all this is not new. Throughout history, Jews, when necessary, have sacrificed idealism to survival. They will curry favor and concessions from the governing class for these very same pragmatic reasons. It augurs badly for the radical and the left-liberal in this country.

The harsh reality of American life for the Jew is that he is *no longer considered an oppressed minority group.* Though there are pockets of forgotten Jewish poor in New York, Boston and a few large urban centers (whose interests the Jewish Defense League defends), the overwhelming majority of Jews in America are middle-class to lower upper-class and they have the highest median income of any ethnic group in the country.

For example, when the Department of Health, Education and Welfare threatens to cut off governmental funds from certain universities or corporations, it is because these institutions have too few blacks, women, Puerto Ricans, Mexicans, or Amerindians—*not* too few Jews, as might have been the case twenty years ago.

Yes, most Jews have "made it." While they may have been radicals at the turn of the century when they were poor and working class, and ripe for militant (read: union) action, today they are middle-class or better, and have new class interests. And Marx is correct: they will protect their class position. The attack in the 1960s has come from below—from the poor black and Puerto Rican under-class. And it is not anti-Semitism as much as class conflict and ethnic/racial rivalry.

But for the Jew, it is not so simple, nor is the situation a new one for the Jewish people. They find themselves as the historical "middlemen," the *luftmenschen* of time. As Arthur Waskow in *The Bush is Burning* points out:

> The Jewish grocer might charge blacks high prices because the non-Jewish bank was charging him high interest—but the blacks were likely to focus on the immediate oppression. The Jewish teacher might jam suburban English down black throats because a non-Jewish educational Establishment had jammed it down his own throat—but the blacks were likely to focus on the immediate oppression. Similarly for Jewish social workers, Jewish doctors...

Occasional anti-Semitic outbursts led Jews to respond with fear—to a defensive anti-black upsurge. It revived painful memories of Auschwitz and Treblinka and the Six-Day War. The result: a widespread feeling that the Jewish people were alone, able to depend only on each other, because the world would abandon them on a whim.

This is the main reason for the American Jews' slide into conservatism.

The upcoming election, as I've said earlier, will give Nixon a large Jewish vote, but there exist divisions here also. An interesting "coalition" of Jewish men of wealth and poorer, lower-middle-class Jews (including a high percentage of Orthodox Jews) will vote for Nixon. The former because of McGovern's economic program that threatens them; the latter because of his too-close identification with radical blacks and youth, and both because of his supposedly "soft" stand on Israel. Younger, college-educated students and professionals, especially Jewish intellectuals, will vote for McGovern exactly *because* of his "radical" economic and social plans and because Israel is not that important to them.

This mini-generation gap among Jews points out that the more assimilated Jew will vote for McGovern; the more traditional will go for Nixon. The three key predictive variables then are (young-old), economic background (blue-collar-professional) and religious identification (traditional-assimilated).

What is the alternative? The one that seems logical is to do with young activist Jews and non-Jews are doing. Go against one's class interests, one's own particularistic framework; begin to make alliances with other groups (not only blacks, but Appalachians, Italians, Poles and other working- and middle-class groups) and begin to confront the real power centers—*which are not essentially Jewish:* banks, corporations and government. Force *them* to stop the ecological, political, military and economic "mutilation" of so many people.

What I am saying is that a new synthesis has to be found and put into action. It is based on two goals: (a) pluralistic accommodation, and (b) new working coalitions cutting across the barriers of race, religion, class and ethnicity. This won't be easy.

The Jew, like all white middle-class Americans, is in many ways also oppressed, but he has not defined that oppression as consciously nor as militantly as have blacks, Puerto Ricans, Chicanos and the activist young.

The consumer, the commuter, the suburbanite, the urban pedestrian are all oppressed—ecologically, financially, physically—assaulted in many ways. Not as bad as the lower class, but bad enough.

I don't like to see blacks fighting Jews, or Puerto Ricans fighting blacks, or Chicanos fighting Anglo-Americans—over jobs, housing and community power—when an "invisible" third party is the real culprit. And that third party is an irresponsive or irresponsible government, whether it be local, state or national, a government which has not changed or changed fast enough to please the clamoring masses.

It is a question of priorities. It is still guns before butter when people are begging and fighting over bread-and-butter issues—like jobs, income, housing, safe streets, clean air and healthy food—issues that cut across classes and ethnic groups. Let me put it in the form of an analogy: I don't like to see brothers and sisters fighting over a little toy when the father, if he had the desire and the imagination, could provide toys for everyone, especially when he is the richest father in the world. One flawed jet plane that falls flaming into the sea could have paid for a lot of toys.

This is the message that Christian and Jewish activists are trying to tell their elders, both Jewish and Christian.

Is anyone listening?

October 1972

My Secret Days and Nights in the Jewish Defense League

The Jewish Advocate, May 2, 1985, p. 15.

* * *

Editor's note: Dr. Jack Nusan Porter is a long-time Jewish activist and the author/editor of 18 books and monographs, mostly on Jewish subjects. He is founder and president of The Spencer Group, a Newton-based real estate consulting, development, and mortgage-brokering company.

Like a bad penny, Meir Kahane seems to be showing up everywhere. He's a troublemaker, and I'd like to tell you how it was 15 years ago when I was a troublemaker, too, as a member of his Jewish Defense League.

I've never admitted it publicly, and most of my liberal friends will be shocked. But my involvement in the JDL explains some of the appeal of Kahane. Today, I'm a real estate consultant and developer; back then I fancied myself to be a Jewish rebel.

In 1969, when I was a grad student in sociology in Evanston, Illinois, at Northwestern University, the JDL was organizing to protest the treatment of Soviet Jews. There were legitimate groups like the Student Struggle for Soviet Jewry, but the JDL had made a name for itself by using militant tactics such as chaining themselves to the Soviet consulate gates in New York City, engaging in sit-ins on the streets in front of the consulate, smoke-bombing and stink-bombing Soviet artistic appearances, and eventually escalating to the bombing of Sol Hurok's office.

There is a recent movie called *Kaddish* about a young boy named Yossi Klein who was involved in similar demonstrations. He is a son of Holocaust survivors. I am, too. That movie was my story in many ways. It was that guilt and that confusion that led me to temporarily abandon my ideals that I had learned in Ichud Habonim, the Labor Zionist Youth Movement of my early years, and join the JDL.

A friend at Northwestern's Hillel told me of semi-secret meetings of the JDL to plan and carry out direct action. Since this was the era of angry Vietnam Vets, fiery SDS radicals, and militant Black Panthers, it was easy to model our tactics on the anti-ROTC and anti-government techniques of the day. The only difference was that this was going to be the Jewish Right using left-wing tactics against the Jewish Left and other targets.

I vividly remember my first late night meeting in the Rogers Park section of Chicago. There were six of us plus several Dobermans. The apartment belonged to someone who loved guns—and Jew who loved guns was a stranger bird indeed. There were guns in special cases lining the wall—shotguns and even machine guns. I was both frightened and fascinated by the fact that here were armed Jews. It was, in my fantasy world, like the Warsaw Ghetto.

My cohorts included a Jewish soldier direct from Vietnam, a Jewish cop, and assorted other Jewish macho types. There was also my Hillel friend. Coming from a small "shtetl" like Milwaukee, I had never seen such Jews before—so different from my Jewish professors and fellow intellectuals at the University of Chicago and at Northwestern. We thought we were tough, but we were powder-puffs compared to these characters.

The Bolshoi Ballet was coming to the Civic Auditorium, and we were going to disrupt it. We knew there would be the usual Jewish, Polish, and Ukrainian protest groups with their placards plus rabbis and their "Sunday School" students. How could we disrupt the ballet, spilling all those people into the street and into the demonstrations? Now, that would get us not only all five Chicago TV stations but also national media like *Time*, *The New York Times*, ABC, CBS, and NBC. We cackled at how easy it was going to be to get the media out and the Jewish community all worked up. We definitely manipulated the media. They knew it, and we knew it, and it was quite easy to do.

We wanted people to leave peacefully and safely, but how could we disrupt and still do that? Heckling and shouting would just get us thrown out and the show would go on. We thought of throwing a smoke bomb on stage but felt it might blind or stagger people.

Even worse was a tear gas attack, which would most likely cause a riot. We decided on hydrogen sulfide liquid—stink bombs—and my Hillel friend and I volunteered to do it. Why? Youthful idealism and naiveté? Who really knows?

That evening we dressed up in suits just like any other respectable theatergoer, bought tickets, and went to our seats. In our pockets were small vials of the evil-smelling stuff. In the middle of the first act of the ballet, we were to walk up the aisle in the dark and slowly pour out the liquid onto the carpet, then casually walk out the building, and watch the amusement that would follow.

I saw my friend doing it, and then I did it, but something went wrong. Someone shouted, "Long live Soviet Jewry!", and I just ran up the aisle into the men's room after pouring a little on the carpet. To this day, I'm not sure why, but I smashed the vial against the bathroom wall and ran out the door to the street.

The plan succeeded—finely dressed patrons, many in fur coats, came out calmly but deliberately, swearing under their breath. The performance was ruined. They opened the doors and windows to let the stink out.

It was my first and last act for and with the JDL. I decided then and there that not only was violence wrong but the JDL itself was wrong for deceiving naïve students and confused (and sometimes scary) Jewish tough guys with glib speeches and easy answers. I think the JDL and Kach stink in more ways than one, and I'll explain why.

There is a crazy irony to this. Several years later, I joined a group here in Boston called *Breira*, and we held a national convention in Washington, DC. JDL members marched, harassed, yelled through the windows, and generally disrupted our peaceful gathering. Once they even tried to storm through the doors.

I went into the lobby to see what was happening, and a man in his 50s—not a young man—ran up to me and bellowed, "You damn self-hating Jew"—"You traitorous pig," and then spit in my face!

I was never so shocked in my life…nor so angry. I could have destroyed him right there. Luckily, we were pulled apart by a policeman and several Breira people. Since then, I've not only had a disagreement ideologically with the JDL but a palpable disgust.

Kahane may be an engaging man, but he preaches hatred of others, and he attracts, both here and in Israel, the worst hooligan elements of the Jewish community. As a Holocaust survivor, they remind me of the Jewish policemen and the Jewish tough guys who worked with the *Judenrat* and the SS. We now have our own Jewish fascists and racists.

We live a democracy that does not need such vigilantism. The American Jewish community and Israeli society have overwhelmingly repudiated Kahane's philosophy. Kahaneism is a repudiation of everything our rabbis have taught us about righteousness. It is a disgrace to the memory of our prophets who preached social justice and equality. Kahaneism will pass but not without a great deal of pain and shame.

May 1985

Letters: Kahane in New York

The Jewish Week, April 5, 2019, p. 6.

* * *

Thank you for that great story about Meir Kahane ("Days of Rage: Kahane in New York," March 8) by Jonathan Mark. Like Mr. Mark, I too was enthralled by the JDL in 1968 for a short time, even engaged in some "direct action" against the Moyseyev Ballet when they visited Chicago, but as I got to know the members and learned about Kahanism, I saw their true colors: losers, racists and weirdos, very confused Jews who had to prove their machoism in a world of goyim.

I do remember a few memorable lines from Kahane, however. Mr. Mark quotes one famous one from a 1971 talk Kahane gave. When Moses came upon an Egyptian beating a Jew, he didn't, in Kahane's telling, set up a committee to investigate the root causes of Egyptian anti-Semitism; he smote the Egyptian. In another instance I remember Kahane telling me, "Jack, if I could have 10 leftists like you, I could run the country."

He always admired committed Jewish radicals who he could turn around to his way of thinking, but what was his way of thinking? Racism, violence, xenophobia, fear of Muslims. It kind of feels like people we know today. Plus, I am shocked at Israel. At one time, they outlawed [the Kahanist] Kach [party]; today, in a new mask, Israel accepts racist political parties.

Jack Nusan Porter
Boston

April 1, 2019

VI. Neo-Nazism and Neo-Fascism

Neo-Nazism, Neo-Fascism, and Terrorism: A Global Trend?

Judaism, Summer 1982, pp. 311-321.

* * *

Introduction

The late comic Lenny Bruce once described a Nazi rally as two Nazis and 500 Jews with all the Jews looking around wondering why there are so many of them there. The point is that we should not exaggerate the numbers or power of the anti-Semitic and racist groups in the United States and Canada. Over the Labor Day weekend in 1980 the American Nazi parties held a national conference in Raleigh, North Carolina, and only 75 delegates from around the United States, Canada, and Europe attended. Five years ago, when I first began my research on neo-Nazis, they held a similar "party congress" in Milwaukee, and then, too, only 75 showed up, and these included a few wives and children. Their numbers have not grown by much since then.

Though the neo-Nazis parties are tiny, we can view right-wing groups as a series of concentric circles with the most respectable people in the center and the least reputable fanning outward. The center contains responsible conservative powers that dominate the Republican Party today, i.e., people like Ronald Reagan and William F. Buckley. They are not anti-Semitic, anti-Israel, or racist, though some of their policies do dovetail with the extreme right. In a circle around the Republicans might fall the "Moral Majority" of Rev. Jerry Falwell and similar groups. They, too, are not anti-Semitic (thought some might quarrel with that), nor are they anti-Israel. In fact, they are among Israel's staunchest allies. Still, many liberal Jews are uncomfortable with both their evangelism and their conservative politics. Outside of them might fall the non-violent but extremely right-wing groups such as the New Christian Crusade Church, the Liberty Lobby, and perhaps the John Birch Society. Way, way out on the periphery are the very dangerous right-wing: the KKK, the Minutemen, the National Renaissance Party, the National States' Rights Party, and similar fringe groups. And even further out, in a deviant class all by themselves, are the neo-fascist motorcycle gangs, Waffen-SS groupies, and sexual and religious Aryan clubs.

The point that I am making is that there is a continuum of conservative and right-wing thinking in this country. Some of it is very powerful but quite respectable in appearance; some of it quite weak (luckily) but extremely racist. While Lenny Bruce was correct in one way, George Santayana's aphorism must also be remembered. To paraphrase: those who forget the past will be doomed to relive it. Did not Hitler begin with small groups of disgruntled army veterans, motorcycle bums, and other cult followers, and did he not eventually gain the support of the more respectable, more powerful military-industrial upper-class? There is a connection between the extremes of my concentric circles. The same economic, social, and political forces that elected a Republican president also contribute to the rise of right-wing, neo-fascist extremism. I will explain what I mean later in the article, but first I would like to detail some of the new trends that are taking place, and while I do not have my baggage packed yet, there is cause for alarm.

New Alliances and Coalitions

A neo-Nazi paper, *The New Order*, published a front-page article proudly proclaiming that a "historic first" had taken place on April 19, 1980. The Ku Klux Klan, the National States' Rights Party, and the National Socialist (Nazi) Party of America had gathered in rural Johnston County, North Carolina (about 30 miles outside of Raleigh) for a public rally, complete with cross-burning. The occasion for this demonstration of "white racial unity" by three of the most prominent racist groups in the state was to show public support for the fourteen men on trial in Greensboro, North Carolina, who were facing murder charges in the killings of several members of the Revolutionary Communist Party on November 3, 1979.

The neo-Nazis do not know their own history. This was not the first time that the KKK and the American Nazis have worked together in this nation's history. I have uncovered historical data that shows cordial relationships between these two groups as far back as the 1930s and '40s. In a book published in 1943 by John Roy Carlson called *Undercover: My Four Years in the Nazi Underworld of America*, there is a picture taken on August 18, 1940, on the grounds of the German Bund Camp Nordland, showing KKK leader Arthur Bell shaking hands with August Klapprott, vice-president of the German Bund (the American Nazis of that time). Right-wing leader Edward James Smyth engineered this joint Nazi-Klan meeting forty years ago.[1]

A similar coalition was recently set free after a jury trial for the killings of five Communist members, including a Jewish doctor. Fourteen neo-Nazis and KKK members were charged with five counts of first-degree murder and conspiracy to commit murder but were set free because the jury regarded communists as worse than fascists. This coalition is a serious matter because, in the recent past, American neo-Nazis have usually worked alone and, while the KKK and the Nazis both have similar political planks ("white power," a new social order, a deep hatred of Communism, an abhorrence of Blacks and Jews, an Aryan Culture, an "unpolluted race," strong centralized leadership, and a new social order), the emphasis on the Nazi uniform has caused rifts within both neo-Nazi groups and between Nazis and Klansmen. While I believe that the swastika and other Nazi regalia will continue to divide these two groups, history—both past and present—has shown that extremist groups can unite, given the right circumstances.

Another development is the increased relationship building among Nazis around the world. Delegations of neo-Nazi groups from Canada, England, and Belgium have come to the USA to meet with Nazi leaders, and this situation should be watched, since it points to the international roots of extremism. People in the "white world" (Western Europe, Canada, South Africa, Australia) are coming under increasing pressure from high-energy bills, high taxes, and unemployment. They are fed-up with bilingual education, affirmative action, equal opportunity, unregulated immigration

---

1   John Roy Carlson, *Undercover* (New York: E.P. Dutton, 1943).

patterns, and the impotence of their countries' foreign policies. They do not like Blacks, Arabs, Cubans, Iranians, Mexicans, Filipinos, "boat people" and Jews. They want easy answers to complex problems. The time is ripe for a world-wide resurgence of fascism. In periods of great economic and political stress, insecure people look for strong leadership, some great white hope who will magically transform their world into sweetness and light—white light.

Increased Political Sophistication

The KKK, the neo-Nazis, and the other extremists have discovered the power of the ballot box. Instead of marching around in white robes, brown shirts, or whatever costume they have on hand, they are becoming more sophisticated in style and tactics. One KKK leader, David Duke, summarized this change on TV with the pithy clarion call of "out of the cow pastures and into the hotel lobbies." So, along with cross burnings and the goose-stepping, they have begun to run for office and to appear on radio, television, and in newspapers with their message. They have also increased their attempts at recruitment on army bases, in high schools and college campuses. Some examples:

- A neo-Nazi named Arthur Jones campaigned vigorously for mayor of Milwaukee in 1976 and won 5,000 votes in the primary against the popular liberal incumbent Henry Maier.
- In 1974, Jesse Stoner, chairman of the National States' Rights Party, ran on a platform calling for the eradication of Blacks and Jews and came in fourth out of a field of ten candidates in the Georgia lieutenant governor's race. He amassed 71,000 votes.
- Neo-Nazis have run for alderman in Chicago, for school boards in San Francisco and Milwaukee, for mayor of Houston, and for governor of Georgia.
- In August 1980, Tom Metzger, a KKK leader and Nazi sympathizer, surprised political analysts and won the 43rd Congressional District in Southern California, the most populous district in the United States. As the Democratic Party nominee, he faced the Republican incumbent, Claire Burgener. With fewer than 50 volunteers on his staff and less than $10,000 in campaign contributions, he was defeated by Burgener, who got 253,949 votes to Metzger's 35,107

(14%). Though expelled from the Democratic County Committee, Metzger is still a member of the Democratic State Committee.

- In Detroit, Gerald Carlson defeated the official Republican candidate in Michigan's 15th Congressional District to face the Democratic incumbent in the fall of 1980. The Michigan Republican Party was so embarrassed by this victory that it asked voters to vote for his Democratic opponent, William Ford. Carlson is a former member of the Ku Klux Klan, the John Birch Society, and the American Nazi Party and ran a campaign based on primarily a single issue: "white superiority" over Blacks and Jews. He lost to Ford but got 53,000 votes (32%) to 68% for Ford (who had won with 80% in 1976 and 75% in 1972).[2]
- On May 6, 1980, Harold Covington, one of the major leaders of the American Nazi Party, got 56,000 votes in the North Carolina Republican primary for State Attorney General. Campaigning with virtually no money and no neutral media coverage, he garnered 43% of the total vote and lost only narrowly.

Nazis and KKK members, including both men and women members, have been appearing recently on national network TV shows such as those of Tom Snyder, Phil Donohue, and Hour Magazine. They often polish their act so as to appear like any other political group, but under strenuous questioning from the host and audience the racism and violence come out into the open. Still, millions of people are exposed to at least some of the philosophy of these neo-fascist groups. I predict that, within a few years, a neo-Nazi or Klansman (or woman) will win election at a state level.

Intellectual Apologetics

One of the most outrageous developments in this sudden turn to the right has been the outcropping of fascism on college campuses and the legitimation of right-wing thinkers by eminent scholars and academics. Again, looking at history, this is not unique. The late Max Weinreich, in his 1946 book, *Hitler's Professors*, documented how German scholars, in conspiracy with German politicians and military, did their utmost to spread Nazi anti-Jewish theory and practice to the occupied and satellite nations and

---

2   See *Jewish Currents* (January 1981): 46.

to any other country within their reach.[3] In an essay in *Jewish Currents* (February 1978), Karen Sacks echoes that theme. She feels that a new *Rassenscience* has emerged in recent years. For example, among today's Social Darwinists, the Nobel Prize winner William Shockley advocates sterilization bonuses for poor Black women and, along with Professors Richard Herrnstein and Arthur R. Jensen, Shockley claims that poor people are dumber than the rich and have more children; hence allowing them to reproduce will lead to "genetic enslavement." While Shockley's work has been dismissed by geneticists and other scientists of the National Academy of Sciences as "unworthy of serious consideration," Richard Nixon's top scientific advisor, Edward David, supported Shockley and publicly berated the National Academy of Sciences for its stand. This "new eugenics" has serious genocidal implications.[4]

Equally alarming is the case of Noam Chomsky, Ferrari Ward Professor. of Linguistics at MIT. Chomsky has recently written a preface to a book by a French historian, Robert Flaurisson, who claims that the Nazi gas chambers never existed and that the facts about the Holocaust and the number of victims have been grossly exaggerated. Flaurisson was dismissed from his post as professor at Lyons University in the wake of the scandal caused by one of his previous books on the subject. Chomsky states in his preface that while he does not share Flaurisson's views he does favor freedom of expression and claims that the controversy over this subject will help reveal the real truth and extent of Nazi atrocities in countries which were not subjected to Nazi occupation. Interestingly, Flaurisson is a member of a leftist group in France and his new book was published by a left-wing publishing firm close to the Trotskyist movement.[5] Chomsky is, of course, also sympathetic to leftist views. It is ironic that these apologetics and the subsequent stamp of legitimacy come not from right-wing intellectuals but from the left.

These are not the only examples of academic support for neo-Nazi and neo-fascist views. Austin J. App, former associate professor of English at LaSalle College, Philadelphia, is the author of numerous neo-Nazi pamphlets, one, for example, called "Did Six Million Really Die? The Truth at Last." The French author, Paul Rassinier, a pioneer of this revisionist

---

3   Max Weinreich, *Hitler's Professors: The Part of Scholarship in Germany's Crimes Against the Jewish People* (New York: YIVO, 1946).
4   Karen Sacks, "The New 'Rassenscience,'" *Jewish Currents* (February 1978): 4-12.
5   Edwin Eytan, "Chomsky Writes Preface to Book Denying Nazi Atrocity," *Jewish Advocate* [Boston] (December 18, 1980).

approach, speaks of "The Lie of Auschwitz." Northwestern University professor (of electrical engineering) Arthur Butz calls his book *The Hoax of the Twentieth Century*, meaning the death camps and the extermination of millions of Jews among others. George Pape, president of the German-American Committee of Greater New York (a cultural organization with over 50 branches in the metropolitan area) objected to the introduction of teaching the Holocaust in the school system with the words: "There is no real proof that the Holocaust actually happened." Elie Wiesel has noted:

> The Holocaust and its memory are now being assaulted, with increasing fury, in many quarters... Why are the professors of history not speaking up in outrage?... Why hasn't the academic community boycotted Arthur Butz at Northwestern? Why haven't students walked out on him?[6]

Terrorism: Left and Right

Over a decade ago, S. M. Lipset rightly analyzed the penchant of the extreme left and the extreme right for targeting similar terrorist attacks. What he wrote back then echoes strongly what seems to be happening today:

> Although many conservatives (e.g. Barry Goldwater and some of the contributors to William Buckley's magazine *The National Review*) are now strongly pro-Israel, the extremist right, like the extremist left, remains very hostile, an attitude linked to their continued anti-Semitism. Thus, *The Thunderbolt*, the organ of the racist National States Rights party...supports "a strong Arab stand against the brutal aggression of Israel." Gerald L. K. Smith's *Cross and the Flag* repeatedly condemns Israel for crimes against the Arabs. The Italian neo-Fascists strongly back the Al Fatah and (like the New Left), reprint much of its propaganda. The fascist magazine *La Nation Européenne* also supports Al Fatah and advertises its publications. The German National Democrats, in their paper, *Deutsche Nazional Zeitung*, take a similar pro-Arab terrorist line. I do not think it would be unfair to say that the revolutionary fascist right and the revolutionary communist left

---

6   Elie Wiesel, "What Really Happened to Six Million Jews?", *Jewish Digest* (April 1978): 36-38. Originally appeared in the *London Jewish Chronicle*.

have similar positions with respect to Middle East conflict and the role of Al Fatah.[7]

My research has verified Prof. Lipset's conclusions, but with some new wrinkles. American neo-Nazi and KKK publications and leaders continue to spout anti-Zionist and anti-Semitic rhetoric and have attempted a few feeble efforts at coalition-building with the Palestine Liberation Organization (PLO). However, given the historic antipathy toward Communist and other socialist groups in the USA, I do not see such coalitions having much of a future here. However, on the matter of Israel, neo-fascist groups have attempted contact with the PLO.

For example, *The New Order* of September-October 1980, a neo-Nazi paper published in Lincoln, Nebraska, printed an article on the front page under the headline, "Nazis vs. Jews and Niggers," which stated that on July 9th (1980), the Chicago unit of the NSPA held a rally in Chicago's Daley Civic Center and that, prior to the rally, the NSPA (Nazi) Stormtroopers joined with members of the Palestine Liberation Organization in a march denouncing Israeli "imperialism and torture of the Palestinian people." The article noted that the Nazis were well-received by PLO members and that they promised to work together in the future. The article ended with:

> For obvious reasons, the Jew-dominated news media were horrified at the idea of the two worst enemies of the Zionists joining together in a united front.

We will see more attempts by right-wing groups to smear Israel and blame it for America's problems. Thus, anti-Zionism will be coordinated with, or at times mask, anti-Semitism. However, I have not uncovered *terrorist* coordination between KKK/neo-Nazi groups and the PLO, but it could occur in the future. The situation in Europe is different. There, a great deal of terrorist activity has taken place in Italy, France, Germany, and Belgium, and definite connections have been made between fascist groups and Arab terrorists.

Ironically, according to a report by Jacques de Vernisy in *Le Matin* (Paris), Palestinian terrorism, which used to preoccupy the police and security forces, is now regarded as only a peripheral part of this new wave. The report notes that, while attacks are perpetrated by Palestinians, it is

---

7   S. M. Lipset, "The Left, the Jews, and Israel" in his *Revolution and Counter-Revolution* (New York: Doubleday-Anchor Books, 1970), p. 398.

often as mercenaries and not in the service of the PLO! The same holds true for Libyans, Iraqis, and others. What we have is a situation whereby "free-lance" terrorists sell out to the highest bidder and are called in by any group that can afford their fees (as high as $30,000 per month).

For example, in Antwerp, twenty-five-year-old Abdel Wahid tossed a grenade into a group of Jewish children preparing for a trip to camp, killing one and wounding seventeen. The next day an anonymous phone caller to the press agency, Belga, claimed responsibility in the name of the PFLP (Popular Front for the Liberation of Palestine). But the PFLP, from its head-quarters in Beirut, immediately denied participation.

In Paris, the three men arrested for the unsuccessful assassination attempt on ex-Iranian leader Shapour Bakhtiar claimed that they had acted on behalf of the PLO and that Yasser Arafat had personally ordered the liquidation of Bakhtiar. The PLO and Arafat denied responsibility. It is also possible that the infamous bombing that killed several people at the Synagogue in Rue Copernic in Paris may not have been carried out by neo-Nazis but by Arab terrorist mercenaries.

At the end of 1973, after the Yom Kippur War, the PLO realized that terrorist operations were detrimental to its cause and so it has turned more to diplomatic action. Even the infamous Black September, responsible for the 1972 massacre of Israeli athletes at the Munich Olympic Games, has been dissolved. Nevertheless, some Palestinians do not approve of this new diplomatic strategy and, after years of terrorist acts all over the world, they remain unable to change. They have therefore deserted the ranks of the PLO to put themselves at the service of others, either out of revolutionary friendship or out of financial interest.[8]

The scope of terrorism is beyond his short article, and it is complex indeed. Soon after the Paris bombing, several reports stated that far-right and far-left terrorists might join forces. For example, *Newsweek* (Oct. 13, 1980)[9] contained several shocking quotations from Italian intellectuals: Professor Paolo Signorelli, a radical rightist, called for "the union of revo-lutionary forces from the left and right in a single popular movement." And Mario Guido Naldi, editor of the right-wing journal *Quex*, said, "You have to remember that a revolutionary is closer to us under any circumstances than a conservative." An essay by Thomas Sheehan in *The New York Review*

---

8   Jacques de Vernisy, "The New International Terrorism," *Jewish Digest* (January 1981): 3-7. Originally appeared in *Le Matin*.

9   John Brecher, "A Wave of Neo-Nazi Terror," *Newsweek* (October 13, 1980): 71.

of Books (Jan. 22, 1981) discusses the rise of what he calls Eurofascism, and he mentions that two members of a highly militant neo-Nazi group in Germany, led by Karl-Heinz Hoffman and thirty other European fascists, were training in the Falangist camp at Aquru, northeast of Beirut. Furthermore, Italian, French, and German neo-fascists are cooperating on terrorist activities and have been aided by mercenary Arab terrorists. All of these are shocking developments that need further verification.[10]

Cause and Effect: The Synergy of Left and Right

What accounts for this upsurge in fascism and terrorism from both the left and right—the Baader-Meinhof Group and Red Brigades on one hand and the KKK, European National Fasces, and neo-Nazis on the other? Events are running away from theory. Traditionally, sociological theory says that fascism attracts the unemployed, embittered white working class. But what explains the entrance of students, intellectuals, and the educated upper-middle class into right-wing extremism? The rise of both the left and the right is due to the tensions and frustrations of a society. Unstable economic conditions, inflation and recession, caused in great part by dependence on Third-World and Arab oil countries and the subsequent loss of power and prestige in world affairs, are among the major factors. The West must face the bitter truth that it is becoming increasingly impotent in relation to its political and economic crises. In fact, many people are even tired of "crises." They want to see a return to a Wilsonian approach in foreign policy wherein the United States will once again be the great teacher to the wayward world. This can lead to two results: hawkish militant assertion of America's power or a more difficult, diplomatic accommodation to the new realities. Many Westerners are unable to cope with the latter. They see diplomacy and accommodation as appeasement, as a sign of weakness. They look to strong leadership and a return to simple answers, thus setting the stage for both conservatism and its more extreme brothers-in-law—fascism, neo-Nazism, racism, and anti-Semitism.

Prof. Gregory Winn of the University of Southern California has written a fascinating paper analyzing the drift towards alienation and, for some, towards terrorism among young West German students.[11] His conclusions

---

10 Thomas Sheehan, "Italy: Terror on the Right," *The New York Review of Books* (January 22, 1981): 23.

11 Gregory F. T. Winn, "Terrorism, Alienation, and German Society," paper presented at the Third Annual Meeting of the International Society of Political Psychology (Boston, Mass.), June 4-7, 1980.

bear repeating not only to explain left-wing activities among German young people but right-wing ones as well. Why and how any person moves in a left- or right-wing direction are complex and difficult questions, but what makes them even more difficult is that the same factors that drive a person to become a member of the Red Brigade can also lead him/her to join the neo-Nazis. The fact is that we have a world of over-educated, under-employed young people, and during economic crises that is an explosive combination. Prof. Winn has two main categories—societal and ideological factors that can lead to terrorism.

A. *Societal Factors*
1. Contempt for the "consumer society" and the welfare state and its rejection *because* of its prosperity and political success.
2. An effort to force democratic societies to crack down harshly on dissent, thereby further alienating leftist and moderate sympathizers. This would bring about a more fascist state—which is democracy's "true colors" anyway. This cynical approach, held by some leftists, hopes to hand the state over to the waiting arms of the right wing. After this move is effectuated, there will come a "true" proletarian revolution.
3. Frustration resulting from lack of job opportunities and over-education of its students, resulting in not only loss of jobs but also dissatisfaction with available jobs.
4. Frustration with a society that is overly taxed, formally rigid and overly regulated.
5. Disillusionment with a society because of the corruption of its political leaders, the similarity of party policies, and bugging/surveillance sandals.
6. Alienation and frustration from "achievement pressures" in the society. The greater pressure to achieve starts young, and has led to tremendous increases in maladaptive behavior—suicide, drug and alcohol abuse, psychiatric breakdowns, and cultism.
7. One could also add—anger directed at Black, Oriental, and Third-World immigrants (who are often better targets than Jews). These people are seen as a threat to jobs when, ironically, they were brought to the country to take menial or dangerous jobs that local citizens did not want. In the United States, these immigrants could be Cubans, Mexicans, or Vietnamese; in France, they would be Africans, Algerians, and other Arabs; in England, they might be

Pakistanis, Indians, and Africans. Throughout Europe, there is antipathy to Turkish, Yugoslavian, Greek, and Italian *gastarbeiter*, and it has led to government restrictions on civil liberties and immigration in both America and Europe.

B. *Ideological and Psychological Factors*
1. A playing out of nihilistic, anarchistic theories best typified by Bakunin for leftist terrorists or mythic, compulsive, authoritarian theories best typified by Spengler and D'Annunzio.
2. A link between idealism, romanticism and terrorism, inspired by a deeply imagine and romantic view of the ideal society. For neo-Nazis, this would be an Aryan society peopled by strong, lean, blue-eyed men and women; for leftists, a society of strong working-class heroic peasants and workers. In both cases, it is a society ruled by the powerful and survived by the most violent.
3. Terrorist violence is based on purely criminal instincts without any reference to any form of revolutionary theory or strategy. As of now, this terror has been mainly from the left (PLO, Baader-Meinhof, Red Brigades, IRA, Weathermen, Symbionese Liberation Army, Red Guards), but, today, right-wing "counter-revolutionary" violence has appeared and will prove even more dangerous.
4. Family alienation and rejection of paternalistic authoritarianism (by leftists) and rejection of paternalistic liberals and welfare statists (by rightists and leftists).
5. A lack of individual purpose (anomie) compounded by *boredom*, especially in democratic, permissive societies.
6. A natural urge to express violence as a means of ridding oneself of suppressed feelings of impotence.
7. And last, the fear of simply being an "ordinary" citizen without identity, a cog in the machine of mass society, a blob in the gray, mundane welfare state. The desire is to achieve something, anything, even violently, in order not to be seen as a "nothing." This last theory could help explain not only left-right terrorism but such disparate acts as the Jonestown deaths (and other cults), the killing of John Lennon, and the hijacking of planes and buses.

Conclusions

While all of these terrorist groups are small in number, they are dangerous for two reasons. First, they can inflict a great deal of damage, greatly out of proportion to their numbers. But most important, they can (and this is their intent) push the government to take steps to counter the violence. This can lead to police-state tactics and the abuse of civil liberties. Thus, all citizens suffer because of the acts of a few. Make no mistake about it. The true enemy of both left and right fascists is the moderate center. The true target is democracy. The acting out of violence is an utter gasp of futility and pain. Terrorism is the act of the impotent, not of the strong; the imprisoned, not the liberated; the frustrated, not the integrated. It is simply theater, a means of attracting attention.

What can we do? First, as distasteful as it may seem, one thing we can do is to listen to the demands and try to change what can responsibly be changed. While the tactics of terror speak for few, the ideology and politics behind the terror may speak for millions. We must listen to the voice of terror. At the same time, we must support strong anti-terrorist laws, and we must train strong anti-terrorist police forces. To understand the terrorists best, we must put ourselves into their minds and think like them. That, the experts tell us, is the only way to understand them. We must also protect precious democratic freedoms despite the provocation. If governments give way to police states in order to catch terrorists, they will hand the terrorists a victory. Most of all, we have to attack the unglamorous conditions that breed terrorism: unemployment, racism, poor housing, discrimination, etc. … the unfinished agenda of the Johnson and Kennedy years. It is difficult simultaneously to root out terrorism and to uphold freedom and justice, but both must be on our agenda. We have no choice.

Summer, 1982

A Nazi Runs for Mayor: Dangerous Brownshirts or Media Freaks?

Present Tense, Vol. 4, No. 4, Summer 1977, pp. 27-31.

* * *

In Milwaukee, the coming of the Nazis uncovered mountains of emotion.

NAZIS A DILEMMA FOR JEWS, read the headline of a lengthy news story in the *Milwaukee Journal*, the city's leading newspaper.

"Rarely, if ever, in the history of the Milwaukee Jewish community has a single issue provoked more dissension, wrought more anger, or spawned more discontent than that which has arisen as a result of the surfacing of the National Socialist White People's Party here," wrote the editor of the *Wisconsin Jewish Chronicle.*

These articles, which appeared two years ago, pinpointed a phenomenon that is worrying some Jews in the United States, being ignored by others and rousing a few to anger and even violence. And beyond the reactions of Jewish communities and individuals, and other Americans, lie thorny legal questions rooted in such constitutional rights as the freedoms of speech and assembly.

Actually, the National Socialist White People's Party—formerly the American Nazi Party—has probably no more than 400 members in some dozen chapters around the country. (The name was changed to stress the

"Americanness" of the Nazis and to downplay their German roots.) They have gained no apparent power or influence; their loyalists are universally regarded as beyond the pale of respectability. But—perhaps because some media people recall that Hitler's Nazis started out as a small group composed mainly of lower-class hoodlums, or more likely because the media are always on the lookout for the sensational—the American Nazis have often been featured on television and in the press, and thus have gained widespread "visibility."

Milton Ellerin, of the American Jewish Committee, whose job it is to keep track of them, found that "Since the Yom Kippur War, units of the NSWPP have flamboyantly picketed foreign embassies, the White House, bookstores, theatres and Jewish houses of worship; appeared in full Nazi storm trooper regalia before Boards of Education and City Councils; distributed literature and defaced public buildings with propaganda stickers in downtown business areas; and publicly announced the opening of new national headquarters to at least three cities."

Founded by George Lincoln Rockwell in the early 1960s, the American Nazi Party was shaken by the August 1967 assassination of its founding "führer" and drifted into obscurity. The 1973 Yom Kippur War and its succeeding oil embargo gave the Nazis a new impetus for growth. The group remerged several years ago under the leadership of a new commander, Matt Koehl, and began an aggressive campaign for political legitimacy. Since then, American Nazis have been involved in scores of incidents in cities as diverse as Milwaukee, San Francisco and St. Louis. They gravitate to areas and issues that are intense, sensitive and interracial in composition—integration in Milwaukee (two Nazi women ran for the school board this past April 5th and lost) and San Francisco, busing in Boston and Louisville, for instance—which they hope to exploit for their own political purposes.

Jewish (and non-Jewish) responses have been, and still are, mixed. In San Francisco last April, a crowd of Jews burned down a Nazi store situated up the street from a synagogue. In St. Louis, television viewers, incensed over the publicity given the Nazis on a talk show, called in and complained to the management. In other cities, Jews and other citizens have engaged in educational programs, rallies, and coalition-building to stop the Nazis.

The history of the American Nazis' activities in Milwaukee, then—including the effort by Arthur Jones, the party's public relations director, to capture the office of mayor in the 1976 election—is instructive. The reactions within Milwaukee's Jewish community to the incidents, episodes and threats; the ensuing political and legal developments, and the still unanswered questions merit thoughtful consideration.

Two major issues were involved. One was the impact of the Nazi group's acts on the Milwaukee Jewish community. The other was the effort to contain the grass-roots Jewish effort that was mounted in the general community, and its results.

In Milwaukee, a city of 691,000, with a long tradition of Socialist mayors and racial and religious harmony, the coming of the Nazis uncovered mountains of emotion, but nowhere more so than in the Jewish community of 25,000.

The first incident to receive notice occurred in September 1974 when the Nazis began distributing their literature at several racially mixed grade schools and high schools. According to a later report by City Attorney James Brennan to the Milwaukee Common Council, "As a direct result of the distribution of Nazi literature, approximately eighty fistfights occurred between students and members of the NSWPP as well as among students themselves." Under disorderly conduct ordinances, the City Attorney's office prosecuted members of the party who distributed the material, but the case was lost in County Court because the judge ruled that their action did not constitute disorderly conduct. His decision was appealed to the Circuit court of Milwaukee County, but was affirmed.

Almost a year later, practically every literate citizen of Milwaukee was aware that the Nazis were actively operating in their midst. As a result, from August 1975, when the Nazis set up a booth at a state fair, to February 1976 when Arthur Jones lost his bid to become mayor, the city was in turmoil and the Jewish leadership was divided into two major camps.

One camp advocated an activist-confrontational strategy, while the other warned that such tactics could only gain more publicity for the Nazis and could eventually boomerang against the Jews. One group wanted to use confrontational but mostly legal methods (rallies, keeping watch on Nazi homes, etc.), while the other advocated educational and "behind-the-scenes" maneuvering. The activist camp saw the Nazis as a growing, threatening menace and called for intensive public demonstrations and resistance, while the "non-activist" camp considered the NSWPP more or less a nuisance element, well under the control of the police and the FBI.

"In the middle," wrote Lawrence R. Tarnoff, editor of the *Wisconsin Jewish Chronicle*, "stands the majority of the Milwaukee Jewish community, concerned and confused, uncertain if they should view the Nazis as the

Gestapo incarnate…or as an insignificant band of street hoodlums wearing the trappings of the Nazis as a means of satisfying their sick quest for notoriety and public disdain."

What intensified the confrontation was that the site of most American Nazi activity took place in Milwaukee's West Side, a working-class neighborhood where elderly and middle-aged survivors of the Holocaust live. With its Hasidic *shuls*, Orthodox synagogues, Kosher "meat clubs," delicatessens and communal centers, this is the most visible Jewish community in the city. The most frequent targets of the Nazis were several West Side congregations made up primarily of concentration camp and ghetto survivors—easy prey for Nazis who accosted and harassed them on their way to services.

Concern, a local newsletter issue by the Concerned Jewish Citizens, an organization of West Side neighborhood Jews most affected by the Nazi activities, reported a spate of incidents during the last four months of 1976. Among them were these:

- A fifteen-year-old Nazi tried to run an auto over a Jewish schoolmate.
- Nazis demonstrated in front of Jewish stores, calling for a boycott of Jewish business.
- *White Power*, the Nazi newspaper, was surreptitiously distributed throughout the city.
- Windows in several synagogues were shattered.
- Nazis threw eggs at the car of Rabbi Israel Feldman.

On January 1, 1976, a firebomb was thrown at the Home of John Dorpat, a local Nazi. He strode into Congregation Agudas Achim later that day, brandishing his swastika armband and cursing the Jews inside. (Dorpat was later charged with disorderly conduct and given a 90-day sentence, but it was waived and he was granted a year's probation on condition he not participate in Nazi activities or loiter near Jewish homes and institutions.)

On that same day, Arthur Jones, a former University of Wisconsin student who was also a Vietnam veteran, stated on television that Jews were responsible for the Dorpat bombing and said: "They will pay for it." Soon after, Jones announced his candidacy for mayor of Milwaukee by filing 1,900 signatures with the Electoral Commission, and campaigned vigorously with paid commercials on radio and television and advertisements in the *Journal* and the *Sentinel*, another Milwaukee newspaper.

Meanwhile, City Attorney Brennan was pressing his case. He asked the Assistant City Attorney, David Felger, to research the law and draft an ordinance that would prohibit distribution of "hate" literature—a difficult task because such an ordinance would have to achieve a delicate balance between an individual's right of freedom of speech and a community's protection from hatred and violence bred by such material.

Felger contacted attorneys general in all fifty states and found an appropriate ordinance in the 1949 Illinois Penal Code. Its constitutionality had been upheld by the United States Supreme Court in 1951 in *Beauharnis v. Illinois*, in which the defendant, Joseph Beauharnis, had been indicted for distributing "hate" literature.

The ordinance, applying to the spoken as well as the written word, amending a chapter of the Milwaukee County General ordinance "relating to unlawful activities by racial or national groups and providing a penalty for defamatory conduct on county property" and known as a "group libel" ordinance, was passed by the Milwaukee County Board of Supervisors in December 1976. A similar ordinance for city property, proposed by Brennan, and known as the "Brennan Ordinance," was introduced in the City Common Council and was defeated last March. Both caused intense debate and conflict among Jews and civil libertarians.

Some Jewish organizations and the Milwaukee American Civil Liberties Union (ACLU) thought the "Brennan Ordinance" would be ruled unconstitutional and would be rejected by a higher court. A few dubbed it "anti-labor"—saying that it could be used against union members who picket. But other Jewish groups, especially those on the West Side, rejoiced when it was proposed. Strongest support for the "anti-Nazi ordinance"—as some people called it—came from the Concerned Jewish Citizens (CJC), who had called for tough measures against the Nazis, and from the coalition of Organizations Against Nazism (COAN), an alliance of groups including the Jewish War Veterans, the Polish Army Veterans, the NAACP, the Veterans of Foreign Wars, the Zionist Organization of America, the Latin American Union, the Wisconsin Board of Rabbis, Women's American ORT (ex-officio) and several other labor and fraternal groups.

CIC and COAN were opposed by the Milwaukee Anti-Defamation League (ADL) and the Milwaukee Jewish Council (MIC). Attorney Robert Friebert, associated with the ADL-MIC, called it a "wretched piece of legislation" that "ten years from now could be used against us." Writing in the *Wisconsin Jewish Chronicle*, he said, "The specter of the Nazis is a disgusting specter, but do we throw out everything we believe in to go after one group? We do ourselves a tremendous injustice if we support this ordinance."

The ADL refused to support the ordinance for three reasons: it was unconstitutional; it could boomerang against the Jews, labor unions, or other groups, thereby engendering more calumny against the Jewish community, and, most importantly, the court trials that would result from enforcement of such an ordinance would give anti-Semitic extremists an opportunity to have a forum for dissemination of their ideas in the press, radio and television. The ADL also supported the Wisconsin CLU position that the Nazis were entitled to legal defense in the courts.

Esther Leah Ritz, a prominent Jewish leader and member of MIC, proposed that the ADL ask David Felger, who had drafted the "Brennan Ordinance," to withdraw it from City Common Council consideration, saying that it would be a "disaster for the Jewish community if constitutional rights were abrogated."

On the other hand, Burton Polansky, a well-known Milwaukee lawyer and president-founder of COAN, said that the Brennan ordinance culminated a year-long struggle for enactment of a group libel ordinance by his coalition and he believe it would be upheld by a higher court, just as the one in Illinois had been.

He declared:

> We have discovered that at times an "extra ingredient" is necessary in order to stop such people as the Nazis—confrontation, not just backstage politicking. We in the Jewish community have become too "professionalized." We have too many "professional" spokesmen for us—too many "court Jews"—and this is demeaning to us as Jews and as Zionists. We need grass-roots neighborhood activity or otherwise we become weak and powerless. We end up pleading or letting our so-called leaders plead for us. In the end, we receive a benign smile and then they throw the petition in the garbage.
>
> For example, we felt it would be intolerable for the Nazis to march on our Jewish Community Center [August 30, 1975]. They came with fifty-six storm troopers plus a dozen or so followers. The police were there in full force. The Nazis marched up and down the sidewalk yelling "Hitler Lives!" and "Dump Israel!"

The fact that we stood two feet from the Nazis and with our chests pushed out, protecting our JCC, that made me feel good. I felt we had to legally form an organization, and out of this came COAN. We printed our own newsletter because the local Jewish press was antagonistic to us and refused to print any information on Nazi activity on the West Side—vandalism, beatings, etc. The general press printed it, but the Jewish press wouldn't.... Instead, people came to us, not them, when they were abused by Nazis in one way or another.

Then there was the equally pressing issue of a Nazi running for mayor. Never in the history of this country had an avowed Nazi run for mayor on a Nazi program. How was Milwaukee to respond?

At the beginning of this eventful year, Arthur Jones campaigned vigorously and on February 17, 1976 received nearly 5,000 votes in the mayoral primary against the liberal and progressive incumbent Mayor Henry Maier. Jones finished in fourth place, but Professor A. Clarke Hagensick of the University of Wisconsin–Milwaukee determined later that many "Nazi" votes were really anti-Maier votes. Then, too, Milwaukee mayoral candidates run as independents rather than on party lines, and many who chose Jones did not know he was a Nazi. Maier, a popular and effective mayor, overwhelmingly won renomination with nearly 70 percent of the vote. It was a lopsided victory, and Maier's opposition would have been all but forgotten had he not run against a Nazi. (Maier later easily won reelection in April 1976 to a fifth term of office over his closest rival—a young challenger name Jan Olson.)

Jones, a youthful, "Aryan"-looking blond, was born in the quiet town of Beloit, Wisconsin and majored in political science at the university. After his honorable discharge from the Army, he moved to Milwaukee, where he worked as a machinist and metalworker. During the election he was employed in a fast-food chain store.

In his well-financed campaign's television announcements and large newspaper advertisements, he proclaimed himself the "white people's candidate," a man who would "with...courage and honesty...stand up as a white man for the white race." His campaign material was festooned with pictures of the American flag and the Nazi swastika, "the ancient symbol of the white race," as he put it. He declared that, if elected, he would "do something about it." The "it" referred to the Nazi Party program. It stood for tough crackdowns on crime, and opposition to all forms of gun-control, busing and "reverse discrimination." The party was also against "unnecessary spending," and in favor of "fiscal responsibility," and believed "in a government of, by and for the people of Milwaukee—not special minorities, sell-out politicians, social experimenters and Communist subversives."

His tone was virulently anti-black and anti-Communist, but anti-Jewishness was toned down. The Nazi literature used in his campaign was very similar in style, content and format to the campaign literature distributed by Richard Johanson, a 31-year-old native of Oakland, California, who ran for the San Francisco Board of Education in November 1976 and received even more votes than Jones—about 9,000. Johanson also sought election as the "white people's candidate" on the Nazi Party ticket. He lost.

Thus the Nazis posed an enormous dilemma for the Jewish community. The issue was over tactics, not goals. All Jews were committed to eliminating or neutralizing any "Nazi threat," but they were badly divided about exactly how to do it.

But aside from tactics, there was another issue, one that every group in society faces: Who speaks for a people or group? In whose name are policies made? And who should represent such a people or group? In the Jewish community, there has often been a split between the leadership and the "grass roots," between the organized community leaders and neighborhood people most affected by a social problem.

The very fact of the Nazi presence poses a challenge to liberal democracy, the tolerance of the courts and the law, civil liberties and community goodwill. It is a test, ultimately, of American principles. Do the Nazis have a right to exist? To form a party with the avowed aim of genocide and expulsion of other American citizens? To disseminate such views? And, most importantly, does the government tacitly legitimate such a group when its candidates run for public office?

For television, radio and the newspapers, the Nazis presented other difficulties. In an honest and critical self-appraisal in the *Milwaukee Journal* during the height of the Nazi activity, Richard H. Leonard, the paper's editor, wrote:

> On the one hand, we are reluctant to publicize an aggressive group
> with a philosophy opposed to the principles on which this nation
> was founded, but on the other hand, we have a responsibility
> to keep the public informed about what this group is doing.

Experience has taught us that organizations of this kind don't disappear simply because they aren't getting publicity. In fact, some prefer not to have the spotlight of public attention focused on them. Others will accelerate their activity in an effort to obtain attention. Either way, the job of the newspaper is to cover the Nazis in a forthright manner that will place them in their proper perspective in the community.

Robert H. Wills, editor of the *Sentinel*, maintained that the press did not create the Nazis, and pointed out that their policy was to cover the Nazis as a news event "because the public wants to know what is going on." He also stressed that the Nazis might have gone completely unnoticed had it not been for local Jewish groups that opposed them, thereby creating a news event where none might have existed before.

And Carl Zimmerman, director of communications for WITI-TV, echoed the same sentiments, but felt that "Nazi activities could develop into something significant that could affect the rest of the country."

The Nazis pose a real dilemma for American Jews. On the one hand, they are a tiny, ineffectual and unimportant force in political affairs, little more than a nuisance element to both the American people and to the Jewish community. Yet, because of the memory of the Holocaust and the understandably nervous Jewish reaction to threats of anti-Semitism, a few insignificant Nazi fools can stir up more trouble than they are worth. It reminds one of the old joke told by the late comic Lenny Bruce: "What is the definition of a Nazi rally? Answer: Two Nazis and 100 Jews, and all the Jews are looking around, wondering why there are so many Jews there!"

So cool heads must prevail. Anti-Nazi violence, such as the Jewish Defense League advocates, is counterproductive and will give the Nazis what they in fact desire: more publicity. Established Jewish defense organizations and grass-roots Jewish neighborhood groups, such as the Concerned Jewish Citizens, must try to work together, bearing in mind, however, that both groups may perceive the problem and its resolution differently and may even have irreconcilable differences. Still, it is a healthy sign to see these indigenous groups in operation. They bring vitality and élan to a Jewish community. For Jewish Holocaust victims and their children, it is psychologically healthy to take part in anti-Nazi rallies and demonstrations.

Moreover, it is impossible to stop such grass-roots neighborhood groups. They react from an immediate need. They are often living in transitional neighborhoods. They are often the elderly, the working class and the "forgotten" Jews. If established Jewish groups will not work with rather than against them, then they will turn to the more militant and more violent JDL in time of trouble.

This is the immediate lesson that this case study has to teach Jewish leadership in Jewish communities threatened by Nazis or other trouble-makers. It is wasted energy for Jews to fight other Jews when, in fact, there are a multitude of tactics—political, legal, educational and demonstrative—that can be used to fight anti-Semitism. No one Jewish group has *all* the answers.

Summer 1977

Art Jahnke

Neo-Nazis in the USA:
An Interview

The Boston Real Paper, April 16, 1981.

* * *

Sociologist and author Dr. Jack Nusan Porter lost twenty-five relatives, including two sisters, to the Nazis during World War II. The son of a Jewish commander of partisan forces in the Ukraine, Porter has spent the last two years studying the neo-Nazi movement in the United States. Porter's research was funded by the Memorial Foundation for Jewish Culture, which is largely financed by the money from German reparations.

AJ: First of all, how many Nazis are there in the United States?

JNP: The total of hard-core members in the United States is probably not more than five hundred. Altogether there are maybe two thousand.

AJ: Why should anyone worry about a few hundred crazies?

JNP: Well, it's true that they attract only very few people, but enough that they can cause mischief, especially if they get into terrorism, as they have in Europe. And when they start running for office, as they already have here, you have to educate people about the Holocaust and fascism. Hitler started with just a few motorcycle bums, a few disgruntled army veterans, and a country that, like ours, had been economically weakened and lacked strong leadership. So if a depression hits this country, we better get worried.

AJ: How old is the Nazi movement in this country?

JNP: There are two Nazi parties. One is called the Ausland, which is the overseas branch of the German Nazis. Until the end of World War II they were fairly strong. I found in my research that the connection between these Nazis and the Ku Klux Klan goes back to the thirties. I have a photograph of a Ku Klux Klanner and a German Bund Nazi in a rally in the late thirties.

After World War II the movement went into decline and was resurrected almost single-handedly by George Lincoln Rockwell. He built them up to a few thousand before he was assassinated by another Nazi.

AJ: We never hear anything about a Nazi party in this country. What names do the Nazis go by?

JNP: The big one is the National Socialist White People's Party, and there is also the National Socialist Defense Force. The key words are National Socialist. There is even a gay Nazi group called the National Socialist League.

AJ: Which of those groups do we have in New England?

JNP: There isn't too much activity in Boston, but Providence, Rhode Island, has a very active neo-Nazi group, and they do something really terrible. If somebody who is Jewish dies, they will send a sympathy letter signed "the Nazi party." They also send out Christmas and Hanukkah cards. They like to get Jews uptight. They use Jews, and they use the Left to get people to attack them. They are very happy to have three thousand people attack them.

AJ: How do the Nazis go about legitimizing such racist ideology as theirs?

JNP: Racist theories are legitimized by many people in the public eye. I'm very upset right now with Noam Chomsky, who is a Jew and a leftist. Chomsky wrote the preface to a book by a French historian, Robert Flaurisson, who claims that the Nazi gas chambers never existed and that facts about the Holocaust have been greatly exaggerated. Flaurisson was even dismissed from his post as a professor at the University of Lyons in the wake of a scandal caused by the book. Chomsky does state that he doesn't share Flaurisson's views, but he favors freedom of expression.

AJ: What kind of people are attracted to the Nazi parties?

JNP: The Nazis attract a lot of young people, and I mean even fourteen- and fifteen-year-old kids. They attract the embittered, the unemployed, plus a few eccentric upper-class intellectuals. They also get a lot of bikers. Bikers seem to like all the Nazis regalia. In fact, one of the problems the Nazis have is that they can't seem to attract a better class of person.

Apply this to a larger scale and you see that the social and economic reasons that Reagan came to power also explain the rise of the neo-Nazis and the Klan. High unemployment, economic problems, a vacuum in leadership, a sense that the welfare state is one gray mass. People don't want to be part of that. They want to do something that will change the world.

AJ: Speaking of changing the world, what can you tell us about John Hinckley?

JNP: Hinckley was a member of the National Socialist White People's Party for a while, but he was too radical for them. If you're too radical for them, you're either an FBI agent, a provocateur, or just a crazy nut.

AJ: What kind of counter-Nazi forces do the Nazis have to worry about?

JNP: There are people who work very quietly trying to eliminate Nazis. Some of them are Jews and some are not. Some assassinate them. Some use blackmail and some use bombs. There are a lot of crazy people out there.

AJ: In the last year we've had at least two Nazis run for political office, and we've seen the desecration of synagogues on Long Island, New York. Are the Nazis growing in ranks, or are they just growing bolder?

JNP: There really hasn't been much increase in numbers in the last five years, but they are becoming more respectable. When they can take off their uniforms and get in a suit and run for office, this is a very dangerous situation. They are pulling the wood over people's eyes. The Moral Majority has some good points, about family and other things, and the Nazis say some good things, too. They want to end unemployment, too—but beneath all that is genocide.

1981

VII. Radical Zionism

My Days and Nights in Habonim

This essay is original for this book. Compare it to the essay "My Days and Nights in the JDL," and you will see a world of difference. Light vs. Darkness.

* * *

My experiences in Habonim were my childhood. Instead of going to a yeshiva to study, my parents sent me to Habonim camp in southern Michigan. My brother went to a yeshiva in Skokie, Illinois, and my sister went to a Beis Yakov School for Girls in Chicago. Thus, we had different upbringings. Mine was secular, socialist, and ardently Zionist; theirs was religious, non-socialist, and somewhat Zionist.

Habonim in the 1950s attracted a diverse crowd of children of survivors, artistic and marginal kids, and of course children who were the offspring of Labor Zionist parents. Labor Zionism, going back to the 1920s, was quite strong in the Midwest, especially Chicago, Detroit, Cleveland, Milwaukee, Madison, and Minneapolis.

One of the reasons for this was that strong Labor Zionist organizations like LZOA, Farband, and Pioneer women were organized decades earlier, some by the fabulous and energetic Golda Meir of Milwaukee, later to become the first and only female prime minister of Israel. She and her cohorts traveled all over the country, but especially in the Midwest, setting up Labor Zionist outcroppings. Second, the Midwest had a strong socialist, progressive and trade union tradition (Milwaukee, for example, had socialist mayors as late as 1951, and Madison has a socialist mayor at this very moment in 2020, Paul Soglin.)

Habonim was led by families. It was several hard-working families that helped it survive, and they passed on the traditions to their children and grandchildren. I remember the Melroods, especially Paul Melrood and his wife and their beautiful home. I wish I could remember what he did for a living to have such a nice house. Our house was old compared to his home near Capital Drive, with its huge picture windows overlooking an expansive lawn, flagstone walkways, and a sunken living room and fireplace. Paul was a gracious man and active in all the Labor Zionist groups like Farband as well as being quite the Yiddish thespian. There was also, alongside the Hebrew culture of Farband and Pioneer Women, a Yiddish culture with plays and concerts. The charming Paul Melrood and the beautiful Bess Lerner were active in what was called the Perhift Yiddish Theater.

There were also the Barland, Faber, Orenstein and Arbit families; in Madison, the Minkoff family; in Minneapolis, the Paradise, Schwartz and Yablonski families; in Detroit, the Kutnick and Salinger families; and in Pittsburgh, the Frank family.

The "jurisdiction" of Midwest Camp Habonim in Three Rivers, Michigan, ran as far west as St. Louis, Missouri, and as far east as Pittsburgh. East of Pittsburgh, people went to Camp Galil near Philadelphia or to Habonim camps in New York State. West of Missouri, from Colorado to California, kids went to camp near Los Angeles. There were also camps in western Canada, near Vancouver. Back then there were 8-9 camps; today, surprisingly, there are still six Habonim/Dror camps, and they are doing very well.

People thought that, in a post-Zionist era where the Likud Party had taken over Israel, a socialist Labor Zionism would close down. True, the city *Kinnim* ("nests" in Hebrew) declined and nearly disappeared, but the summer camps held fast. They may have had to downplay the "socialist" aspect, but they have emphasized other issues that liberal and progressive parents want: political activism, community organizing, climate change, *tikkun olam* ("repair of the world" in Hebrew, a Judaic concept of renouncing idolatry in Orthodox Judaism and generally acting beneficially to society's well being in other Jewish denominations), crafts and Scouting, as well as Hebrew, Jewish and Israeli history and politics.

Habonim camps attract activist parents and activist kids. Not surprisingly, Habonim "graduates" have included journalists such as Leonard

(Label) Fein, J.J. Goldberg, Ken Lucoff, and David Twersky, as well as actors and comics like Sacha Baron Cohen (from British Habonim) and Seth Rogen (from such movies as *The 40-Year-Old Virgin* and *Knocked Up*), plus academics such as Hasia (Schwartzman) Diner and the present author, both of us from Milwaukee *Ken* ("nest" in Hebrew) Lachish.

Also, Lyle Zackler, a founder of the LGBQT community of Israel, should be included. Zackler, who died young from a heart attack on a Tel Aviv street, was a charismatic but flawed leader. The son of prominent Chicago Zionists, he was also a closeted homosexual who acted inappropriately with young campers. My first encounter with homosexuality came when I was a *madrich* (counselor, leader) at Camp Tavor in the early 1960s—way before gay liberation had come to prominence—when Lyle was asked to leave camp because he had asked a camper to have sex with him. I still remember the day his parents arrived to take him home. We sadly said goodbye to him, but no one ever said the word—gay—or anything. It was an act without a name. All we knew was that he did something "wrong"; exactly what, no one said.

I wish that later in life I had had the opportunity to talk to Lyle and get the complete story, but he died too soon.

There was a movement in the 1960s to change all names to locations in Israel, so Midwest Camp Habonim became Camp Tavor, named after a hill in Israel, similar to the one at camp, though, of course, much higher, and Milwaukee's Camp Habonim became *Ken* ("nest") Lachish (the alma mater of Hasia Diner and myself, as mentioned above), named for an ancient city in northern Israel. I was elected *Rosh Ken Lachish*, a kind of president, in 1961, and I still have a mimeographed newsletter from the summer of 1961, when I was only 16 years old and a junior at Washington High School. (This was way before Xerox machines; we used rolled-up messy ink pads to run off newsletters). I recounted several issues facing our *Ken*:

> This past year has its disappointments and frustrations as well as its high spots…but three things have occurred this past year which hadn't happened in quite a while. They are as follows:
>
> 1. We've had for the first time separate *madrichim* (leaders) setting up and maintaining their own meetings.
> 2. We've had the responsibilities of the *Ken* distributed among the *chevra* (the group).

3. The meetings themselves are much more balanced. We've had, besides *shira* (song) and *rikud* (dance), *sichot* (discussions) and occasional *mifalim* (projects, like art or fund-raising). But now is the time that we should examine our disgruntlements as we look to a brighter year in which these malapropisms will and shall be rectified...

The unique thing about Habonim was that, at every level, we kids (with the help of adults at times) ran the movement, and we considered ourselves a "movement," not an "organization." (I can see where subconsciously I was becoming a sociologist—I instinctively knew the difference.) An organization is static and run by adults *for* kids; a movement is active and radical and run *by* kids themselves. Of course, we had leaders (*madrichim* they were called, Hebrew for "those who direct or show the road"), and at every level, older, more mature *madrichim* led younger ones; it gave us all a lot of responsibility. Just look at my letter to the *Ken*—it is very mature, already citing Cicero and using several French and Latin words (*en masse, merci beaucoup*), as well as hifalutin English words like "malapropism," "ameliorated," and "disgruntlement." I was one smart kid, but at 15 or 16, where did I learn all those fancy words?

The ethos of Habonim was as follows:

1. *Hakshama Atzmit*—Self-realization of your dreams
2. *Chalutziut*—Pioneering spirit
3. *Kupa*—Sharing—from each according to his ability; to each according to his need.
4. Socialism—democratic, not autocratic
5. *Aliyah*—moving to Israel—the highest form of self-realization was making *aliyah* to *kibbutz*, not the city
6. Labor—work and labor are not only good but holy. All work should be praised. Labor is good and important, no matter what kind it is.
7. Community-building
8. Secular Judaism
9. *Tzofiut*—Scouting, camping, very much inspired by Lord Baden-Powell's Boy Scout Movement
10. Love of the Land of Israel, the Bible, and its history

Compare this to the Revisionist creed of the Betar Movement, right-wing Zionism:

1. Capitalism
2. Self-defense
3. *Hadar*—manliness and grace under fire
4. Secular Judaism
5. *Aliyah*

The differences are stark, yet there are similarities: Both Habonim/Dror and Betar have a love for the land and the history of Israel, of scouting, of work, of manliness, and of grace under fire, but they differed over socialism and self-defense. Betar was always more violent and more prone to use firearms; Habonim/Dror was more apt to use nonviolence, restraint, and diplomacy, yet would naturally resort to guns in order to protect their country. There were "heroes" on both sides.

Bernie Sanders, in an article in *Jewish Currents*, outlined his admiration for Israel and his defense of socialism. I am similar. I am still a socialist, and I still try to live up to those ideals, but it is not easy. As the late Milton Himmelfarb once wrote, "Jews live like Episcopalians but vote like Puerto Ricans," that is, they vote against their class interests. I once had a net worth of a million dollars yet I still voted like a Puerto Rican—radical and democratic socialist, despite the red-baiting and despite the insults and catcalls.

Sanders made being a socialist "cool" again, and while I call myself a Labor or Socialist Zionist, I am not sure Bernie would be comfortable being labeled a Zionist in this post-Zionist world, and neither would many Israelis. He respects Israel but wants it to live up to its once-progressive ideals.

Israel Needs a Social, Political, and Peaceful Revolution

Jewish Liberation News Service, May 1973.

* * *

On the seventh day following the short but bloody Israel-Arab Six-Day War, there was no rest, no *Shabbat* (Sabbath). The cold-war thaw of the past half-decade has brought to the surface numerous social problems that were long waiting off-stage. A few sensitive Israelis had predicted that when peace "breaks out" there will be *tzores* (troubles). They are correct, but trouble has already begun—even before an official peace has been declared.

Israel has a woman's movement; Israel has a consumer movement; Israel has a student protest movement; Israel has an anti-poverty movement; Israel has a civil and religious rights movement; and Israel has an ecology movement. Though they are tiny groups in most cases, they are, nevertheless, the vanguard of radical change, and these changes are long overdue.

Who could have predicted that Israel would ever have conscientious objectors to war? A Black Panther party? A Jewish Defense League? An Israeli New Left? A feminist movement? Israeli Jews engaging in espionage alongside Arabs? And these scandals and movements and forces for change will continue.

Recently, one of the leaders of the women's and consumer rights movement in Israel, Shulamit Aloni, a fifth-generation *Sabra*,[1] a lawyer, writer,

---

1   A Jew born in Israel.

and ex-Knesset member, visited the United States under the auspices of the Foreign Ministry. In one of her speeches, she said:

> I understand our leaders [in Israel]. After all, how many battles can they be asked to fight in a lifetime? They fought before they came and again after they came. They're old and tired. They deserve to have peace within our borders, but that is impossible. Change is imperative.

I agree 1,000 percent (forgive me, Senator Eagleton). The present Israeli leadership is old—Golda Meir is 75; Zalman Shazar and David Ben-Gurion are over 80; Pinchas Sapir and other Cabinet members are long past retirement age. But age is *not* the issue, because there are clear-eyed and far-sighted visionaries among the "old-guard." The real need is for progressive and provident leadership. The crucial problem in Israel is how to get beyond the "garrison state" mentality that permeates the state.

Before there can be any meaningful radical change *internally*, there must be *peace* with the Arab state *externally*. This is not the place for a far-ranging analysis of this emotional and controversial topic, but I must say that one step toward that goal of peace is the recognition of the Palestinian people's aspiration for a homeland. My position is that a bi-national state (really a tri- or quarto-national state, because too often Christians, both Arab and non-Arab, and Druzes, are forgotten) is a futile and naïve dream. No, a bi-national "workers" state will not work. The only real alternative is a Palestinian state in what is now Jordan.

If you ask me what I really believe, I will say that I am extremely pessimistic; this hot and cold war that now exists will continue for my lifetime; I anxiously await *any* change in the status quo, no matter how insignificant, but overall I am not very hopeful about peace. The entire stalemate depresses me terribly, but I want… As for now, I am concerned about Israeli society.

As I've emphasized, Israel needs new progressive leadership; the Knesset needs more women, more young people, more Arabs, more Sephardim, more Westerners (especially more Americans with an innovative spirit), but especially it needs far-sighted progressive leadership!

The Israeli government, though it has undertaken miracles in absorption, land and water development, and education, is insensitively over-bureaucratized, as any Ephraim Kishon story portrays. The Israeli leadership, a product of intensive change, is now threatened by change, and its reactions on some issues have shown, not only the cracks and fissures within the social fabric of Israel, but also the government's myopic and at times repressive policies. For example:

a. *Golda Meir once called the Israeli Black Panther Party "a bunch of delinquents." Compare this with what another leader, Elie Eliacher, said in January 1972 at an assembly of Sephardic delegates to the 28ᵗʰ Zionist Congress, attended by many top officials and religious leaders: "Two Israelis cannot survive. Our history has proved it. We cannot afford to have one happy, prosperous Israel reaping all the advantages of our eventful period while another Israel lacks the most elementary conditions of life, living in slums, underfed, underclothed, struggling on an income close to the dole, unrepresented in our national forums... The Black Panther movement is only a symptom of things to come which can and must at all costs be prevented."*

b. *Amos Kenan, controversial Israeli journalist, has had his play censored because the government is offended.*

c. *Lilith, a critical English-language journal edited by (mostly American) students living in Jerusalem, is censured because a comic strip by David Geva—called "Super Golda," with premier Meir caricatured as a tough "super-man"—incurred the wrath of an Israeli bureaucrat.*

These and other examples should point out to the reader that much more attention must be paid to internal social problems and to internal civil liberties, despite the concerns of *aliya* (immigration), *klita* (absorption of immigrants), *bitachon* (security), and development.

Change is possible in Israel. It has a democratic socialist tradition. It has (I strongly hope) the flexibility and apparatus for social change. It has a tradition of civil rights for minorities. It has a *Halacha* that must be flexible enough to adjust and adapt to a new world, a world of rapid and dizzying change, a world entering "future shock."

Like all modernizing nations, Israel is following, in many ways, the American pattern of development: consumerism, a higher standard of living, plus all of the problems that highly technological societies face— pollution, urban decay, increased population, inadequate housing and transportation, a widening gap between the rich and the poor, alienation and post-affluence social movements—drugs, juvenile delinquency, counter-culture sects, anxious minority groups who want to enter the "good life" or a productive life beyond mere material goods.

I see Israel where America was in the early '60s. Nevertheless, it is in much better shape than America to solve its problems and to integrate its dissident minority movements. But will it? Or will it react in a crass and unyielding manner? When Golda Meir called the Black Panther Party in Israel a "bunch of delinquents," I knew then that Israel was in trouble, and my estimation of Ms. Meir's political acumen plummeted.

Israel needs new leadership. It needs new ways to protect human rights; it needs to allow peaceful dissent and even a bit of disruption; it needs to *listen* well to the voices of protest; it needs to adopt a constitution and a bill of rights (it has neither) granting civil liberties; it needs to change the legal structure of marriage and divorce to adapt to a new lifestyle; it needs to increase and enforce human rights, especially for women and especially in the area of jobs, marriage, and divorce.

Israel must undertake the excruciating task of deciding what kind of state it wants to be—a secular Jewish state, an orthodox theocracy, or some viable compromise?

Many Jews, both in the diaspora and in Israel, will oppose the tide of social change. Some have said, "What's so pressing about women's rights or consumerism? There are more important issues. We need to collect money for national security." This sentiment is expressed by many American Jewish leaders. Though money is extremely important, it is not the solution to every problem.

I am reminded of the words of the late great Martin Luther King, Jr.: "Philanthropy is commendable, but it must not cause the philanthropist to overlook the circumstances of economic injustice which makes philanthropy necessary."

These words are too often forgotten by men of wealth. These Jewish leaders (and their wives) do not even recognize their own male chauvinism and anti-feminist emotions. (In Israel, they would be called *basar lavan,* Hebrew for "white meat," because "chauvinist pig" is not kosher.)

These movements, especially those dealing with women's rights (divorce, marriage, etc.), will be staunchly opposed by religious traditionalists, who feel that separation of synagogue and state would be disastrous and would undermine and completely "eliminate" religion. Civil divorce and marriage plus equal rights for women would only reflect the reality of the state—a state in which over 50 percent of the citizens (the majority) are *not* Orthodox, yet are coerced to abide present rulings. There should be civil as well as religious marriages and divorces. The choice should be left up to the individual, not the state.

It is said that, since the destruction of the Temple, only fools make predictions. Still, I would predict that the majority of citizens would still have Orthodox religious marriage rites. Only a few would opt for civil marriages, but it would be the individual's choice, not the state's.

The major reason why religious traditionalists will oppose the civil and women's rights movements is because *religion and politics are intertwined in Israel.*

The religious parties will oppose these movements not simply on grounds of *Halacha*, but for reasons of *realpolitik*. They stand to lose enormous political and economic power if civil liberties are extended to everyone, regardless of race, sex, religion, or national origin. Therefore, I can well understand their opposition—it is the *sine qua non* of power. They might lose control of the enormous religious apparatus that has developed—the rabbinical courts, the slaughterhouses, the *mohelim* (ritual circumcisers), the religious schools, and *yeshivot.*

In short, what makes the conflict so difficult and so deserving of the wisdom of a Solomon is simply because of this double-barreled problem of loss of political power *and* infringement of *Halacha.*

I call for a radical transformation within Israeli society. I am not a political organizer, and I am not an Israeli citizen. This internal revolution can be undertaken only by Jewish, Arab, Christian, and Druze citizens within the Israeli state. I am simply an intellectual and an outside social critic, writing from afar. This article is *not* a detailed political program; it is *not* a precise manual for strategic intervention; it is simply a "call to arms," a declaration for action, action that I believe is long overdue.

I do, however, have a few "guidelines." The term "revolution" is used in a variety of ways. Some equate it with any profound social and political change, some with a "storming of the palace" form of *coup-d'état*. Others in a more restrictive sense use the term to mean an attack on the moral-political order and the traditional hierarchy of class statuses which commences when existing institutions lose their legitimacy and can no longer function without wide-scale repression.

The concept of revolution is very broad, and this short discussion will not do it justice. But, in short, what is necessary is a *long-term*, concerted, political and economic action combined with innovative cultural change—revolutionizing the way people live in their daily lives and the way they relate intimately with each other. This is not revolution in the historic meaning of the term, but a slow drive for radical change using both traditional and novel means. Or, as radical theoretician Richard Flacks has described it:

> The revolution in advanced society is not a single insurrection. It is not a civil war of pitched battles fought by opposing armies. It is a long, continuous struggle—with political, social, and cultural aspects inextricably intertwined... It is not simply a socialist revolution, if by that one means the establishment of a new form of state power... It is more than that. For it must be a revolution of those whose lives are determined by those decisions. It is, in short, not a revolution aimed at seizing power but a revolution aimed at its dispersal.

One last point: Many Jews wish to muzzle criticism of Israel or feel that any deep critique of Israel plays into the hands of its enemies. To these Jews, I ask them to listen intently to the words of Noam Chomsky, who, in a recent *Ramparts* (January, 1973) article, wrote the following:

> Surely it is obvious that a critical analysis of Israeli institutions and practices does not simply imply antagonism to the people of Israel, denial of the national rights of the Jews in Israel, or lack of concern for their just aspirations and needs. The demand for equal rights for Palestinians (as well as women, Sephardim, etc.) does not imply a demand for Arab dominance...or a denial of Jewish rights. The same is true of critical analysis that questions the existence of the state institutions in their present form.

I call for a social, political, and non-violent revolution in Israel, a kind of (Charles) Reichian "greening" of Israel. To some, this demand seems incredible; to others, it smacks of treason. Yet, I make this demand because I *love* Israel, and I criticize Israel because I *love* it. To silence criticism is to silence freedom. This is *my* message to Israel on its 25th anniversary.

1973

The End of Zionism?

Do the recent elections in Israel in September 2019-2020 show the end of the Zionist dream, or the renewal of that dream? Many believe we live in a post-Zionist era, that Zionism has no meaning anymore. But first let me explain what Zionism meant in the past:

1. *Aliyah.* David Ben-Gurion said that the only true Zionist is one who moves to Israel. It should be noted that he changed his tune after strong pushback from American and world Jewish leaders, and since he depended financially on these "givers," he backed down. But it is a pillar of Zionism.
2. *Cultural Zionism.* I learn Hebrew, *rikud* (Israeli dance), and *shira* (Israeli songs), and that's my attachment to both Israel and Judaism.
3. *"Cardiac" Zionism.* I feel for Israel in my heart. I love Israel but would never move there.
4. *"Check-book" Zionism.* I give money, so leave me alone.
5. *Labor or Socialist Zionism.* Left-wing, dovish, and similar Zionism.
6. *Revisionist Zionism (Betar, Likud).* Right-wing, reactionary, and conservative Zionism.
7. *Religious Zionism.*
8. *Secular Zionism.*
9. *Anti-Zionism,* yet still Jewish: *Haredi* (fundamentalist Orthodox Jewish); anti-Zionist and Communist; or Bundist, socialist, Yiddishist, supports Israel but is anti-Zionist.
10. *Canaanites:* Anti-Zionist and anti-Jewish Israelis.

So, you see, it's complicated.

And what makes it even more complicated is that anti-Semitism arose in the reign of U.S. President Donald Trump (2016-2020). More Jews were killed during his presidency than since the Shoah.[2] What complicates things is when anti-Zionism turns into anti-Semitism. So, let me delineate the various forms of anti-Zionism. They range in people's minds from simple criticism of the Israeli government to support for the BDS (Boycott, Divestment, and Sanctions) Movements to the total elimination of a Jewish state (genocide):

1. Criticism of Israel and its policies regarding the settlements, the Palestinians, or the status of Jerusalem.
2. Support for a single-state solution which would make Jews just another part of the state.
3. Support for the BDS movement which is seen as undermining not just the West Bank settlements but the entire state of Israel.
4. Support to oust all the Jews from the Middle East; in short, genocide against the Jews and Israelis.

The question is: When does criticism of Israel slide into anti-Zionism or anti-Israel sentiments? In short, what is free speech, and when does it end? The issue is especially acute on campuses where Israelis or pro-Israeli speakers are routinely shouted down. But this is also true for right-wing or conservative speakers, not just Jewish or Israeli speakers. Conversely, left-wing Jewish or non-Jewish speakers have been shouted down by right-wing students. It is very difficult to teach on campus today.

Deborah Lipstadt, in her book *Antisemitism: Here and Now* (2019), basically takes my position—or I take her position—that criticism of the policies of Israel is *not* anti-Semitism, but when that criticism slides into the demonization of Israel, of questioning the very legitimacy of a Jewish state, then it becomes anti-Semitism or worse. But this begs the question: What is a "Jewish state"? Is it a state only for Jews, a religious state, or a secular democratic state for all religions—Christian, Muslim, as well as Jewish? There are pitfalls and dangers for any one of these choices. And these questions go back to the late 1940s and the time of Judah Magnes and his idea of a "bi-national" state or even earlier to the 1940s and Hannah Arendt's discussion of the "crisis of Zionism" (Arendt, 2007).

2　The Holocaust.

Back then, the crises were how to fight the Nazis at the same time as fighting the British in Palestine; this dilemma was solved by David Ben-Gurion—"we will fight the British as if there were no war; and the war as if there were no British." (The actual words were "to fight the White Paper," a document limiting the entrance of Jew to Palestine from Nazi-ravaged Europe.)

Today, the struggle is more complex and includes what is called "inter-sectionality," a fancy term that means we are not just talking politics but race, class, gender, sexual orientation, transgender, and disability. Plus, the Left and Right on campuses are equally strong today. The Right will disagree with that statement, but it is true: campuses have strong right-wing students who will shut down left-wing speakers as easily as the opposite.

When I was active in student protest in the 1960s, the Left and Liberal students were in control while conservatives like YAF (Young Americans for Freedom) were small in number and marginalized as weirdoes. Today, there is parity: right-wing and left-wing students are both strong in number, and each would like to cancel the other out. Plus, political correctness has taken over on both sides.

At Harvard, where I have been affiliated since 1982, I have to be very careful, especially around Black students and especially around Black women so that what I say conforms to the "proper" norms: sensitivity to speech (female as well as male idioms), dress (especially hair style is now a sensitive issue); touching (no touching or hugging); and definitely nothing that smacks of "harassment" or "insensitivity" to Blacks or women.

White and older (and also Jewish) teachers like me have to be practically eunuchs, and that is why so many of my generation have opted to retire from academia. Naturally, I exaggerate a bit. Of course, I can teach and be friends with students, but the norms have changed. Discussions of Jews, Israel, Blacks, women, gays have all become very difficult; one has to treat these subjects very carefully. And it starts early; already in grade school, junior high and high school, teachers and administrators pound away on Martin Luther King Day on how "we whites" have to be super-sensitive about our "inherently white male power." It's almost masochistic, and if you don't abide by the norms, you will be isolated and eventually fired.

But to return to the question: Do we live in a "post-modern" or "post-Zionist" world? Answer: Yes, indeed we do.

But what is Zionism today?

Is it the *chalutz* in a *kova tembel* (sun hat) and khaki shorts tanned from work in the orchards, returning home, taking a nap, spending a few hours with his kids before they go to sleep in the communal children huts, and then he and his wife or girlfriend go dancing the *hora* into the night?

Is it the modern Orthodox family who packs up their children, sells their home in the suburbs, and moves to Israel so they can live an "authentic" Jewish, meaning an authentic spiritual life?

Is it the *haredi* with *peyos* (ear locks) who follows his *rebbe* to *Eretz Yisroel* so he can be close to the graves of the prophets and the Holy Temple?

Is it the hi-tech entrepreneur who moves to Tel Aviv to start up his latest company?

Is it the retiree from New Jersey or Milwaukee who moves to *kibbutz* to be closer to her children and away from the cold and snow?

Is it the intellectual, the writer, the artist, or the amateur archaeologist who wants to return to the Holy Land to write, to explore, or to read his/her poetry?

And yes, is it the Mormon or Evangelical Christian who moves to Israel to walk in the steps of Jesus, Peter, and John?

Of course, Zionism is all of these people, and that's what makes Israel so complex, so frustrating, and so authentic. The Arab and Muslim world has finally come to the conclusion that the Palestinians cannot make up their minds about a two-state solution; they had their chances and blew it; so they have become frustrated with them and have turned to Israel, and a new relationship is emerging with Saudi Arabia, Oman, Qatar, Abu-Dhabi, and Dubai. If Iraq and Syria were more stable, they might also move in that direction. Only Iran, not the people but its fundamentalist rulers, is opposed to Israel.

So, a new dawn is rising for Zionism and for Jews, and new forms of Zionism will emerge in its wake.

Sources

Arendt, Hannah. "The Crisis of Zionism" in Jerome Kohn and Ron H. Feldman (eds.), *The Jewish Writings*. New York: Schocken Books, 2007, pp. 329-337.

Berenbaum, Michael (ed.). *Not Your Father's Antisemitism.* St. Paul, Minn.: Paragon House, 2008.

Chesler, Phyllis. *The New Anti-Semitism.* New York: Jossey-Bass, 2003.

Lipstadt, Deborah E. *Anti-Semitism Here and Now.* New York: Schocken Books, 2019.

Pollack, Eunice G. *From Antisemitism to Anti-Zionism.* Boston: Academic Studies Press, 2017.

Tenorio, Rich. "Best-selling author warns internal turmoil may be biggest threat to Israel." *The Jewish Journal* (of the North Shore of Massachusetts), February 3, 2020, p. 5. About the thoughts of Israeli writer Ronen Bergman.

Troy, Gil. *The Zionist Ideas: Visions for the Jewish Homeland—Then, Now, Tomorrow.* Philadelphia: The Jewish Publication Society, 2018. Also see Noah Lucas, "Is Zionism Dead?" in Jack Nusan Porter, *The Sociology of American Jews* (Lanham, Md.: University Press of America, 1978, 1980).

Weisman, Jonathan. *Semitism: Being Jewish in America in the Age of Trump.* New York: St. Martin's Press, 2018.

(Note: While my spell-check feels that the correct spelling is "anti-Semitism," some authors use "antisemitism" without any hyphen. I have used the forms that the authors used, but I use the form "anti-Semitism" throughout this book.)

VIII. Radical Poetry and Prose

The Ten Commandments of the Holocaust

1. Thou shalt remember everything and understand nothing.
2. Thou shalt record everything—memoirs, diaries, documents, and poetry.
3. Thou shalt teach it diligently to thy children. As Rabbi Emil Fackenheim has said: the survival of Israel is now a sacred duty.
4. Thou shalt teach it to the Gentiles and to their children because thou art often at their mercy.
5. Thou shalt not heap abuse upon the children of the ungodly. Though the wicked are to be punished, their children must be forgiven.
6. Thou shalt not judge the victims.
7. Thou shalt not place one set of idols (the Heroic) above another (the Cowardly). They are to be judged equally before the Lord. As Reb Eli Wiesel of Sighet has said: There is a time to remain silent, so therefore know when to be silent.
8. Thou shalt not lose faith. Amidst all thy doubt and confusion, I, the Lord your G-d, am here among thee.
9. Thou shalt not dwell heavily upon the sadness of the past. Rejoice, for thou hast survived while thine enemies have perished.
10. Thou shalt not turn away from thy brothers and sisters; instead, reach out and build a paradise on earth so that life and love can prevail.

Jack Nusan Porter, 2002

The Radical Poetry of Jack Nusan Porter: Introduction

I wrote these early poems in the spring of 1966 and fall of 1967 while at the University of Wisconsin–Milwaukee, at the height of the anti-war movement. Maybe I wrote them because of the stress; maybe because of the boredom in class; but, in any case, there they sat for over forty years until now, and then I added a few more poems written in the summer of 2009.

Few have seen them; fewer have heard them. Morgan Gibson, English professor at UW–M wrote the following after I showed him the early poems:

Mr. Porter—

Thanks for letting me see these. The long poem ("The Children") is the most interesting because the words are the most *active.* Other poems (and the last two sections of that one) are flabby, need surgery. But you are on to some interesting effects and I'd welcome you into a class—especially the poetry writing class, given again in the spring of 1967… (original emphasis)

(signed) Morgan Gibson

This was, however, enough incentive to keep writing. Sadly, I never took the course. I graduated in June 1967 with a major in sociology, but I always loved my English courses, especially one taught by Mrs. Katherine Whitcomb on twentieth-century American literature (Theodore Dreiser, T.S. Eliot, Ernest Hemingway, William Faulkner, and Robert Frost—poetry, short stories, and novels). I've always loved short stories, going back to Edgar Allan Poe, Saki, and the "Porters"—Katherine Anne and O. Henry.[1]

---

1   William Sydney Porter was O. Henry's real name.

Later, Dan Burnstein and my cousin Alan Porter have been an inspiration for me to write and not worry about censorship, or how "bad or good" they are—just write and get good advice.

Mystic

Dedicated to Rabbi Shlomo Carlebach

Hush! Mushroomed room,
Hot faces, old and lean,
Curled heads, crow's feet
Common, summoning strengths
To gain access to the mystic's
Inner dialogue and to the external
Music of a God and a flaming faith.

    His sex-stringed voice gnarled about the chamber.
    The thick skin of indifference
    Broke and unleashed the flood gates of joy

The mystic tore into the
Gap and exulted his advantage.
The voice subdued and devoured,
His disciples gained momentum,
Embrace the message,
The flame, and then—the faith

The Children

I.

Disintegrating sarcophagi, laden
With oppressive dust,
Shrouding ancient tombs,
Long hidden from weak eyes.
Huge white granite

Blocks release the
Occult of time, of
Horus and Ibis, of
Monarchs in slim boats, of
Slaves supporting sun-gods, of
Crocodiles and cats whose
Emerald eyes gleam and
Mutely question.

II.

And Ramses withered, the
Slow unctuous wheel turned;
Tablets decreed, rosaries of formulas,
Unformulated, untested.
By fire glazing, a wall of
Vaporous sulphur, vipers.
Reed seas bowed, shuffling;
Nachson choked and prayer-filled
Went under.
Scar-bleached souls, quibbling
Plunged onward and straggled
To *terra cane.*
Thieves, bloody beggars, pearly virgins,
Pious merchants, carrying
Bloodstones and bread.

III.

Push on, children, while
Suns consumed flesh,
Baked in fear, scorpions
Yellow and twisted, flick out and
Inflame dusty sandals.

IV.

An old man leans on a rod,
Divining rod, and crooks his flock

To a rock-encrusted enigma.
A lone flaming rock, a precipice,
A scriptural conclusion.
A midwife bleats and struggles,
Crying out to the old man.
But tar and pool are forgotten, a
Microcosm relinquished.

V.

Red replaced reed and
Rock replaced rod.
Miasma of doubt pervades.
Dusk comes and destroys the stain.
Sabbatical wisps of warmth,
Nipples and teat, succor for all,
Mothers release, and fathers, anxious, unbend.
And then, the manna descended,
Small glossy fruit,
Caterpillar dew,
Eaten in haste like the
Unleavened bread, afraid of the
Force that drove them to eat,
Scraping the ground, the shrub, and the
Rock, then wearily praying to idols of wood,
Their focus unreal, unknown, and unruled.

VI.

The Sabbath departed.
The old man, aflame, carried
His burden and strode on alone.
He reached the summit of
Vision and found an eagle's nest and
A dove. The dove, white,
The eagle, gone.
He then grabbed two rocks and
Burned God's thoughts upon the heights,
Prematurely wept, and descended to the
Plain and to the orgy of the scene.

VII.

The children danced, reveling in
A new game.
The old man coughed and spat,
Shattering his thoughts upon the
Dust.
The clouds grew dim while the
Children played. They knew
No fear;
They reveled on, the bronze
Burned, the children laughed.
Their laughter flowed through the desert,
The world turned on its axis,
The dove flew away,
The eagle returned,
And the children are still laughing.

Ode to Amerika

Observations on the "Chicago 7" Trial, 1969-1970

Judge Hoffman, self-hating, Magoo-eyes, and $100,000 judge-ship:

Before you stand two Jewish lawyers, advocates of love; three Jewish men, not boys—Jerry Rubin, Lee Weiner, and Abbie Hoffman (no relation except by an historical quirk); a Black brother, Bobby Seale, Black Panther, musician, waiter, and artist; Tom Hayden, Rennie Davis, John Froines, and Dave Dellinger.

They know now what it is to be a nigger, a kike, and a scapegoat.

The prosecutors are Jews.

The defendants are Jews.

The Judge is a Jew.

And a Holy Presence stands over this trial that is labeled an abomination and a circus.

I see Jerry Rubin walking into court, kissing his wife-lover, and on his clothes is pinned a six-cornered yellow star—and instead of a gas-chamber, he receives a contempt-of-court citation for mocking the judge and Amerikan justice.

Tears and blood run down spectators, reporters, wives, and children as police and marshals grab, hit, evict, and otherwise bring down the wrath of pigs on the long Judeo-Christian faces and arms and legs of struggling and kicking Jews and Jewesses and non-Jews and non-Jewesses who all are one, who all suffer together, being young and alone and long-locked and defiant in the eyes of pig-judge, pig-politics, and stiff unfeeling world.

AMERIKA,

You who were the ethical center of the universe,

You who saved the remnants of my family from Nazi-pigs,

You who salvaged the Western world from itself,

Stand alone today, resting on your fuckin' John Wayne laurels while your leaders cut down the manhood and womanhood of us all.

AMERIKA,

You who kills Panthers and Vietnamese,

You who allows Biafrans and Black children to die,

You who sucks dry the lands of the world with your Rockefellers, Fords and Agnews,

AMERIKA,

You have sunk to your knees in depravity and desolation, and today...

You dare to sit in judgment over

Two lawyers and

Eight defendants and

They and I spit in your fuckin' face and

Call you the ethical center of hell!

POWER TO THE PEOPLE!

Chicago

February 1970

What is a Jewish Radical?

It is not being a "communist" or even a "socialist" but being at least what is euphemistically called a "progressive"—that is trying to transform the world, to have a vision of what we call *tikkun olam*—the mending and healing of the world.

It means, as Marx says, to get at the "root" (*radix*) of the problem.

It means spending $5,000 on a bar mitzvah but giving a tithe (10 percent) of all of your gifts to charity. But then again, it's hard to be a Jewish radical and have $5K to spend on a bar or bat mitzvah. In fact, it's hard to be any kind of radical and live in a $350,000 house as I do.

It's being a "tough Jew" yet compassionate.

It's worrying about the working man, woman, and child.

It's fighting anti-Semitism, knowing that the ADL cannot do it all.

It's cringing at the word "JAP" or "Jew me down."

It's bringing Harry Braverman's *Labor and Monopoly Capital* to Palm Beach for light reading.

It's never having to say you're sorry.

It's demystifying everything all the time.

It's loving the masses.

It's loving people.

It's hating mean-spirited people like Newt Gingrich or Jesse Helms.

It's not fearing social change.

It's being a good sociologist.

It's having the sociological imagination: connecting your personal troubles with society's problems and knowing that it's not *your* fault.

It's believing in God, unlike so many atheistic radicals.

It's being an "outsider" to the Jews and a Jew to the "insiders."

Well, to be a Jew is *always* to be an "outsider."

It means being too radical for the Jews and too Jewish for the radicals.

The eternal progressive outsider.

It means to be a *mensch*.

It means listening to all three Marxes—Karl, Groucho, and my friend Michael.

It means to have "the American God of Money Slapped in Your Face," as the late d.a. levy, a dead poet, once wrote.

It helps to be working-class or to come from "trash."

It's hating bullshit.

Eldridge Cleaver once said, "There's some cold shit on the ground."

"And there's chicken shit, bullshit, and big elephant shit (like they teach at Harvard or MIT)"—Fritz Perls said that.

It's people taking themselves very, very seriously.

It's remembering everything and understanding nothing.

It's teaching the Torah diligently to our children.

It's avoiding *lashan hara*, the evil tongue.

It's not losing faith.

It's believing in the sun, even when it is not shining.

It's believing in love, even when feeling it not.

It's believing in God, even when she is silent (adapted from an inscription on a cellar wall in Cologne, Germany, where Jews hid from the Nazis).

March 14, 1995

The Jewish Poet

This article was originally published in *Jewish Currents*, Vol. 29, No. 1, January 1975, pp. 16-23. Later it was reprinted in *The Jewish Radical*, 1986, and *The Jew as Outsider*, 2014, by Jack Nusan Porter.

* * *

"When I'm dead, you ought to give more attention to live poets."
— d.a. levy

d.a. (Darryl Allen) levy was a "poetpublishereditor" who lived a short fast bittersweet life and then shot himself to death in his Cleveland apartment on November 24, 1968. There were people who said he might have taken over the mantle of Allen Ginsberg if only he had lived longer, but...

levy was among the many "new left" poets that emerged out of the '60s. He takes his place alongside Diane di Prima, Jane Stembridge, Todd Gitlin, Michael Rossman, Don Lee, Nikki Giovanni, and others, black and white, who have placed art and literature at the disposal of the people, for the liberation of the oppressed.

levy, like so many artists, was deeply influenced by older "gurus" of the left: Paul Goodman, Allen Ginsberg, Gary Snyder, and Alan Watts.

He was born in Cleveland in October, 1942 (a Scorpio), grew up, decided to commit suicide at seventeen, changes his mind and began to read and write; graduated in 1960 from James Ford Rhodes High School, didn't have the money for college, joined the navy, spent seven months and three days there, talked his way out, returned to Cleveland, became the charismatic personality behind Cleveland's avant-garde in and around the University Circle area, was mocked, hounded and arrested the final years of his life. His father, Joseph Levy, was a shoe salesman; his mother was a Christian.

In Cleveland he edited the *Marijuana Quarterly* and *The Buddhist Third Class Junk Mail Oracle*, wrote a lot of poetry, inspired *ukanhavyrfuck-incitibak*, and helped a lot of poets.

Morris Edelson, editor of the Madison, Wisconsin paper *Quixote*, poet, a good friend to writers, and a kind of Max Brod to levy's Kafka, wrote the following in a short intro to one of levy's collections, *Private No Parking:*

> ...(levy) was invited in 1968 by *Quixote* to spend some time in Madison.
>
> he came, slept at Grace and Dave Wagner's, visited some Freshman English classes and Comparative Literature Department meetings, gave a non-reading and taught/didn't teach a class: it was a Free University class in telepathy, d.a. never went but the class met anyway, thinking he was trying to tell them something. he was.
>
> after the month in Madison, d.a. went back to Cleveland – some say he killed himself, others say the pigs did it because they had sent him up before for reading his poetry to people. TO THAT SENTENCE HIS ATTITUDE WAS ONE OF DEFIANCE NOT SELF-PITY. Yours?
>
> levy becomes now a memory, a target, an energy...levy's death released his poems for a lot of people – I liked them a lot better when he was alive.

A cult has sprung up in the past five years since his death. Death as the final success. Like Lenny Bruce, most people didn't appreciate levy until he died. He didn't make it as big as Bruce or Marilyn Monroe or Janis Joplin or Jimi Hendrix. They haven't written a play or a book about his life yet, but they may.

America, without question, is a little crazy and a little different. In Russia, they take poets much more seriously than here. There, if they don't dig what you're doin', they send you to Siberia, or shoot you, or put you in a mental asylum. Here they give you five minutes on the Johnny Carson show...if you're not too much of a threat to the State. If you are, they arrest you and drain your time/resources/energy with trials, outrageous bail, writs, appeals, etc., and then you're usually acquitted and set "free."

If that doesn't work, they make you turn inward and kill yourself. Do the job yourself; it's less trouble for the state.

Like Baudelaire, Joyce, D.H. Lawrence, and Andre Gide, levy too was harassed. Throughout 1966 and 1967, his arrest and trial made him a *cause célèbre* in Cleveland. On November 28, 1966, the Cuyahoga County Grand Jury secretly indicted levy on charges of "publishing and disseminating obscene literature," which carried a fine of $200-$2,000 and 1-7 years in jail, or both. He eluded the police for a few weeks, but finally gave himself up. He was released on parole and eventually the charges were dropped. levy was a symbol for the entire counterculture-drug-psychedelic world that Cleveland's "moral entrepreneurs" wanted to demolish. The obscenity charges were only a ruse. They carried more hard-core magazines in the porno stores near the Asphodel Bookstore (where levy worked) that were more "pornographic" than anything levy ever wrote. Those porno stores weren't touched by the police. People like Allen Ginsberg, Tuli Kupferberg, and the Fugs came to Cleveland to raise bail and hell.

Some say levy's final act of suicide defined Cleveland…and defied it. It might have, but I don't glorify or romanticize suicide. I don't mean to moralize, but suicide is against God's law and against Jewish law. There must be a good reason for that. There are a lot of "death trips" around, and the 1960s produced even more: speed, smack, revolutionary suicide, personal suicide. Little insidious trips: overwork, overworry, overeating, overbreathing. If we look closely, we all have them: everything we do that's no good for us kills us a little.

For levy, life got to be too much, too thick and heavy, too frightening and too powerful, or maybe it was more simple: he committed an act of free will. He saw a fucked-up world and then just dropped out. But he died long before he died. He lived death; he felt death; he carried death around with him. It was his steady companion:

> …it is always a question of
> finding a way to die
> that is acceptable to the
> mass media
> so the people can hear you
> when you insist that you
> death was their failure to provide
> you with a meaningful life.

What is it that turns off so many people to America? (Like Listerine, I love it and hate it…twice a day.) But not the poor or the working class—they seem to love America, to glory in it. They're the real patriots. No, I mean the affluent, suburban, well-educated white kids—Jewish, Protestant, or Catholic, One of the things that turns their rage out and then inward is a tremendous feeling of frustration, disappointment, and a naïve expectation that America is somehow different—the gap between creed and deed…and then the lies, bullshit and more lies.

Our teachers (parents, presidents, senators, mayors, etc.) lied to us. Columbus didn't "discover" America; George Washington was a slave driver; Betsy Ross never existed; Benjamin Franklin was a double-agent; Abe Lincoln wasn't too happy about freein' "his niggers," for if he could have, he would have liked to have kept the country united and the blacks as slaves; FDR didn't lift a finger for the Jews; Eisenhower was a twerp whose greatest talent was not getting America involved in a war; Jack Kennedy (o'holy Kennedy) was the man responsible for the Bay of Pigs and the oppression of Castro; his brother Ted is an irresponsible driver who should be in jail for negligence and involuntary manslaughter; and Nixon, dear Nixon, would have sold his own momma to get re-elected. Will the high schools' civics books mention Watergate? My Lai? Chicago?

What the '60s did to me, to you, to levy, and to everyone of our generation (and others) was to destroy our heroes, our history, and (to some degree) our hopes. We've now got to start again (this time with patience); for some, like levy, the trip was too much, so he split, but he left us a bit of his vision.

Our disillusionment blinded us from a fact: our "leaders" are *human*; scandal and corruption *is* business as usual. America has a great p.r. job to live up to but it hasn't always done it. The working class knows this: they aren't astounded by Watergate, they *know* all political leaders are on the take. To them, in short, leaders may be corrupt and incompetent (and still human), but *basically* the country is good and democratic and noble.

For the political and cultural "left," the entire *system*, not simply its leaders, has to be scrapped and replaced with some kind of (as yet undefined) noncompetitive, nonexploitative socialist state.

Probably, levy saw such contradictions and barriers for a proletarian revolution because his vision owes as much (may be more) to Paul Reps, Alan Watts, and Phillip Kapleau as to Karl Marx or Chairman Mao.

Mike Kaplan, once an SDS leader, now a Hillel counselor at the University of Wisconsin–Milwaukee (radical politics is becoming theologized) knew levy and said this about him:

I was impressed with the man. He was a very sensitive guy. He had a personal vision, but he wasn't trapped in it…and other people could see it too. He wasn't an obscure poet, or so private that no one could understand him. He truly meshed the personal with the political.

But levy was criticized by the New Left for being "decadent" and not concerned enough with the proper working class ideological dogma. It was a common attack, one that Abbie Hoffman, Jerry Rubin, and John Sinclair also had to put up with. The Yippies tried to bridge the gap between the drug-oriented/inner consciousness/hippie faction and the non-drug/community-organizing/Marxist-radical faction. I don't know if they succeeded. levy stayed on his own track without necessarily putting down either.

Morris Edelson probably laid it down better than anyone:

He was a lovable guy and he didn't claim to be the revolution or the greatest, as did some young poets he knew… But the revolution was on his mind, the state of the nation was his concern, his poetry had big topics and a large, honest way of looking at things. An article in the Maoist "Literature and Ideology" first issue criticizes him at length for not being a Marxist and for thinking that inner consciousness could affect power structures. d.a. didn't have their steady, simple faith, being caught more in the ugliness and death all around him, cut off from his own tradition by the grotesque travesty it had become in America. He did feel that the country was his enemy in an immediate sense, and, being acute, he put little faith in long-term strategies and planning that went by the book. So his poems may not sound consistent—they speak of a new consciousness, which we have associated with the hippie line, and they speak of sabotage, which we think is unusually anarchistic. They point beyond life in several places, and the narrow Marxist here can say they are decadent. But d.a.'s need was for an immediate sense of overcoming the shit and hell of life, and vague references to the future and rising revolutionary consciousness weren't enough for him.

To me, d.a. was not a political message-bearer so much as a teller of stories that were true up to the moral. He told clearly, with wit and anger, the experiences of his generation, of himself as right in the middle of the forces bearing on his country. Politically he was valuable because he put it better than others (no claim that he was in control of everything or above it or outside it) and because he was involved in trying to attack the oppression that threatens everyone. His example of courage and persistence inspired people.

levy's poems were terse and muscular and specific. He didn't play games nor did he prattle about his integrity. His Madison work interested me because it not only included the description of oppression and the desire for love that his other work had, but it commented on the efforts groups here were making in an attempt to change society. We need that dimension of comment on our work; we need a public poet who is unprotected by a grant or an official status, whose attention goes beyond lousy self-consciousness...

A moody, curly dark-haired, shy, thin, worried, restless, pale, nervous man, levy was constantly searching for *THE WAY* out of the maze. His poetry was a form of self-analysis. To change society, change yourself first. To be a radical is to grasp the matter by the root. Now the root of man/woman-kind is man/womankind itself, and the real meaning of revolution is not so much a change in management but a change in man/woman:

This is what i've been
trying to say – if you
attack the structure –
the system – the establishment
you attack yourself

KNOW THIS!
& attack if you must
challenge yourself externally

but if you want a revolution
return to your childhood
& kick out the bottom...

this is not a game
your childhood
is the foundation
of the system...

if you want a revolution
do it "together"
but don't get trapped in
words or systems

people are people
no matter what politics
color or words they use
& they all have children
buried in their head

if you want a revolution
grow a new mind
& do it quietly
if you can…

Though he was into a search for inner consciousness and other maps, still he was wary, wary especially of the "phoney psychedelic advertisements" of California poets, mystics, and sensitivity leaders who came East bearing gifts:

he came here
just like a tourist
is this the best
california has to offer?...

i had to tell him
we didn't need
his undeveloped love
images…

california, don't send
your myths to us

your dream mecca
is a whorehouse
painted with phoney
psychedelic advertisements

we have a different game
still undefined, we spend

our mornings wandering the
soft hills of Ohio
looking for the
hidden words
that grow here
without the help of
your artificial
inner sunlight.

levy spent his whole life in Cleveland except for a month or so in Madison. He had a Midwestern simplicity; he lacked the light sunlit optimism of the West; he lacked the academic cool of the New England and New York writer/poet. The coasts got the media play, but Cleveland was different; it had different problems, a different lifestyle than Berkeley or Boston. levy decided to stay in that city, a city that most people think isn't worth shit, just a ramp off I-90.

There was a Yippie-like thrust to his poetry, for he was trying on different hats, finding new ways to show life's absurdity and still keep from having the cops and the system come down on his head too hard:

Last week I threw 75 university ashtrays
into the lake – sailed them high into the air
like clay pigeons Pow Pow

sealed ten parking meters with Elmers glue
and tonight some hippy will call me a creep
and the r(R)adicals will try to take my
conscience with words about war

the system is going to fall I'm sure
next week I'm putting plaster of paris
in the toilets of city hall
I'm just making sure it doesn't fall on me.

There must be a million ways to protest a war
economy other than getting your head
beaten to dust for television audiences
I don't let the pigs get between me and
the enemy anymore

In my pocket 100 student subscriptions
to Time Magazine and 100 unknown addresses
there must be a million of us who drop tacks
in official parking lots – let them have
their special reserved spaces…

The allusions and the tactics seem dated today, but the questions levy (and the left) raised are, to use the language of Watergate, still operable. People may wear a suit a tie, but they must still listen to an inner voice: do it as best as you can (you may fail at times) but DON'T GET CO-OPTED:

you might call me a hypocrite, but inside
I know who my enemy is and I know who
protects him.
I don't smoke pot or talk against the system
I'm just helping it along
the mysterious road of suicide.

But in the end, levy was not pushing a "heavy" trip on anyone. As Morris Edelson pointed out, levy, like Elie Wiesel, was a teller of tales. If they ring true and touch you, so much the better:

note:

peace & awareness
like two small birds
trying to leave the planet
because they are tired of dying

im not advocating anything

I don't want to leave the impression that all of levy's poetry was bitter or angry or polemical—it wasn't. He was capable of some beautiful tender lyrical moments:

Once at Edgewater Park
I sat on the breakwall
& unbuttoned a young girls
blouse –

her bra was white like the
snow of the himalayas
& her mouth was full of flowers

the first time i balled
was on Memorial Day

it was something else
Last O
oh

d.a. levy was a religious poet on a religious search. As an outsider, as the wandering Jew, he could see what others had overlooked. As a Jewish rebel *par excellence*, he felt cut off from mainstream Judaism, wanted to return, was repelled, and began to seek other old/new paths towards self-realization, mostly from the eastern religions. He was part of a long line of rebels/heretics from Jesus to Spinoza to Marx to Kafka to Lenny Bruce:

im a levy of the levites
yet in Cleveland
i have painted myself
        celtic blue
& am feeling
something like an outlaw
the druids give me soup
& think im a lama.

His "outsider" status was centered on the fact that levy was the off-spring of an intermarriage. (His wife, too, I believe, was not Jewish.) His mother was a Christian, his father a Jew. Though technically, according to the Orthodox *halacha*, levy was not a Jew, still his Jewishness mattered to him. He had a "Jewish heart":

i am a levy of the levites
and last week
a fanatic jew in the heights called me a
halfbreed
because my mother was a Christian

i am a levy of the levites
& last week a rabbi
thought i was kidding

when i told him
i was interested in judaism

god i think yr sense
of humor is sad
& perhaps you are also
feeling something
like an outlaw

god i am wondering
for how many years
have the jews
exiled you
while they busied themselves
with survival

Like a true Hasid, levy took his prayers and supplications straight to God, with no distracting middleman. Yet deep in his heart, he felt that even God was not listening and that the Messiah was not coming. This lack of faith was levy's fatal flaw. (Nihilism and resignation are not the way.) Yet, his vision was prophetic and accurate; he clearly saw the dilemmas of being a Jew in America. In his three most "Jewish" poems—"new year," "poem to michael Solomon" and "sitting on a bench near TSQuare"—he brings these cries out:

they want to pay $2 at the box office
& call it faith
walk out if its a bad movie…

…their holy cities
will not stand if built with
american money & the real jews
here cannot walk into a temple
without vomiting

...& now i wonder how many jews are
destroyed in this country each year
my father with his lonely eyes
trying to return home
only to have the american god of money
slapped in his face.

Where is God? What does He want? What does He want of us? levy asked the right questions. Rather than find a *rebbe* (not a rabbi) and study; rather than find others, a community, and search on, he was among these very people he mentions in his poems, those Jews who were "destroyed." Rather than rebuild, he destroyed himself, thus finishing the job that American society and the Jewish community had started.

January, 1975

IX. Radical Cinema and Media

Revolution and Rebellion in Film

Unpublished essay, circa 1972

* * *

The films of the 1960s student protest—*The Strawberry Statement*, *R.P.M.*, *Getting Straight*, *Zabriskie Point*, and others—have become quaint period-pieces. In fact, they have become just another genre in American filmmaking, like the western, the gangster movie, and the Hollywood musical. It's not only that these "revolutionary" films were trite, repetitious, and even boring, but they were deliberately detrimental to the making of a radical social and cultural transformation in this country. The documentaries of a *Cadre* or *Newsreel*, the semi-documentaries of a *Medium Cool* and *Uptight*, or the films of Jean-Luc Godard (*La Chinoise*, *Sympathy for the Devil*) are consciousness-raisers; the Hollywood versions are consciousness-deadeners—or at best, consciousness-confusers. Their purpose is to distill all emotion into trivia; all political struggles into a kind of glamorous upheaval. It would have even been better if these films showed a simplistic solution—the good guys vs. the bad guys, like gangster films in the 1930s, but directors and writers did not even do that.

Instead, there is confusion and alienation. Everyone's a loser; the cops are hit with rocks, the students are beaten bloody, everyone's trying to have sex right before the big "bust" (or during it, as in *Getting Straight*), the administrators are bumbling fools, and the teachers are bumbling idiots. The final outcome is that there is no outcome—just more chaos. The first casualties knocked off were the issues—racism, university expansion, ROTC, the Vietnam War, and imperialism. Who needs to explain the issues? Just get a few picket signs—that's the message.

The late Herbert Marcuse warned in his *One-Dimensional Man* that the great power of the technocratic society is what he calls "repressive des-ublimination." It's simply the ability of going through the motions of change without any real or purposeful change in the structure of society. In short, it turns reality into plasticity. It's not merely that these films (or the media generally) distort the reality of oppression; it goes beyond this. It is that technocracy itself has the capacity to provide satisfaction in a way which generates submission and weakens the rationality of protest. In the crudest example, it's like someone seeing a movie like *Getting Straight* and saying, "Man, now I understand campus protest."

Luckily, this submissiveness and weakened rationale may not happen. Why? One reason is that Hollywood can't pull the wool over anyone's eyes any longer, it can no longer present unrealistic presentations of life and still be believable. We've seen too much television and too much live action in the streets to be taken in by a Hollywood glossy. Yet, my particular worry is that there are gullible people in this world who believed that *The Strawberry Statement* is THE STATEMENT on student protest. My concern is real, since the technocratic society will utilize every device to stifle the insur-rection and revolt that threatens it. Not only will it use direct violence to repress, it will use the more subtle means of a "repression tolerance," a tol-erance that in itself is repressive.

Films like *Zabriskie Point* or *R.P.M.* are cinematic versions of what the revolution is *not*, just as *Playboy* is an example of what sexual freedom is *not*. The exploitation of radicals has become, like that of sex or rock groups, just another commodity to buy or sell. Like any commodity, you can reject it or accept it; you can turn it off or turn it on. The trouble is that the radical transformation of a society is not a commodity. No sales pitch can end the repressive nature of the political, judicial, ecological and social system of a nation. One cannot buy and sell it—one can only struggle for it.

The alternative is to make one's own movies, boycott the existing "rev-olutionary" movies, or get Hollywood to make the equivalent of a *Battle of Algiers*. I see one or two hopeful signs for Hollywood, especially with some of the younger directors or older men like Nicholas Ray, but it's only a slight hope. The major point is to understand the plastic image and to develop an alternative image to replace what Hollywood gives us.

Rebellion is very American. Whether it be the rebellion of the anti-hero (Humphrey Bogart), the adolescent (James Dean), or the deviant (Andy Warhol), it is easily understood and place in its proper sociological cubby-hole. Revolution, however, is seen as very un-American, very un-democratic, and therefore very frightening to most Americans, Thomas Paine and the Boston Tea Party aside. Revolution means radical transformation of the institutions of a society, redistributing and democratizing power, wealth, and influence.

The key that unlocks the door that answers the questions that explains America can be put into one simple word: *contradictions.*

This country/world/age is governed by its contradictions. To understand the contradictory values, assumptions and ideologies of America is to understand and thereby change America.

The American Creed, or better yet, the "John Wayne Syndrome" on one hand, and the "James Dean/Andy Warhol/Abbie Hoffman Syndrome" on the other, are antagonistic and mutually destructive values that are at odds with one another, and leads foreign observers to see us as both aesthetically fascinating and morbidly violent; naïvely adolescent and maddeningly arrogant; benignly tolerant and relentlessly oppressive; and hell-bent on destroying the universe…but with a smile on our lips and a wink in our eyes.

How will we reconcile the following: a creed that states all men are created equal and the screw-the-other-guy rush up the grease-pole of success; a creed that states that all races and religions should be free and our own deeds of genocide (the Amerindians); concentration camps (the American-Japanese during World War II); and slavery (Blacks); the Protestant ethic of work, self-control, and frugality with the ethics of spontaneity, openness, and spend-spend-spend; the ethics of violence and corruption versus the ethics of innocence and good humor; the ethic of deferred gratification and the quest for gratification NOW, freedom NOW, peace NOW, power NOW, and love/sex NOW.

The dialectic between these forces has erupted already and will continue to erupt. As the great novelist Elie Wiesel has told us—the issue is not so much to seek answers, but to ask the right questions, and the questions, contradictions, and struggles that the militant and the young (both in age and in spirit) have asked and fought over, will be with us for a very long time.

A Hollywood studio has yet to produce a revolutionary film that adequately grapples with these questions.

Yet, surprisingly, on another level, Hollywood can indeed be seen as a revolutionary force, both for oppressed people in this country (Blacks, Indians, poor Whites) and in newly developing countries in Asia and Africa. It is one of the unpredictable consequences of mass media.

In 1956, President Sukarno of Indonesia announced to a large group of Hollywood executives that he regarded them as political radicals and revolutionaries who had greatly hastened political change in the emerging Third World nations. Hollywood gave poor oppressed people an expectation of life that did not jibe with their own reality. The gap between what they saw in a Doris Day film and their own destitute lives caused a certain tension to appear, which in turn led to a revolt when this tension was properly manipulated by political agitators.

As Marshall McLuhan (1966:257) noted:

> What the Orient saw in a Hollywood movie was a world in which all the *ordinary people* had cars and electric stoves and refrigerators. So the Oriental now regards himself as an ordinary person who has been deprived of the ordinary man's birthright.

To most Americans, this theory doesn't hold. To them, this aspect of film is subliminal, a kind of reverie. But to deprived Americans, movies and T.V. act like a time-bomb, setting in motion tensions and expectations that ultimately lead to confrontation and political revolt.

In political science and sociology, this is known as the *theory of relative deprivation*. In this theory, truly oppressed and completely repressed people do not revolt. Only when there is a glimmer of hope, only when some reform has emerged, then does revolt occur. In a sense, a little freedom begets a little more freedom; some reform begets more reform. Politically, if you give oppressed people an inch, they'll take a mile.

As I've said earlier, American movie-makers have always been better at producing liberal, reform-minded movies. Politically, I call them rebellion movies. They are not revolutionary.

For example, since its origins, cinema has developed films of social consciousness reflecting the bitterness and the joy of the personal dilemmas confronting mankind (and womankind).

One of my favorite films is King Vidor's *Our Daily Bread*. Made in 1934, this Depression-inspired film about a group of families who return to the soil, to simple pleasures, and to communal living in order to survive economically, has lost nothing in its message to the generation of the 1960s and 1970s.

The 1930s sparked a new kind of Hollywood realism as both sound and the Depression conspired to introduce a naturalistic style in setting, writing, and performance. The social-problem film was prominent in the Thirties. The most impressive of this type of film—actually, it is a genre of its own—was the gangster/G-man theme.

During this decade, there was widespread public indignation over the prevalence of crime in America and the inability of the police and FBI to effectively deal with it. This indignation was sharpened by the famous Lindbergh kidnapping early in 1932. The Lindbergh case gave the federal government the opportunity to have jurisdiction over crimes which hitherto had been wholly under state jurisdiction.

The late J. Edgar Hoover, the resourceful head of the FBI of the Department of Justice, saw his chance and began to use his office as a means of catching gangsters and bank robbers.

Thus began the long procession of public interest in such "Public Enemies Number 1" as Al Capone, John Dillinger, "Pretty Buy" Floyd, "Baby Face" Nelson and so many others.[1] It is difficult to say who the real heroes were—the gangsters or the G-men. An actor like James Cagney would play both roles—the bounding young G-man and the notorious killer. Films like *The Public Enemy* (1931), *Scarface* (1932), *The Front Page* (1931), and *Little Caesar* (1930) are excellent examples of this sort of social problems type of cinema dealing with the sociology of crime in America.

Arthur Knight (1957:238) points out that the studios quickly brought to the screen not only a staggering succession of gangster films (fifty in 1931 alone!) but equally sensational exposés of other social problems: rackets, political corruption, prison brutality, bank failures, and newspaper scandal sheets. The tendency was then, as it still is today, that the fabric of society was still sound, so blame was heaped on isolated individuals rather than on the power structure itself or on those who controlled the state.

---

[1] It is interesting to note that Dillinger's only federal offense up to the time of his murder on July 22, 1934, in front of the still-standing Biograph Theater in Chicago was the interstate transportation of a stolen car. It is also ironic that Dillinger's last act on earth was seeing a movie at the Biograph. Reality and fantasy merged beautifully. He probably saw a newsreel of himself and FBI's search. Today, the Biograph Theater specializes in movies of the 1930s, especially gangster films.

Audiences seemed to find reassurance that everything could be solved by the jailing or killing of a brutal warden, a hoodlum gangster, or a power-hungry politician.

Though many films of this genre were cheap exploitations, one, *I Am a Fugitive from a Chain Gang* (1932), based on an actual case, was so shocking that an aroused public forced a reformation of the chain-gang system.

The election of Franklin Delano Roosevelt in 1933 injected a much-needed dose of optimism to the country and to films. Musicals, which only a short time before had been singing "Brother, Can You Spare a Dime?", were now shouting out that "Happy Days are Here Again."

The reformist trend of the New Deal also explored other themes besides gangsterism, prisons, and back-to-the-soil movements. It dealt with bigotry and anti-lynching laws in *Fury* (1936), *Winterset* (1936) and *They Won't Forget* (1937); with the desperate plight of migrant workers, *The Grapes of Wrath* (1939); and with films upholding the belief in democracy and the honest democratic way of life, John Ford's *Young Mr. Lincoln* (1939) and *Abe Lincoln in Illinois* (1940), as well as such biographies as *The Life of Emile Zola* (1937).

"Underlying all these films," Arthur Knight (1957:242-243) explains, "was the awareness that our cultural and intellectual freedom was a precious heritage that the growing forces of fascism both at home and abroad were threatening to destroy."

The rise of Germany's Hitler, Italy's Mussolini, and Japan's warlords brought an end to this fascinating and terribly important decade. It spanned the stock market crash of September 3, 1929, to the rumblings of World War II in September 1939. It was an era very similar to our own turbulent sixties and seventies. The class of political ideologies, trade unionism, socialist parties, communist and anti-communist forces, the forces of law and order versus the forces of change, liberal reform versus radical change, and "future shock" were all characteristic of the age. It is a wonder that widespread revolution did not take place during the Depression. Aside from the Civil War, this era was the greatest single threat to the stability of a still young nation.

Yet the nation survived without revolution. Why? The most salient reason is that the common people still believed in the country's ideals. There was still hope for democracy, for the good life, for the Horatio Alger success story.

Movies such as *My Man Godfrey* (1936), *Footlight Parade* (1933), *Easy Living* (1937), Busby Berkeley's *Gold Diggers of 1935* (1935), and Ernst Lubitsch's *Monte Carlo* (1930) and *Trouble in Paradise* (1932) were all escapist films that gave people hope against the depression of unemployment, hunger and fear. Revolutionary filmmaker Jean-Luc Godard noted: "Even a Lubitsch comedy of the thirties [was still] a reflection of the American capitalist way of life at that time."

The essential issue, the basic structure of the society, was not questioned. Aside from Roosevelt's reforms and America's entry into World War II, it is my thesis that it was movies and other mass media that helped cool out revolution in this country! An individual could fight the intolerant and oppressive elements in a society, but in the end, the society itself was vindicated. Clean up the house, but don't destroy its foundation, because the foundation was still sound, went the reasoning.

A delectably served slice of Americana, *Meet John Doe* (1941), is a perfect example of the strong individual, played by Gary Cooper, who rallies the populist fervor of the people to fight greed, corruption and arrogant power. And the people prevailed, and so did society. It is in this way that movies have, until this very day, undercut the revolutionary thrust. As long as the majority of citizens still have confidence in this country's Constitution and Bill of Rights, and as long as citizens feel that only "minor surgery" is needed to repair major social problems, then there will never be revolution here in terms of a seizure of power *à la* Cuba or China, especially so in a wealthy, complex, technocratic society like America. It is still a mighty powerful and mighty flexible nation.

I would now like to go back to an earlier issue and elaborate what the essential differences are between the revolutionary and the rebellion film. These differences are not at all subtle; they are profound, and they revolve around two central points.

One, the *intent* of the director is most important. The mass media is an extremely important part of revolutionary struggle. Cinema is part of this struggle, and a revolutionary film is on the side of the revolution. The intent of the director, of the filming staff, and most importantly, the money that produces the film—all must be concerned with political change first, artistic quality second, and profit-making a distant third. One can see that a revolutionary Hollywood film is a contradiction in terms. Hollywood means profit, and if a theme can be exploited for profit, so be it. The corporate and banking sources that back a film are not ready to commit political and economic suicide for the sake of a dogma that not only they don't believe in, but of which they are bitter enemies.

The McCarthy Era of the early 1950s is a bitter example of what side the major studios are on when the chips are down and when the political pressure is applied.

The directors, producers, and staff of rebellion films are usually liberal reform-minded citizens, working within the confines of powerful studios/ corporations and their own political timidity. They make revolutionary statements on film at great personal and monetary risk.

The second most important difference is, of course, the *political theme.* The rebellion film portrays a social problem in a vacuum, cut off from the larger society. The revolutionary film portrays an attack against the entire society. The hero (or heroine) of a revolutionary film is a rebel *with* a cause; the hero (or anti-hero) of a rebellion film is a *Rebel Without a Cause.*

The James Dean-type rebel is an example of adolescent frustration. The anti-hero makes no important linkage of his personal problems to wider societal issues. As I hope to make clear, the leitmotif of this entire book is the sociological imagination—a crucial political and well as academic task of making such links.

If these links are not made, then what is portrayed is simply a personal thrashing about, a confusion, wherein adults are quick to retort: "He'll grow out of it," and into benign respectability.

Many people in the sixties had hoped that student and Black protest was nothing more than collegiate/plantation shenanigans, like panty raids, but they soon found that the questions raised were much more serious— the quality of life, freedom, sex, morality, imperialism, oppression—and could not be dismissed so easily. Only outright repression or repressive tolerance could be used.

A revolutionary film is not a toy for personal amusement or escapist entertainment, but a vital and dangerous tool for social change.

Bernard Weiner (1972:14) has also made clear that a political film is a difficult as well as a dangerous task:

> In a renewed age of ideology, we should not be surprised at the large number of political films, that are now making their appearance. We also should not be surprised that many of them are aesthetic, and even political disasters. Few political directors can resist the

temptation to slide over the fine line which separates high political art from mere agitprop. After all, the ostensible objective of the political film is to educate and alter people's behavior, so it is very easy to become too didactic, or to caricature the enemy in one-dimensional venality.

The danger for political filmmakers in being overzealous advocates of the revolution is that nobody will come to see the films other than those who are already convinced. The result is that the films influence and educate nobody, and the process becomes a circular rite of ideological masturbation.

Weiner goes on to say that American political films, especially those dealing with the campus or youth revolution—*The Strawberry Statement, Getting Straight, R.P.M., Joe, WUSA, Easy Rider,* and others—were just so much Hollywood illusionism, almost totally divorced from reality. I might also add that the first three were also *financial,* as well as political, disasters.

Even foreign directors who depicted the political revolution in America failed ignominiously, for example, Antonioni's *Zabriskie Point* (which Pauline Kael called a love affair between the hero's Cessna and the heroine's Packard). However, Giuliano Montaldo's *Sacco and Vanzetti* and Bo Widerberg's *Joe Hill* were at least admirable failures. at least an attempt was made to display the reality of radical organizers of two generations ago. American directors have virtually ignored the radical and labor heroes in their own back yard.

Only two fiction films by American directors, according to Weiner, are infused with integrity and honest vision: Paul Williams' *The Revolutionary* and Robert Kramer's *Ice.* They succeed because the former is set in some time-past of unspecified locale and the latter in some time-future, so neither has to deal with time-present America. This is a curious reason. I still believe it is possible to make a revolutionary film in present-day America, but it must be subtle; it's too easy to get heavy-handed in one's self-righteous advocacy of violent social change or in counter-cultural lifestyles. Movies like *Putney Swope* and Emile de Antonio's *Millhouse: A White Comedy* are both black humor (and for *Putney Swope* this is a pun) that hit hard although a bit too heavy at times.

Putney Swope, a black junior executive of an advertising firm, is elected chairman because nearly everyone on the board thinks no one else will vote for him so they do, and consequently, he turns the ad agency into a revolutionary force. It is a brilliant premise, but somehow fails because of confusion over political direction.

The best political films, or at least the most powerful and exciting, come not from America, not from Western Europe, and not even from China (though Godard would disagree here), but from the third World: Gillo Pontecorvo's *The Battle of Algiers* (again, Godard would disagree) and *Burn;* Octavio Getino and Fernando Solanas' *The Hour of the Furnaces;* and three Latin American films: Miguel Littin's *El Chacal de Nahueltoro* (*Jackal of Nahueltoro*), Jorge Sanjinés' *Yawar Mallku* (*Blood of the Condor*), and Tomás Gutiérrez Alea's *Memorias de Subdesarrollo (Memories of Underdevelopment).* According to Pauline Kael in *The New Yorker,* Solanas' film is:

> …[the] movie equivalent of a revolutionary manifesto…perhaps the most spectacular example of agitprop moviemaking…an emotional assault. A movie like this is a gun in the struggle and a far more effective gun than Godard's revolutionary movies because though it may aim at both the heart and the mind, it strikes the heart.

Littin's *El Chacal de Nahueltoro* (*Jackal of Nahueltoro*) is set in Chile and is based on the true story of a peasant, born and reared in rural poverty, who, in a drunken rage, kills a mother and her five children. He is pursued, caught, and convicted. During his imprisonment, he rehabilitates himself through study, work and religion. He is sentenced to death and becomes a mass media celebrity. The movie is not simply a strong case against capital punishment, but an indictment against poverty, exploitation, official hypocrisy, greed, corruption, and the misuses of the media, and ultimately led to the election of Marxist president Salvadore Allende.

Sanjinés' *Yawar Mallku* (*Blood of the Condor*) is set in Bolivia and depicts the abject poverty and daily humiliations of the Bolivian Indians, both in the village and in the city, and the scandalous news that the U.S. Peace Corps clinic, in connivance with the racist military junta, is sterilizing Indian women without their knowledge when they come for treatment. Because of U.S. pressure, the Bolivian regime refused to permit it to be shown. Violent street demonstrations, however, forced a revocation of the ban, and to date over one-third of a million Bolivians have seen the movie. Such is the power of the people.

Alea's *Memorias de Subdesarrollo (Memories of Underdevelopment)* is set in Cuba in 1961 and 1962, around the time of the disastrous Bay of Pigs invasion and the Cuban Missile Crisis. It is also a time when the Cuban middle classes begin to feel the pinch of revolutionary change. Many in fact, scramble to get out of the country—"to go north," as they say in the movie. The main character, Sergio, sees his wife off at the airport. They are surrounded by tearful faces. Many leave Cuba with genuine regret. The film is part documentary and part fiction. Newsreel footage shows Bay of Pigs prisoners marching down a road, preparations for the defense of Cuba, a T.V. speech by Castro, and American newsreels of policemen beating up Black demonstrators, all mixed in with stream-of-consciousness memories that give this film its impact.[2]

Though "Third World" films are often amateurish in technique, over- and under-exposed, sometimes trite and lacking in tension, they do exude an authenticity that compensates for their faults. There is no time for frills; the need for revolutionary change, whether in South America, South Africa, the Arab States (including Palestinian films) or in Asia, is deemed too important for such things. Lack of money can also account for this lack of polish.

To conclude with a quote from Bernard Weiner (1972:16);

Third World films emerge not from the typewriter of some well-paid, intellectually liberal scriptwriter, but from the gut-level anger and emotion of an oppressed people.

These…films are by no means perfect, and they tend toward much more sentimentality and didacticism than the white West is comfortable with—but we must remember that they are not produced for us. They are made out of the harsh reality of daily life—and their aim is to educate and influence their countrymen to the need for organized resistance to imperialism and further cultural degradation.

---

2   For those interested in showing these films, contact Third World Cinema Group, 244 West 27th Street, New York, NY 10001. For more on such revolutionary films, see William Murphy's incisive analysis, "Two Third World Films" (1972:14-16).

Dalton Trumbo and the
Hollywood Ten: Their Legacy

Unpublished piece.

* * *

Trumbo, 2015. Directed by Jay Roach. Written by John McNamara, adapted from the 1977 book by Bruce Cook. With Bryan Cranston as Danton Trumbo, Michael Stuhlberg as Edward G. Robinson, Helen Mirren as Hedda Hopper, David James Elliott as a befuddled and ambivalent John Wayne, Diane Lane as Trumbo's supportive wife Cleo Fincher, Dean O'Gorman as a defiant Kirk Douglas, John Goodman as Mr. King, a B-movie maker, Louis C.K. as Trumbo's fictionalized friend Arlen Hird, and German actor Christian Berkel as the comically dour director Otto Preminger. 2015.

Trumbo (the documentary), 2007. Directed by Peter Askin, based on the play *Trumbo* by Christopher Trumbo, Dalton's son. With readings by Joan Allen, Brian Dennehy, Michael Douglas, Paul Giamatti, Nathan Lane, Josh Lucas, Liam Neeson, David Strathairn, Danny Glover, and Donald Sutherland.

Red Hollywood, 1995. Directed by Thom Anderson and Noel Burch. Digital video, color, 114 minutes.

The movie *Trumbo* follows Dalton Trumbo's life quite accurately and closely follows the documentary *Trumbo* that was made eight years earlier, while both *Red Hollywood* and *Trumbo* the documentary finally tell us the real story of...yes, "Red Hollywood." Coming on the heels of urbane, progressive and brilliant émigrés, escapees from Nazis to Hollywood; given the impact of the Depression, poverty, class conflict, and racial unrest, the Spanish Civil War of 1936, and the rising tide of Fascism and Nazism, the Communist Party in the USA, along with the other socialist and democratic-socialist movements, attracted many people and many Jews. Ninety percent of the Communist Party (CP) membership in Los Angeles was Jewish!

Red Hollywood, shown at the Harvard Film Archive in the fall of 2015, is an intelligent work that carefully unfurls thematically organized scenes from more than fifty features written by the Hollywood Ten, and ties them together with interviews of these legendary writers, including several with a still-defiant Abraham Polonsky. The directors of this rarely seen film maintain that the Hollywood Ten writers used film as a media for promulgating both latent and overt themes of racism, anti-Semitism, xenophobia, and war.

Why, then, do we have two films and the resurrection of a third about this man and his friends and enemies, many of who called him the most brilliant screenwriter in movie history? Probably because, if anyone could have broken the back of J. Parnell Thomas, Joe McCarthy, and the Hollywood blacklist, it would have been Trumbo. He was such a damn good writer that Hollywood simply had to ignore his involvement with the Communist Party and end the blacklist.

There were no winners in this tragedy; only losers. And there were good and bad on both sides. Each reacted in his own way; each made mistakes; maybe they all did. Maybe they should have been proud of being Commies and said so instead of invoking the First or the Fifth Amendment. How different it was just 15-20 years later when an Abbie Hoffman or a Jerry Rubin or a Dave Dellinger or an Angela Davis proudly proclaimed themselves Communists, Socialists, or simply radicals, some in jest like Jerry and Abbie, some real like Davis or Dellinger. None hid behind constitutional "rights."

But in the 1940s and 1950s there was a different mindset in how to handle one's involvement in the CP; one year we were friends with Russia, the next deadly enemies. It made no sense. And it was all pure poppycock. The Russians, aside from some minor espionage, made no real dent in the security of America. It was all hyper-hysteria. But it destroyed many lives.

Who helped Trumbo break the list? First, Kirk Douglas and *Spartacus* in 1958; next, Otto Preminger and *Exodus* in 1960. Finally, Present John F.

Kennedy went to see *Spartacus*, and Hedda Hopper was finished when that happened.

It was also ironic that the man who put Trumbo away for a few years in prison in Kentucky was also his co-prisoner at the same time in the early 1950s. J. Parnell Thomas went to jail for tax evasion while Trumbo was in the same prison for contempt. How ironic!

The Hollywood Ten, also known as the "Unfriendly Ten"—or, as Elia Kazan snidely remarked, "one or two had talent, the rest were simply unfriendly"—were ten mostly Jewish screenwriters and directors. The real question is not whether they were Communist but whether they really influenced Hollywood films? Did they sneak into movies a "secret code" that could infiltrate the hearts and minds of American citizens? The answer is both yes and no.

I found the documentary *Trumbo* very moving, seeing that it interwove letters read by well-known actors, interviews with Trumbo's children and friends, and archival photos and documents of the time, all deftly compile to tell the true story of Communism in Hollywood. Finally, let us admit it, Hollywood was filled with socialists, Communists, progressives, and left-liberals, and it still is. Ronald Reagan, Adolphe Menjou, Robert Taylor, and Hedda Hopper were in the minority politically, but they scared the shit out of the (mostly Jewish) Hollywood producers and studios.

There are powerful scenes in both *Trumbo* the movie and *Trumbo* the documentary of Hedda Hopper browbeating Louis B. Mayer (whom she had slept with when she was a beautiful young starlet); John Wayne feeling a bit ambivalent (good for him) when confronting Trumbo; and Trumbo's encounter with Edward G. Robinson.

And lurking to the left of J. Parnell Thomas slithers Richard Nixon; but Bobby Kennedy was also there on the side of McCarthy, so everyone was covered with the slime of McCarthyism. (Even a Sunday evening, December 6, 2015 TV tribute to Frank Sinatra courageously pointed out that the Kennedys cut off Sammy Davis Jr. from meeting with them because of his white wife, Swedish actress May Britt. Sinatra was furious, but what could he do? Even the Kennedys' hands were dirtied by prejudice and red-baiting. No one was immune except for some brave individuals, many unknown.)

Some in Hollywood quietly supported Trumbo, lending him money. The movie shows a contrite Eddy Robinson, first supporting Trumbo, then caving in as his career disintegrates, and naming names. Trumbo never forgave him, even when Robinson came crying to him, begging for forgiveness.

As one scholar observed, "Virtually overnight the atmosphere in Hollywood became one of terror. Lives were wrecked, careers destroyed, marriages and families shattered as friend betrayed friend, sometimes after swearing devotion the night before."[3]

And let us not forget the Jewish aspect of all this, which is somewhat muted in all three films. One wag once said, "Russia fears three things: AIDS, Jews, and Ronald Reagan" (they thought Reagan would bomb them—this was in the 1980s), and America in the 1940s and 1950s also feared three things: homosexuals, Jews, and Joe Stalin.

An engrossing 1929 article by the great U.S. muckraker and journalist Upton Sinclair (1878-1968) entitled "Communist 'Criminals' in Los Angeles" first appeared in *The Nation*, the oldest liberal magazine in the United States, and discussed the case of Yetta Stromberg, 19, who was charged with a crime of discussing Communism and had her students make a red flag with a hammer and sickle. She was convicted, ironically, in San Bernardino Superior Court. The movement against the "reds" started several decades before the trials of the "Hollywood Ten." Sinclair discusses several other Jewish Communists as well in his essay. At the time, Jews made up an estimated 90 percent of the Communist Party's membership in Los Angeles.[4]

But what emerges from these films is that these men (and they were all men on trial; very few women writers are mentioned) were indeed members of the Communist Party, and many, especially their leader John Howard Lawson, led successful strikes against the studios. Walt Disney was especially incensed when his workers went on strike—how could they do that to Mickey Mouse's creator?

The Hollywood moguls wanted to both re-assert their power over their "writers" and to quash Communist-led union organizing. I think those were more salient reasons for the suppression than lefty screenwriters inserting subtle pro-Communist sentiments in films.

---

3   Ronald L. Davis, quoted in Gerald Horne, *The Final Victim of the Blacklist: John Howard Lawson, Dean of the Hollywood Ten* (Berkeley: University of California Press, 2006), p. xvi.

4   Tony Michels (ed.), *Jewish Radicals: A Documentary History* (New York and London: New York University Press, 2012), pp. 129-132.

But what is the legacy of Trumbo and the Hollywood 10? And why do these moves appear at this time to delight and impress audiences today? What is it about the *Zeitgeist* that beckons us back in time? These are interesting questions. I don't necessarily have an answer; maybe a reader can tell us why Trumbo, John Howard Lawson, Ring Lardner, Jr., Adrian Scott and the others are still relevant today.

In the 1950s it was the fear of Communism taking over our society, of Hollywood screenwriters "infiltrating" our movies with "secret messages" of liberalism, tolerance, and peace. Maybe we are facing similar tensions today. Fear is stalking our great society: fear of the foreigner, fear of the Muslim assassin, fear of the terrorists ready to commit genocide. Maybe it is also the fear that our planet is becoming overcrowded, polluted, and changing its climate.

Like in the 1940s and 1950s, the right wing, the heirs to J. Parnell Thomas, Joe McCarthy, and yes, two presidents who got their start at those HUAC hearings—Richard Nixon and Ronald Reagan—are ready to pounce on the liberals and radicals and say that they are responsible for our problems. We face difficult times, and those fears could land a Republican in the White House in 2016.

Why Were There No Women Among the Hollywood Ten?

There was no limit to HUAC's inconsistencies. If the friendly witnesses included women (Ayn Rand, Lela Rogers), why was "the other side" (HUAC's term) all males? The committee had enough information on Lillian Hellman and Karen Morley to subpoena them in September 1947—and did so in 1952; why not in 1947?[5]

Women made up about 20 percent of the some five dozen writers, actors, directors, and producers who were blacklisted, yet they were not included in the Hollywood Ten or the Hollywood Nineteen. Why? In general, minorities, such as women, gays, Blacks, were in essence "written out of history"; they were not taken seriously by Congress. Such were the times. It would not be until the radical 1960s when women's rights and female

---

5   Bernard K. Dick, *Radical Innocence: A Critical Study of the Hollywood Ten* (Lexington, Ky.: The University Press of Kentucky, 1989), p. 3.

consciousness would emerge, yet among the blacklisted were some of the most prominent figures in American literature.

Perhaps an entire documentary could be devoted to this group of women, some famous, some obscure. They included:

- Dorothy Parker, *née* Rothschild (1893-1967), writer, poet, critic, and screenwriter.
- Lillian Hellman (1905-1984), probably the most controversial of all of them.
- Betsy Blair (1923-2000), actress who was nominated for an Oscar in 1955 playing the mousy girlfriend of Ernest Borgnine in *Marty.* She was married to Gene Kelly, which probably helped her survive, and later to important director Karel Reisz. Like so many black-listed, she escaped to Europe.
- Gale Sondergaard (1899-1985), actress in such films as *The Good Earth* (1937), married to blacklisted Herbert Biberman.

And there were others who were less well-known:

- Marguerite Roberts (1905-1989), one of the highest paid screen-writers in the 1930s.
- Karen Morley (1909-2003), actress.
- Jean Muir (1911-1996), actress. Her son, Michael Jaffe, is a suc-cessful TV and film producer.
- Bess Taffel (1913-2000), screenwriter, who also worked in the Yiddish theater.
- Dorothy Tree (1906-1992), actress and well-known voice teacher, and also a Yiddish speaker. She died of heart failure at the famous Actors Fund of America Nursing Home in Englewood, New Jersey.
- Herta Ware (1917-2005), actress, married to Will Geer, another actor and activist. Geer appeared as a sheriff in Herbert Biberman and Paul Jerrico's classic film *Salt of the Earth* (1954).
- Hannah Weinstein (1911-1984), TV producer and journalist in the UK and the USA, who hired blacklisted writers.

There were others, and there were many wives and daughters who were also active in the Communist Party and in other progressive movements. There were a large number of couples who shared a similar ideology and philosophy and became lifetime partners (Lillian Hellman and Dashiell

Hammett; Gale Sondergaard and Herbert Biberman; Herta Ware and Will Geer).

As late as 1999, there were stories about them; see the December 1999 *Vanity Fair* article on the "blacklist survivors," most of them women. All of the men have died; there are just a few women still alive as of 2016.

Did Jews "Dominate" Hollywood, and Were They Communists?

Hollywood indeed is dominated by Jewish people in the same way that pizza parlors were once dominated by Italians and now Greeks. Is that bad or good? It just *is*. As recently as the 2016 Golden Globe Awards (of the Hollywood foreign press), Ricky Gervais made some jokes about Mel Gibson's anti-Semitic tirades and Jewish dominance in Tinsel City and ended the show with "Oh, Mel and I wish everyone 'shalom."

However, this "dominance" during the Hollywood Ten HUAC hearings caused much concern in the Jewish community. Here is a quote from Gerald Horne's book on John Howard Lawson, *The Final Victim of the Blacklist* (2006: 232):

> …this question of communism was inseparable from the question of Jewishness, an equation that met neatly in the person of Lawson. This, too, was intimidating, particularly to stars, a number of whom were Jewish and many of whom were notoriously insecure with famously fragile egos and notional concepts of self-worth.

Here is what Gerald Horne (2006: 232-233) writes, using the comments of an undercover agent for the US Senate hearings (from the files of an internal security subcommittee report, dated June 18, 1947):

> When a conference on "thought control" was held at the refined Beverly Hills hotel, sponsored by the left, the Senate agent present was haughtily dismissive; it was "the same old crowd, about 95% Hollywood Jews of the 'commie' type…from John Howard Lawson on down".
>
> When Lawson received his L.A. farewell [he was going off to prison—JNP], the [U.S. Senate] agent present was spitting mad. It was a "rabble rousing affair from start to finish," and there were "approximately 3000 in the crowd and it was SOME crowd. About 90% Hollywood Jews and that is speaking conservatively and

advisedly; about 5% Negroes and the other 5% were renegard [sic] whites." While the national anthem was being sung, many of the spew from the gutters of Hollywood did not even remove their hats. It would be impossible for many of them to sing the song because some spoke very poor English and the rest cackled like geese in Yiddish.

Who Were the Hollywood Ten? A Thumbnail Sketch

The Hollywood Ten were chosen, similar to the Chicago 8 twenty years later, for their political use to HUAC people. They were chosen to represent a wide range of strengths and positions, not just political positions but positions in the Hollywood guilds and unions. But there were many other people snared into their nets: Perhaps 50-60 or more.

There was also a "Hollywood 19" or the "Unfriendly 19." They consisted of the following, and once again did not include women. Here is an important quote from Bernard F. Dick's book *Radical Innocence* (1989: 3):

> The nineteen were a curious mix of screenwriters (Alvah Bessie, Lester Cole, Richard Collins, Gordon Kahn, Howard Koch, Ring Lardner, Jr., John Howard Lawson, Albert Maltz, Samuel Ornitz, Waldo Salt, and Dalton Trumbo); directors (Edward Dmytryk, Lewis Milestone, and Irving Pichel); writer-directors (Herbert Biberman and Robert Rossen); a writer-producer (Adrian Scott); a playwright (Bertolt Brecht); and an actor (Larry Parks). In 1947 the only name familiar to the average moviegoer would have been that of Larry Parks, whose ability to capture Al Jolson's mannerisms and lip-synch his songs in *The Jolson Story* (1946) is still a marvel of verisimilitude.

But the "19" were whittled down to "10" for the following reasons:

- The Hollywood Ten were high-profile and successful screenwriters (and one director).
- They were well-known organizers and "agitators."
- None of them had served in the military (for example, Paul Jarrico was excluded because he had served).
- Their non-service could then be used as an example of an internal "Fifth Column" of traitors.

- Plus, several were involved in the making of *Crossfire*, a film that examined anti-Semitism. This showed that the committee fused anti-Communism with anti-Semitism, that anti-Semitism was an important factor in this witch-hunt.

The Hollywood Ten were as follows: Dalton Trumbo, John Howard Lawson, Ring Lardner, Jr., Lester Cole, Adrian Scott, Herbert Biberman, Samuel Ornitz, Edward Dmytryk, Alvah Bessie, and Albert Maltz. Six of them were Jewish. They were all sentenced to a year in a federal correctional institution, whether in Ashland, Kentucky; Springfield, Missouri; or Danbury, Connecticut; fined $1,000 each and served ten months. That was the usual penalty.

Dalton Trumbo (1905-1976) was arguably, along with Ring Lardner, Jr., the most famous and successful of the "Ten." He was born December 5, 1905, in Montrose, Colorado. He attended the University of Colorado, and his family moved to Los Angeles in 1925. He published short stories and articles for major magazines, and in 1934 he began work for Warner Brothers. From 1936 to 1973, he had about forty screen credits. He wrote many successful films, several of them Academy Award nominees and winners, including *Roman Holiday*, *Spartacus*, and *Papillon*. His association with Kirk Douglas' Bryna Productions in 1958 led to the end of his blacklisting when he wrote the script for *Spartacus*. In 1960, he came off the list with Otto Preminger's announcement on January 19, 1960, that he had hired Trumbo to adapt *Exodus*. Trumbo won an Oscar under the name of "Robert Rich" for *The Brave One* in 1957 and under the name of a real person, Ian McClellan Hunter, in 1953 for *Roman Holiday*. (In actuality, the story is more complex. Trumbo did not write the actual screenplay; he wrote the story on which it was based. Hunter wrote a screenplay, but he was not the only writer. There were at least four others, including two by Ben Hecht and one by Preston Sturges, but Trumbo should have gotten screen credit and at least shared in the Oscar.) He died of a heart attack on September 10, 1976, in Los Angeles.

According to Allan H. Ryskind, Trumbo was a "hard-core [Communist] Party member, a fervent supporter of Stalinist Russia... and an apologist for Nazi Germany until Hitler double-crossed Stalin and invaded the Soviet Union. Yet to this day, he is regarded as a hero in Hollywood." (2015: x)

John Howard Lawson (1894-1977) was often called the "dean" of the Hollywood Ten, and the "enforcer" of the Communist Party line in Hollywood after he was dispatched from New York by Party headquarters to monitor writers (Ryskind, 2015: x). But he was much more: an eloquent speaker, a consummate union organizer, an insightful writer of the craft of screenwriting, a pioneer in early "expressionistic" playwriting (*Roger Bloomer* in 1923; *Processional* in 1925), as well as a prolific screenwriter (*Dynamite, Bachelor Apartment, Blockade, Algiers, Action in the North Atlantic, Sahara, The Jolson Story*, and *Cry, the Beloved Country*). He should be counted up there with Trumbo and Lardner as among the most important writers and political figures of that era, yet he has been often overlooked.

Born on September 25, 1894, in New York City to a wealthy and assimilated Jewish family, he enrolled in Williams College in northwestern Massachusetts in 1910, at the age of 16, the youngest member of his class. He died on August 14, 1977, in San Francisco.

Ring Lardner, Jr. (1915-2000) came from a distinguished American literary family. His father was a famous raconteur and humorist; his brother John Lardner was a sports columnist; and not one but two brothers, David and Jim, died as war correspondents in Europe: David in Germany, and Jim as a volunteer in the Abraham Lincoln Brigade in Spain. Lardner was born August 19, 1915, in Chicago and attended Princeton University. In 1936, he began his career as a publicist for David O. Selznick, and from 1937 to 1947 he worked regularly as a screenwriter in Hollywood. He won an Oscar for *Woman of the Year* in 1943 before the blacklist and another one for the movie *M*A*S*H* in 1971 after the blacklist. He was one of the most successful post-blacklist writers. In 1986 he wrote the script for the program on April 7 at Avery Fisher Hall, New York, commemorating the fiftieth anniversary of the Spanish Civil War (1936-1986).

Lester Cole (1904-1985) was born June 19, 1904, dropped out of school, and in 1925 was an assistant stage manager for Max Reinhardt's production of *The Miracle* in New York and on tour. In 1927, he was stage manager of Grauman's (now Mann's) Chinese Theater in Hollywood. In 1932, he was hired by Paramount as a screenwriter, and from 1932 to 1947 he acquired over thirty screen credits. In 1934, he joined the Communist Party. From 1966 to 1985, he taught screenwriting, mostly at San Francisco State University. He died of a heart attack on August 15, 1985, in San Francisco.

Adrian Scott (1911-1972) was born February 6, 1911, in Arlington, New Jersey, attended Amherst College, and graduated in 1934. In 1940, he received his first screen credit for *Keeping Company* (1940) at MGM, and in 1942 he was hired by RKO Pictures, for which he wrote the highly successful *Mr. Lucky* (1943). He then became a producer for RKO and produced *My Pal Wolf* (1944) and the successful *Murder, My Sweet* (1944), directed by Edward Dmytryk. Scott and Dmytryk reunited on *Cornered* (1945), *So Well Remembered* (1947), and the more successful *Crossfire* (1947). Scott died on December 25, 1972, of lung cancer.

Herbert Biberman (1900-1971) was born March 4, 1900, in Philadelphia and attended both the University of Pennsylvania and the Yale School of Drama in the early and mid-1920s. In 1930, he married actress Gale Sondergaard, and they remained married until his death in 1971. His Hollywood period lasted from 1935 to 1947. In 1956, his most famous film, *Salt of the Earth*, about the uprising of zinc miners and their wives in New Mexico, was awarded the International Grand Prize for best film. In 1956, Biberman worked as a land developer. He died of bone cancer on June 30, 1971, in New York City.

Samuel Ornitz (1890-1957) was the oldest of the Ten and known as the "patriarch." In the words of Dalton Trumbo, he was "a man of immense dignity, sincerity and learning." He was born of the middle class in New York City, where his parents were wool merchants. Though he lived comparatively well, he attended the Henry Street School and gradually became a confirmed Socialist. He was a well-known novelist and reformer before he became a screenwriter. His proletarian novel, *Haunch, Paunch, and Jowl* (1923), is well known in Jewish-American literature. The title refers to a man who betrays his convictions and becomes a politician with an expanding waistline and heavy cheeks (jowls). *The Sock: A Play of Protest* is perhaps his most famous work. He died of cancer on March 10 at the Motion Picture Country Home in Los Angeles.

Edward Dmytryk (1908-1999) was born September 4, 1908, in Grand Forks, British Columbia, Canada. He was the only director in the Hollywood Ten and the most successful director of all post-blacklist members. In 1923, he was hired by Famous Players-Lasky (precursor of Paramount) as an errand boy, then worked in Paramount's editing department beginning in 1929, working on such films as Leo McCarey's Marx Brothers movie *Duck Soup* (1933). In 1932, he married Madeleine Robinson. In 1935, he directed his first film, *The Hawk*, and went on to direct twenty-four films from 1939 to 1947. In 1944, he joined the Communist Party, which he left in 1945. In 1948, he married Jean Porter and moved to England to direct *The End of the Affair* (1955). From 1951 to 1975, he directed twenty-five more films. Among his pre-blacklist films are *Confessions of Boston Blackie* (1941), *Counter-Espionage* (1942), *Hitler's Children* (1943), *Murder, My Sweet* (1944), *Back to Bataan* (1945), and especially *Crossfire* (1947), one of the first films to deal with American anti-Semitism. After the blacklist, his films include *The Juggler* (1953), based on Michael Blankfort's novel and starring Kirk Douglas; *The Caine Mutiny* (1954), based on Herman Wouk's novel and starring Humphrey Bogart, José Ferrer, Van Johnson and Fred MacMurray; *Raintree County* (1957), based on Ross Lockridge Jr.'s novel and starring Montgomery Clift, Elizabeth Taylor and Eva Maria Saint; *The Young Lions* (1958), based on Irwin Shaw's novel and starring Marlon Brando, Montgomery Clift and Dean Martin; *The Blue Angel* (1959), based on Heinrich Mann's novel and starting Curd Jürgens, May Britt and Theodore Bikel; *The Carpetbaggers* (1964), based on Harold Robbins' novel and starring George Peppard and Alan Ladd; *Anzio* (1968), based on Wynford Vaughn-Thomas' book and starring Robert Mitchum, Robert Ryan, Peter Falk and Earl Holliman; *Alvarez Kelly* (1966), a western starring William Holden and Richard Widmark; and *He Is My Brother* (1975), starring Keenan Wynn and teen idol Bobby Sherman. Dmytryk died of heart and kidney failure on July 1, 1999 in Encino, California, at age 90.

Alvah Bessie (1904-1985) was born on June 4 in New York City. He received his B.A. from Columbia University in 1924, and in 1938 he volunteered for the Abraham Lincoln Brigade to fight for the Spanish republic. From 1939 to 1943 he was drama and film critic for New Masses. In 1943, he was hire by Warner Brothers and continued his career in Hollywood until 1947. In 1954, he gave up membership in the Communist Party. He died in Terra Linda, California, on July 21, 1985. Among his prominent Warner films were, in 1944-1945, *The Very Thought of You, Objective, Burma*, and *Hotel Berlin*.

Albert Maltz (1908-1985) was born in Brooklyn, New York, on October 28, 1908, and received his B.A. from Columbia University in 1930. He attended the Yale School of Drama in 1931. From 1942 to 1947 he acquired seven screen credits. From 1952 to 1962, he lived in Mexico. In 1960, Frank Sinatra, probably known from an earlier 1945 film *The House I Live In*, announced that he was hiring Maltz to write the screenplay for *The Executive of Private Slovik*, but then reneged. After his blacklist, Maltz wrote four films from 1970 to 1974: *Two Mules For Sister Sara*, *The Beguiled* (as John B. Sherry), *Scalawag*, and *Hangup* (as John B. Sherry). He died on April 26, 1985, in Los Angeles. Maltz was the only blacklisted writer whom Jack Nusan Porter actually met, in Los Angeles in the late 1970s.

Sources

We are just touching the surface of the many archives in this field. Sites as diverse as the University of Southern California, the University of Wyoming, the Richard Nixon Presidential Library and Museum, the Wisconsin Center for Theater and Film, the Wisconsin Historical Society, Southern Illinois University (the John Howard Lawson papers), and the New York Public Library have the papers of these writers and their opponents.

Important books (both pro and con) on the subject include:

Barzman, Norma, *The Red and the Blacklist: The Intimate Memoir of a Hollywood Expatriate* (2003). This is a rare memoir by a female screenwriter and an "enthusiastic Stalinist" according to Allan Ryskind.

Bernstein, Walter, *Inside Out: A Memoir of the Blacklist* (1996).

Biberman, Herbert, *Salt of the Earth: The Story of a Film* (1965). The story of the only U.S. film ever to have been blacklisted.

Billingsley, Kenneth Lloyd, *Hollywood Party: How Communism Seduced the American Film Industry in the 1930s and 1940s* (1998).

Buhle, Paul, and Dave Wagner, *Radical Hollywood* (2002).

Ceplair, Larry, and Steven England, *The Inquisition in Hollywood: Politics in the Film Community, 1930-1960* (1980). This is an oft-quoted reference book.

Dick, Bernard F., *Radical Innocence: A Critical Study of the Hollywood Ten* (1989). An excellent book.

Dmytryk, Edward, *It's a Hell of a Life but Not a Bad Living: A Hollywood Memoir* (1978). Written by the director of *Crossfire* (1947) and *The Caine Mutiny* (1954), who was named one of the Hollywood Ten.

Hearings Regarding the Communist Infiltration of the Motion Picture Industry: Hearings before the Committee on Un-American Activities, U.S. House of Representatives, 1947-1953.

Horne, Gerald, *The Final Victim of the Blacklist: John Howard Lawson, Dean of the Hollywood Ten* (2006) and *Class Struggle in Hollywood, 1930-1950: Moguls, Mobsters, Stars, Reds, and Trade Unionists* (2001).

Kahn, Gordon, *Hollywood on Trial* (1948). This was one of the first analyses of those times.

Koch, Howard, *As Time Goes By: Memoirs of a Writer* (1979).

Lawson, John Howard, influential books on screenwriting: *Theory and Technique of Playwriting and Screenwriting* (1949) and *Film: The Creative Process* (1967).

Leab, Daniel J. (ed.), *Communist Activity in the Entertainment Industry: FBI Surveillance Files on Hollywood, 1942-1958* (c.1991).

Lyons, Eugene, *The Red Decade: The Stalinist Penetration of America* (1941). This is an early anti-Communist tract.

Navasky, Victor, *Naming Names* (1980).

Ryskind, Allan H., *Hollywood Traitors: Blacklisted Screenwriters: Agents of Stalin, Allies of Hitler* (2015). A recent book written by the son of Morrie Ryskind, a Marx Brothers screenwriter, who turned against his fellow screenwriters and testified against them. It's an interesting book, since it gives a perspective on the "other side," of people who actually saw them as "traitors" and "spies."

Sayre, Nora, *Running Time: Films of the Cold War* (1978).

Schwartz, Nancy Lynn, completed by her mother, Sheila Schwartz, *The Hollywood Writers' Wars* (1982). An excellent book.

The Jew as Bourgeois

This essay was one of my earliest, coming out in February 1970 at age 25, while I was a Ph.D. candidate in sociology at Northwestern University in the Midwest during the time that I co-founded the radical Jewish Student Movement in Evanston and Chicago. Philip Roth's *Goodbye, Columbus* (the title comes from the fact that one of the characters went to Ohio State University in Columbus, Ohio) had come out as a movie and presented a rather critical though honest portrait of bourgeois Jewish life. In fact, some critics called Roth's description anti-Semitic. I compared it to *The Graduate* with Dustin Hoffman, an earlier film of the rebellion afoot in the land.

But this was a "soft" rebellion against bourgeois suburban life; the revolutionary form would come quite soon. Another film and book that influenced this one was *Marjorie Morningstar* by Herman Wouk, which was must more muted Jewishly than Roth's novel.

In a way, the JAP (Jewish-American Princess) of Ali McGraw could be seen as a step forward, a strong-willed woman and not a negative stereotype. Compare *Goodbye, Columbus* with *Love Story*, where McGraw plays a doomed Cliffie (a Radcliffe girl) in love with a Harvard jock. *Love Story* was deracinated of anything Jewish, Italian, or characteristic of any ethnic group.

Thus, *Goodbye, Columbus* was radical for its time, and it radicalized young Jews, especially Jewish women, who were rebelling against their image portrayed in the film. I also can't believe I wrote this at age 25. It is some of the best writing I have ever done. This short essay appeared in *Otherstand*, a Jewish radical underground paper in Montreal, on February 4, 1970. Sadly, like most "underground" radical papers, it no longer exists.

* * *

Jack Porter is a Ph.D. candidate at Northwestern University and is a co-founder of the radical Jewish Student Movement.

Ten years ago Philip Roth wrote *Goodbye, Columbus*; recently the book was transformed into a movie of the same name. Though critics haled it as "sensitive and brilliant," "outrageous," and "incandescently alive," to many it was both vulgar and maudlin. Life in suburbia is vulgar and materialist, and today Roth's predictions have come true. To understand this is to understand the revolt of Jewish youth.

The movie, like the book, elicited a torrent of outrage against Roth. Because it was vulgar and maudlin? No, not in itself. But because both Roth and Larry Peerce, the director, reproduced the vulgarity and materialism of a contemporary lifestyle. Moreover, it was the lifestyle of a particular American ethnic group, the Jews. And for giving away such "trade secrets," Roth and Peerce will burn in hell. Why? For the simple reason that they hit uncomfortably close to home. Peerce doesn't even have to strip away the veneer; it's there; it's real…

To go in one generation from poverty to wealth is sometimes a heady brew. Yet it is so American. Some sociologists like Robert Park and Nathan Glazer have argued that the Jews are the most American of all groups and that they exhibit these traits in a more "flagrant" way than all other groups in society.

The Jew is Everyman and more so the Jew is Suburban Man—The American Dream personified. Yes, Jews are a peculiar and fascinating group. Yes, they are even more fascinating to other Jews, especially Jewish intellectuals…like Philip Roth, who has been called by Truman Capote the "youngest and possibly the most brilliant member of the Jewish intellectual 'mafia' of New York."

This "mafia," incidentally, is supposed to center around the literary magazines. *Commentary* in New York City is composed of critics, artists, writers, editors, etc., who reinforce, praise, and publicize each other's work. Some say this literary clique does not even exist; it is unimportant, really. What is important is that the intellectuals who supposedly comprise this group are mainly Jewish renegades from the American Jewish mainstream, revered by non-Jews and other Jewish intellectuals and students, but grudgingly praised and at times criticized by middle-class Jews as "dangerous, dishonest, distorted, irresponsible and self-hating"?

Goodbye, Columbus is about the summer romance between a lower-middle-class Jewish boy name Neil Klugman and an upper-middle-class Jewish girl named Brenda Patemkin. Neil is good-natured, jocular, cynical, yet easy-going and unsure of his future. His only concern is to do what he likes to do at the time that he does it. He has just gotten out of the Army and works in a library in what be called by urbanologists as a "changing neighborhood."

Brenda, on the other hand, is rich, spoiled, sexy, smart, and very sure of what she wants. She is home for the summer from school at Vassar. Brenda could be described (as a fraternity guy from Northwestern told me) as a "New York bitch." This epithet is uttered with as much awe and solemnitude, if not a bit of fear, as vituperance. I may be speaking as a male chauvinist, but Brenda comes out smelling like a...well, it's not like a rose.

Film director Peerce (who, incidentally, is the son of famed cantor Jan Peerce) is more sympathetic to Neil, but it does no good. Neil gets "shafted" at the end anyway. Neil and Brenda fall in love and then, in the course of a few days, into bed. Yet, even their first sexual encounter in the attic of her home is "materialistic" at base. She had been looking in an old couch for some money her father had left her. She found no money, but they make love on that same ratty couch as soon as the search is over.

As I've said, the sexual "thing," the "summer romance," is the moving plot in the film. Though this moon-June genre could have dominated, luckily it doesn't. There is no happy ending, and for this—many patrons wanted their money back. Some viewers, as they left the theater, muttered some obscenities under their breath at Peerce, maybe at Roth, at someone anyway, for that "lousy ending."

What is the ending? Let's put it this way—they don't kiss, make up, get married, and live happily ever after. I give credit to Peerce for sticking to Roth's original ending, and not being influenced by Hollywood-type gimmickry.

But it isn't only the ending that upsets people—especially Jewish people—it's the pretentiousness and banality of the Jewish wedding scene. There is a subplot to the film, and it is the upcoming marriage between Brenda's brother, Ron, and his fiancée. Ron lives in Columbus, Ohio, and goes to Ohio State, and he's a "jock"—a basketball star. You see, after he gets married, it's goodbye Columbus, and hello, Patimkin Kitchen and Bathroom Sinks (as an assistant to his father, the president).

Yes, the wedding is vulgar. Everybody's there—aunts, uncles, cousins, musicians, even a Hasid (where did he come from?)—and there is food. Food is part of a ritual in Jewish life. It is symbolic, and people who eat it are symbols that are brought together in some type of holy bond. That bond is cemented by chopped liver and gefilte fish. And you better eat. If you don't, not only are you considered impolite—you're worse—you're some kind of goy.

Vulgarity implies lacking culture and taste, being crude and boorish. Yet, it also means being honest, and no one is more honest about his life-style and all its shortcomings than Mr. Patimkin. The short scene in the office between Neil and Mr. Patimkin drives this point home. One is vulgar if one is judged by standards that are not vulgar, not crude. It implies a type of social superiority. Yet, it is one thing to be vulgar and not know it and another thing to be vulgar and know it.

Mr. Patimkin knows who he is—he's a "goniff"—a hard-working, working-class man, even if he has a maid and two Cadillacs. His wife and, yes, his daughter Brenda are vulgar, too—yet they will not admit it—for to do so would be too painful—a denial of their dream, the American dream, to be like everyone else, and especially to be like the cool, blond, respected goy; yet knowing that to be this is an impossible dream.

Neil knows this; Mr. Patimkin knows this. And by knowing, they are not only honest with themselves, they see the games that people—newly rich people—play. Mr. Patimkin will play the game, too—knowing he's still basically struggling "pisher" just up from Newark, and not a country-club member in Scarsdale.

Neil will see it and remain uncertain and perplexed—but he will acknowledge that uncertainty, that fear, openly. Brenda may fear her mother—yet try as she might—she is her mother. She thinks she is free, independent—yet she is as "bourgeoise" and materialistic as her family— the Vassar veneer is as thin as glass—beneath beats the heart of a suburban Hadassah committee lady who will marry a "nice Jewish doctor" and raise a few (2.4) kids. And she will never know why; her lifestyle is so dominat-ing—she'll never know.

Neil may have lost a romance. For a guy who is "horny," that can be rough. Yet, he may have been honestly in love with Brenda—he probably was, But, as he said at a dance given by Brenda's friends (that was right before the nude swimming scene, Henry): "I can't go to either extreme." He can't. He'll go back to his library job, even though Brenda and Mrs. Patimkin degraded it. He'll go back confused, but buoyant… I can dig it.

It is easy to make comparisons with another movie aimed at "young people"—*The Graduate*, both dealing with an alienated male meeting a spoiled female and both falling in love and then into bed. But there is a better comparison than this one. It is with a movie of the late 1950s—*Marjorie Morningstar*—adapted from Herman Wouk's novel of the same name.

Natalie Wood, who plays the title role, is like Ali McGraw's Brenda Patimkin; both are restless and unfulfilled "bourgeoise" Jewish women who are trying desperately to break out of the mold of middle-class values and lifestyles that seem to stifle their talents and careers. Yet, both are sisters under the skin, or better yet, they're "mothers" (Jewish) under their Vassar or Hunter College degrees and WASP-like demeanor. Try as they like, they still remain "Yiddishe Mammas," salvaging respectability and surface decorum from a radical, hard-nosed veneer. They are constantly under tension, caught between the complete liberation of their bodies and minds and their desire for security and dependence, even if that security means a return to the quiet sterility of the suburb and the "gilded ghetto."

For the man in the movies—Noel Airman in *Marjorie Morningstar* (portrayed by Gene Kelly) and Neil Klugman in *Goodbye, Columbus* (and yes, even Benjamin Braddock in *The Graduate*)—all struggle for self-identity to a lesser or greater degree, but all remain at peace with themselves at movie's end. They are content; no longer must they "hustle." They've struggled for a career, for a "goal"—they've been rebuffed, or they've seen the absurdity of striving and "playing the game."

Noel Airman returns to his summer resort in the role of social director after his flamboyant flop on Broadway; he is at peace with himself. Benjamin Braddock (Dustin Hoffman) returns to college with an empty degree and an empty future, and he knows it; he is at peace with himself. Neil Klugman returns from an army stint with a library job and a long, hot summer ahead of him, and he accepts it all in a manner that would have Hermann Hesse's Siddhartha smile knowingly. He is at peace with himself.

Knowing that much of our lives is sham and absurd "games" and of playing out roles that we neither enjoy nor wish to continue—yet we do it to please our parents, our wives, our bosses, our community. We've become "organization men" *par excellence*, with image and showmanship and materialism more important than love and sensitivity and acceptance of our lot in life.

It is what C.G. Jung has called a search for individuation or self-actualization, which can be defined as the self-realization of a moral decision to seek self-fulfillment, to become a single homogenous being alive and "at one" with the entire universe. It is a selflessness of the highest order. It is "knowing thyself" and then knowing that much of it is a sham and a fraud.

The reactions to this mode of thought are numerous. You can find it among the hippies living within the hundreds of Haight-Ashbury's in this world; in the drug-induced state of believers and seekers; in the streets and on the college campus among the protesters and the "rioters." Indirectly, it can be sought and found in the movies of Jean-Luc Godard, the journalism of Norman Mailer, the songs of Bob Dylan and the Beatles, the poetic rhetoric of Eldridge Cleaver and Che Guevara, and the novels and poems of Ken Kesey, Terry Southern, and Allen Ginsberg.

It has been called a search for relevance in the hills of absurdity and madness. As Jack Newfield calls it, it is the perception that "adult society is literally absurd, that America is threatening to become a giant lunatic asylum...they [young people] simply don't want to participate in a war that kills a million Vietnamese, attempts to put Benjamin Spock and Muhammad Ali [Cassius Clay] in jail for opposing that slaughter, and then places Ronald Reagan and Lester Maddox in positions of authority over their lives..." Right on, Jack, that's where it's at.

Goodbye, Columbus is not a political picture; none of the above appears in it. Yet, better than any sermon or speech is the statement by Neil that he rejects all extremism: "they are all absurd." Yet while one may disagree with his conclusion, one must note the honesty of self-realization and self-actualization that comes through.

Neil is interested in life—one day at a time—in the black kid who comes to the library, in "laying" Brenda as often and as well as he can, and in somehow not getting involved in the inanity of the suburban life around him.

It seems from this discussion that all the girls are portrayed as pampered "bitches" and that the guys are contented idealists. This bit of "male chauvinism" may be due to the fact that all the authors and scriptwriters are men, and possibly a woman would have portrayed them differently. Yet the final outcome of all these novels and movies finds the woman less secure and less comfortable in her found role.

But this is not the point—the point is that there are increasingly a number of films "exploiting" the youth theme, and contrasting the tawdriness and ostentation of the middle class and *nouveau riche* with the ideals of their children. This contrast has been the subject matter of much of today's literature, and, as Alfred Kazin has put it, it has saved Jewish writing from its "innate provincialism."

The New York clique of intellectuals mentioned earlier, composed of such luminaries as Delmore Schwartz, Saul Bellow, Lionel Trilling, Karl Shapiro, Joseph Heller, Harold Rosenberg, Isaac Rosenfeld, Lionel Abel, Clement Greenberg, Norman Podhoretz, Bernard Malamud, Irving Howe, Philip Rahv, Leslie Fielder, Bruce Jay Friedman, Robert Warshow, Paul Goodman, Norman Mailer, Nate Glazer, Philip Roth, and Kazan himself, have all addressed themselves to the Jewish question, the American question, and the universal question of self-actualization and the ultimate absurdity and dignity of life.

Maybe today it is "in" to make movies like *Goodbye, Columbus*; maybe it is "in" even to be Jewish; yet the questions posed have always been "in." And during our own "gilded age"—these questions are more important than ever. Let me close with a quote from Alfred Kazin:

> There is a real madness to modern governments, modern war, modern moneymaking, advertising, science, and entertainment; this madness has been translated by many Jewish writers into the country they live in, the time that offers them everything but hope. In a time of intoxicating prosperity, it has been natural for the Jewish writer to see how superficial society can be, how pretentious, atrocious, unstable—and comic. This, in a secular age when so many people believe in nothing but society's values, is the significance of the Jewish writer's being Jewish.

February 1970

David Mamet's *Homicide*: A Re-evaluation

This essay is original for this book.

I saw David Mamet's movie *Homicide* years ago (it came out in 1991) and knew it was an important movie, but after seeing it recently in a new DVD release with very useful commentary, I gained an entirely new insight into the film. Of course, my interpretation is tempered by the fact that Mamet has become a neo-conservative, right-wing Zionist, but this movie actually shows a glimpse of that political shift.

Mamet is great at analyzing sociological "slices of life," but his viewpoint is conservative, especially when it comes to Jewish identity. It is akin to Alan Dershowitz, a confused liberal turned conservative. Definitely, *Homicide* presents a conservative, even right-wing slant, on Jewish identity. That puts him out of touch politically with mainstream liberal and radical Hollywood.

However, this is a complex, multi-layered movie with the usual taut "Mamet-style" dialogue and filled with crisp innuendos. Joe Mantegna, in the DVD commentary, says, "No one really talks like this, plus it is not easy to learn Mamet's lines," but Mamet is one of the few screenwriters in Hollywood who has a distinct "voice"—you immediately know it's a "Mamet" movie or play.

The film starts out like any other detective thriller, with a police special unit about to barge into an apartment in order to capture a wanted bad guy and cop-killer, played by Vingt Rames. He barely escapes amidst a blaze of gunfire, and he's on the run.

While the cops are looking for this bad guy, there is a murder of an old Jewish lady in the Black ghetto. Bobby Gold "stumbles" onto the scene and is given the case. He objects. He wants to find the bad guy. He doesn't want "to babysit this old lady's death." But that family has "juice" downtown and wants to find the killer of their mother and grandmother, and since Bobby is Jewish, he gets the case.

Bobby Gold is a Baltimore (where the movie was filmed) detective, played by Joe Mantegna, and his sidekick Sully is played by W.H. Macy, an esteemed character actor whose claim to fame sadly is as the husband of college scandal-monger Felicity Huffman.

So, what's going on? Lots.

- The conflict between Bobby and Sully and the FBI. The Baltimore cops have no respect for the FBI. "They couldn't find Joe Louis in a bowl of rice. They'd fuck up a baked potato," Bobby says in a memorable line.
- The conflict between Bobby and the city's Black mayoral aide Patterson, played by Louis Murray.
- The conflict between Bobby's Jewish identity and the proud identity of the dead Jewish woman's family.
- The conflict between Bobby and a mysterious woman he meets at the *shiva* house who wants him to blow up a neo-Nazi office fronted by a toy store.
- The conflict over a series of attacks by alleged neo-Nazis that sidetrack Bobby from going after the bad guy.

It seems that the old lady was a gun-runner in Palestine for Menachem Begin's Revisionist group, or maybe even the Stern Gang, an even more dangerous right-wing terrorist group that David Ben-Gurion had to suppress in pre-Palestine/Israel days.

So, you get the picture. This is a complex plot, and only a near-genius like David Mamet can pull it off. He likes complicated, secretive, game-driven (cards, poker, gambling) stories, but *Homicide* is his most successful. He went on to make more money writing scripts for Hollywood blockbusters like *The Untouchables*, but he uses the money from those commercial films to make his smaller, more independent, and thus riskier films. Today, he says, it is almost impossible to make his kind of movies. "You need $20 million bucks."

Bobby Gold is "the Jew." He's the "mouthpiece," the guy who knows how to talk, how to negotiate. The department needs him to talk to the bad guy's mother and help them give him up peacefully. It's a typical good cop/bad cop scene. Sully plays the Bad Cop insulting the lady; then Bobby steps in and plays the Good Cop. In a bravura performance, he ingratiates himself with the mother, sympathizes with her, and tells her they'll bring him in alive. "Don't hurt my baby," she admonishes.

Provocative flyers appear on walls after the shooting of the old lady: "Crime is caused by the Ghetto" and "The Ghetto is caused by the Jew" (with a picture of a large rat underneath). There is also the strange appearance of a word, "GROFAZ," and Bobby goes to a local Jewish library and asks scholars there what it means, and one says, "*Grosse Feld Herre Aller Zeiten*," referring to Hitler as "The Greatest Strategist of All Time." Bobby is skeptical, but maybe there really are bad white supremacist groups out there killing Jews and frightening Blacks.

(I might add that, as a Holocaust scholar, I never came across this Nazi phrase, but since the movie came out, I have seen it on posters. Also, the comparisons to another leader who sees himself as the "greatest" is not lost on viewers either.)

The mayor's aide (a young Black man) has a meeting with the Chief of Police (played by a Black man) and the detectives on the case (all white men, by the way), and again, there is a memorable scene between Bobby Gold and the Black aide who says to Bobby, "I don't need you to wax my car. Just do your job and bring him in…you kike."

At first, Bobby, Sully, and the detectives (plus the audience) are stunned. They can't believe they are hearing this. In a complete reversal, a Black guy calls a Jew a "kike," and a fight breaks out between the two of them that takes all their restraint to stop Bobby from punching out the Black aide.

The scenes between Irish Sully and Jewish Bobby are sharp and pointed with the usual Mamet dialogue:

"I gotta babysit the candy store."

"But, Bobby, we need you, baby. You're the mouthpiece. Just look busy (on the candy store thing). We need you, man."

"But they say I'm their people, Sully."

Then things get even more philosophical. Sully asks, "How come you always have to be the first one through the door?

"Why? 'Cuz I'm a Jew. I got to prove myself to them."

What Bobby has to prove is that he's more than a "mouthpiece," more than a talker; he's a macho man. "I was called a pussy 'cuz I was a Jew. They'd say, 'Send a broad through the door if you send a Jew.'"

It reminds me of when, in the 1970s, Nate Cohen played shortstop and I played second base on a team called "The Road Runners," composed of mostly tall Irish guys in Brookline's softball league, and we'd hear things like, "Jeez, those guys play pretty good for Jews." Joe and I had to prove ourselves to these knuckleheads that we were just as good as they were as players.

Mamet says, "Film is myth projected on a bedsheet," and he throws in a lot of sociology onto that bedsheet.

"It never stops," the granddaughter (played by Mamet's wife, Rebecca Pidgeon) says of Mrs. Klein, the murdered old lady.

"What never stops?" Bobby asks.

"The killing of Jews." And she continues: "Do you hate yourself that much?" she asks Bobby.

"You're a Jew." Meaning, be a proud Jew, Bobby, not a self-hating Jew who wants to emulate goyim.

Mamet says he was influenced by Joseph Campbell's book *The Hero with a Thousand Faces* as well as Bruno Bettelheim's *The Uses of Enchantment*. The hero must go deep into the cave (the basement of the building where the bad guy is hiding), and he must confront the Minotaur and find out the "secret." But what is the secret?

It's reminiscent of an earlier encounter in the film with a wild, mentally unstable guy who just killed his wife and kids. The weirdo asks Bobby, "Would you like to know how to solve the problem of evil?"

"No, man, 'cause if I did, then I'd be out of Job…"

In the end Bobby confronts not only the Minotaur in the cave but also his own private demons, his own identity as a Jew.

As Sully says, "It's either a piece of cake or a slice of life."

Sources

Mamet, David. *Homicide: A Screenplay*. New York: Grove Weidenfeld, 1988, 1992. This is the original screenplay, and it follows the movie quite accurately. The quotations by Mantegna are from the DVD commentary section.

A Response to Screenwriter
Robert J. Avrech

Is Hollywood Leftist and Anti-Frum (Orthodox)?

This was a letter in response to Robert Avrech's essay in the Orthodox Union's magazine, *Jewish Action*, Winter 5774/2013. *Frum*, by the way, is short for "religious"; *shomer shabbos* means "observing Sabbath laws"; *shul* means "synagogue"; *daven* means "praying." The letter was never published.

* * *

Regarding Robert J. Avrech's "confessions of a *shomer shabbos* screenwriter" (Winter 2013 issue), it's a shame I have to write this letter, since I very much admired his screenplay *A Stranger Among Us*. It was one of the best and most honest representations of Hasidic life ever put on the screen and arguably Melanie Griffith's best role.

But his comments about Hollywood are off base and inaccurate. There are many "Hollywoods"—there is the "sleazy" porno-driven Hollywood; the politically correct Hollywood; the "sick" jaded Hollywood. But the bottom line is money and how to make quality productions that will make money. That's the *real* Hollywood.

Mr. Avrech's list of seven "messages," for example, is overly simplistic. Does Hollywood make movies for *frum* Jews or Christians where everyone is heterosexual and everyone goes to *shul* or church and *davens* all day? Of course not. Hollywood is a secular place, Mr. Avrech. All seven of your "messages" are mostly untrue. Republicans are not stupid, and Democrats are not glamorous.

Also, one sees many women depicted in a family life and not only in careers. There are also few Torah Jews in movies, for the simple reason that Hollywood is, as I've said, a secular place, not a place for documentaries. As Samuel Goldwyn once said: "If I want to send a message, I'll call Western Union!"

Israel and Zionism, of course, presents a more perplexing concern. True, there is criticism of Israel in the press and in academia, but I can't think of a single Hollywood movie where Israel is denigrated. In fact, just the opposite. There are movies where Israelis are shown to be quite brave. Zionism is often "invisible," but I have heard comments that Palestinians, or better yet, Muslims and Arabs, are also invisible. Hollywood does not like to upset any ethnic or religious group. In fact, Israel or Zionism is rarely mentioned in most Hollywood movies. The last movie that was "Zionist" and positive towards Israel was probably *Exodus*, made in 1960.

These are controversial issues, and Hollywood tends to shy away from controversy. If they labeled every terrorist attack as Muslim, it would not only be unfair to all the good Muslims out there who abhor violence of this type, it would also be untrue (not every terrorist attack is Muslim-inspired), and it would put the studios in great physical danger as well. So they try to keep it neutral and generic, except in movies like *Zero Dark Thirty*, where obviously the attacks came from Al-Qaeda. Ironically, quite often the "bad guys" are Russians.

Yes, Hollywood is a liberal place. That is true. Life is life, and Hollywood is liberal. What's new about that? Yes, gay marriages are supported by the Hollywood elite, but then so do 55% of all Americans.

Also, he writes, "Almost every Hollywood executive director, producer, and writer I've ever met has attended an Ivy League university where secular, leftist thinking dominates…" There are so many errors even in that one sentence. First off, most Hollywood people have NOT gone to Ivy League schools—maybe in the finance or business or social networking side, but not in the creative side. Second, as someone who is at Harvard, I can say that people there are not all secular or leftist. This is crude Red-baiting. There are mostly liberal professors, true, and a few hard-left professors, true, but also some hard-right professors and a lot in the middle. One cannot generalize about Harvard, but yes, in general, academia and Hollywood are liberal bastions, but not leftist, meaning socialist/Communist.

Yes, Hollywood "values" can be inimical to the *frum* life. That is why so many *frum* people don't have TV sets, or if they do, they're hidden in their bedrooms only for the parents to watch. Still, many young *frum* guys and gals do go to the movies, and they are able to filter the "good from the bad."

Is Steven Spielberg such a terrible guy if he supports gay marriage or global warming or is in favor of abortion and against capital punishment? And Steven Spielberg, in my estimation and in my limited involvement in Hollywood, represents, I believe, the "true Hollywood," whatever that is.

I wish Mr. Avrech well, but he's no sociologist. His views on Hollywood are so stereotypical that, if I said the same things about Jews, I'd be called a bigot.

Prof. Jack Nusan Porter
Research Fellow
The Davis Center for Russian and Eurasian Studies
Harvard University

Dr. Porter is a writer, editor, and political activist whose many books include several on Hollywood: *Happy Days Revisited: Growing Up Jewish in Ike's America; Milwaukee and Hollywood;* and, in progress, *21 Screen Treatments for Hollywood.* He comes from a *frum* family; his brother is Rabbi Shlomo Porter from Baltimore, and his sister is Bella Porter-Smith from Minneapolis.

Winter 2013

X. New Directions for Israel[1]

Ten Days on the West Bank: A New Year's Hope for Peace

BEIT SAHOUR, West Bank, Palestine. I recently returned from the West Bank, a term that Israeli radical settlers don't like. They prefer "Judea" and "Samaria"; and Palestinians don't like the term either. They prefer "Palestine." Welcome to the Middle East.

I stayed with the Nimeer and Shama Rishmawi family in this predominantly Christian village. Both Beit Sahour (Canaanite for "magic," I am told) and Beit Jala are Christian towns. They are just outside Bethlehem, or Beit Lechem, "House of Bread or Meat" in Hebrew, but it has Canaanite roots that give it an older translation. However, Bethlehem, which was once 75 percent Christian in 1948, is now only twenty-five percent Christian.

I asked my hosts where did they all go, and they replied that most of the Beit Sahorians moved to America, to Saginaw and Flint, Michigan. Thousands of Christian Palestinians live there quietly, under the radar. In general, sadly, Christians—in this case, Orthodox Christians such as the Rishmawis—are dwindling in number, not only in Palestine/West Bank but also in Iraq, Iran, Syria, Lebanon—in fact, throughout the Middle East.

However, this was Christmastime, and the Rishmawis, who number as many as 800 clan members in the town and throughout the West Bank, were celebrating the pre-Christmas season. One of Nimeer (Arabic for "tiger") Rishmawi's brothers owns a Christmas shop in Beit Sahour next door to his house. Plastic Santas ten feet high are out front; tree decorations and toys of all kinds line the store shelves. I bought three red-and-gold Santa hats. I love Christmas and I'm not Christian.

Nimeer and Shama Rishmawi live in a large stone (what some call "Jerusalem stone") home filled with three generations, their son George and his wife Fida ("sacrifice" in Arabic), and their two lovely children, Bisan and Basin.

Their family goes back hundreds of years, back to the time of Jesus Christ, who roamed these fields and valleys. Shama was an excellent cook, and I will miss her cooking and her family very much. Palestinian hospitality is without equal.

While on the West Bank, I acted as a Palestinian and was treated as a Palestinian until I flashed my American passport. I stood in line at some dozen checkpoints, whether between Bethlehem and Jerusalem, Ramallah and Jerusalem, and other points in-between. Sometimes the lines moved quickly; other times there were delays, especially during the four-day Muslim feast of El-Eid (a festival ironically based on Abraham's attempt at sacrificing Isaac; however, in the Muslim version, Ishmael replaces Isaac). Young kids were not used to the security searches and did not take off their clothes or bags or belts fast enough. Frustrating, but it gave me time to talk to Palestinians.

The checkpoints are like airport security but more intense—for example, Israel has on record every single Palestinian citizen, and they must place their palms down on a pad and their picture and background shows up. If it doesn't show up, you don't go through unless you have a pretty good excuse or the soldier is tolerant that day, and the checkpoints are not manned by Andy Frain guards but by young 18-to-20-year-old soldiers, both male and female.

Palestinians also need a special pass to get to the Jewish side. One of my hosts, Eyad Burnat, was not able to get a pass to Jerusalem, which means he cannot get an exit visa to America to speak, because only in Jerusalem is the U.S. consulate. A catch-22. Can't get to Jerusalem; so can't get to America.

Nimeer had to go to a hospital in Jerusalem but could get only a one-day pass. Shama has not visited Jerusalem in years, yet she is only a 20-minute ride away.

There are worse indignities. I visited the town of Bi'lin, west of Ramallah. Every Friday there is a nonviolent demonstration at a fence that intrudes on Palestinian farmland and olive groves. Demonstrators include not only Bi'lin residents but also many "internationals," people from England, Scotland, Ireland, France, Greece, and even a few Americans and Israelis. I was a rarity: an older American Jewish leader. Few had ever seen one—so rare, in fact, that I was interviewed by Iranian TV, Palestinian TV, French media, and Irish media.

True, at times some kids throw rocks over the fence. There is, however, no way to throw the rocks *directly* at soldiers. They are lobbed over, but the soldiers easily avoid them, plus they have large shields to protect themselves. Also true, at times, some demonstrators tried to pry open this gate that divides the fence. And this is a fence, by the way—not the infamous wall; just a wire fence.

However, soldiers lob many volleys of tear gas, percussion bombs, and even rubber-coated bullets. Some demonstrators have died. No soldier has ever died in Bi'lin. There are also raids. I didn't witness one while I stayed in Bi'lin, but about a month later, five jeeps filled with thirty soldiers and border police came into town to harass the "internationals," hustled them outside in the rain at night, checked their passports, and invaded their living space. No reason; just harassment, since the Israelis are not happy with the Bi'lin website and publicity that the "internationals" bring to the "fence." It's bad public relations for Israel.

I talked to numerous Palestinians and felt neither fear nor intimidation, and they all asked me to take a "message to Obama." Both Muslims and Christians alike have this almost mystical belief that I could bring a message to him, a message of peace and justice in this holiday season. I told them I knew Senator John Kerry and I would bring that message to him and via him to Obama and Hillary Clinton. They trust that I will.

What do they want? First and foremost, human dignity and respect; a reduction of the checkpoints; more easily obtained exit visas and passes to other parts of the region; less arbitrary searches and seizures; more water; but mostly, more respect and dignity. Many Palestinians are "post-nationalist"; they want to go beyond a state and a flag and an army. They want simply respect and human rights.

They blessed me and thanked me and told me that maybe only the Messiah can bring peace to this troubled region. Is Obama their "messiah"? I certainly hope so.

2016

The Future of Israel

One of the biggest issues facing Jews and the world in the twenty-first century is the connection of Jews to Israel and of anti-Semitism to anti-Zionism. But it is not as simple as some pundits make it seem. Again, we have to define our terms.

First, what is anti-Semitism?

Second, what is anti-Zionism?

And third, is criticizing Israel a form of anti-Zionism or anti-Semitism?

I have answered these questions in previous essays in this book (for example, in "The End of Zionism?"), and I cannot do justice to them all in this short essay. Hundreds of books have been written on anti-Semitism and anti-Zionism.

It turns out that, like the definition of Zionism, there are many forms of anti-Zionism, so people are talking past each other. There is no common ground, no common definition for these terms.

My answer is, however, quite clear: if you believe in the sanctity of the State of Israel and want it to exist, then you have the right to criticize. But if you feel that Israel should not exist and you want to destroy Israel, then your anti-Zionism is not simply a critique, it is the end of the Jewish people. In short, it is genocide.

One of the problems facing the Jewish community is the problem with the Left. As Alan Johnson points out in his review of Susie Linfield's book *The Lion's Den: Zionism and the Left from Hannah Arendt to Noam Chomsky* (2019):

Why do so may left-wingers who ostensibly stand for the national self-determination for all peoples demand instead that a single nation-state, the little Jewish one, be brought to an end? Why do they anathematize Jewish nationalism as "racist" and "settler-colonialist," even comparing it to Nazism, while welcoming Arab nationalists and even Islamists as "part of the global Left"…?

There are many reasons for this. The Left may hold Israel up to a higher standard than, let us say, Syria or Saudi Arabia and expect more from it. Or it could be that the occupation of the West Bank has led Israel to be seen as a "colonizer," and that is not a good image to have. Or it could be based, at least regarding Jewish leftists, on self-hate. So the threat from the Left is a serious one. However, I must agree with many Israelis that the biggest security threat is not external—Israel has the capability to protect itself militarily—but internal.

Can Israel survive internally from its own contradictions?

Ronen Bergman, a rising star in the Israeli intellectual scene, in an interview with a Boston-area journalist, said the following:

"I think internal is by far the greatest threat.

…internal shifts inside Israeli society, including the violence, the incitement, the language used [by] one against the other on social media, the disrespect for democracy, the campaign Prime Minister Netanyahu is leading against the very foundation of democracy in order to save his neck from jail…a lot of this is a recipe for disaster.

Divisions exist between right and left, religious and non-religious, between Ashkenazim and Sephardim; differences between Jews and Arabs, secular and religious, between liberals and nationalists. These are deepening. They're not getting better, but much, much worse."

And I would add the widening gap between the rich and the poor; the growing problem of homelessness, gentrification, and poverty; interestingly, Israel, as a country that grew too quickly into affluence, reflects the same problems that the United States faces. Plus, both have leaders facing similar issues: a Prime Minister facing jail; a U.S. President who faced impeachment; both facing huge divisions in the electorate to the point that the election process has broken down completely in Israel and is facing severe divisions in the United States.

Could this mean the beginning of the end of these two major civilizations? Before a civilization falls, there is a long period of chaos. If you tie in climate change, pollution of the oceans and air, serious viruses, and a threatened planet, Israel and the U.S. face not only their own extinction but also the extinction of our entire planet. We will all be dead when that happens, but the sign are here for our grandchildren and their grandchildren to face.

Both countries face a daunting task: not so much who will win the next election, but who will seize the harness of leadership and think globally, not just nationally. Can we as a planet and as a world do that, or is it too late?

Sources

Johnson, Alan, review of *The Lion's Den*, "The Anti-Imperialism of Idiots," *Jewish Review of Books*, Summer 2019, pp. 23-24.

Linfield, Susie, *The Lion's Den: Zionism and the Left from Hannah Arendt to Noam Chomsky* (New Haven, Conn.: Yale University Press, 2019).

Tenorio, Rich, "Best-selling author warns internal turmoil may be biggest threat to Israel," *The Jewish Journal* (of the North Shore of Massachusetts), February 13, 2020, p. 5 (on Ronen Bergman).

XI. New Directions in Presidential Politics

The 2016 American Presidential Race: Where Do the Forerunners Stand on Foreign Policy Issues?

Where do Hillary Clinton, Bernie Sanders and Donald Trump stand on the following foreign policy issues?

The Iran/Saudi Conflict

Hillary will support President Obama's push to normalize relations with Iran as well as keep intact America's close relationship with Saudi Arabia. This delicate dance will not be easy. Hillary has the best chance to maintain it and keep the status quo, which will make most people in the region happy. Trump is very much against the deal with Iran and will try to damage or end it, and this will be disastrous for the region. Bernie will maintain the Obama initiative. The problem with both Bernie and "The Donald" is that they are both outsiders, new to foreign policy and have no "track record," so it is difficult to gauge what they will do. But they could be influenced by advisors.

The Israeli/Palestinian Issue

Again, Hillary will maintain Obama's momentum to curb the West Bank settlements and move both parties toward establishing a peace agreement.

She supports a two-state solution, yet she has advisors who are even more radical to her left who will push Israel harder. Bernie will push for a two-state solution and stopping new settlements on the West Bank and in Jerusalem. "The Donald" is probably the opposite; he is a strong supporter of Netanyahu and will support Netanyahu's policies. Still, he is a pragmatist and a great "negotiator." He will try to get both Israeli and Palestinian leaders to meet and resolve this issue of a two-state solution, but Netanyahu will renege and not follow through. This is a most difficult situation; only the messiah will be able to solve it.

Vladimir Putin/Russian/Ukraine Conflict and the Syrian Conflict

All three will hang tough against Putin regarding Crimea, Eastern Ukraine, and other issues. Putin will respect all three as tough negotiators; he had no respect for Obama. As for Syria and ISIS, "the Donald" will be the toughest against ISIS, as will Hillary. Regarding Bernie, we are not sure how tough he will be "on the ground," so to speak. None will deploy U.S. troops except as advisors. All will strengthen the Kurds, despite Turkish admonitions, as the best defense against ISIS. As for Assad, again, this is a dilemma. Maybe with the help of Putin, Assad will flee to Russia. Will this be better, or worse? Such is the Middle East—you know the old "scorpion-frog tale"—there are no easy solutions to the Middle East.

Refugees

Both Hillary and Bernie take an open, more tolerant policy toward refugees with, of course, security safeguards. "The Donald" will severely limit refugees coming into the United States.

Conclusions

The major advisors to Hillary are from her earlier connections at the White House: former Secretary of State Madeleine Albright, former Defense Secretary Leon Panetta, and my colleague at Harvard, Nicholas Burns, a former undersecretary of state and ambassador to several Middle Eastern countries. (Surprisingly, he served under George W. Bush [the younger Bush] and not under a Democrat.)

Hillary has also been listening to more "radical" advisors such as former Ambassador Thomas Pickering; Anne-Marie Slaughter, the State Department director of policy planning; Sidney Blumenthal, a former aide to Hillary's husband, former President Bill Clinton; and Laura Rosenberger, who has been with the State Department and the National Security Council. But she is her own boss and will make up her own mind.

Bernie and "The Donald" have no known foreign policy advisors, but, in full disclosure, I will be applying for a position in their administrations, as well as in Hillary's, to be either on the National Security Council, Ambassador to Israel or Ukraine, or consul to the Kurdish Autonomous Region of Northern Iraq. (P.S. It didn't happen.)

Sources

"Advising the Democrats," *The Forward* of New York, January 29, 2016, pp. 12-14.
"Jews for Trump," *The Forward* of New York, January 22, 2016, pp. 3-4 and pp. 6-8.
The Forward of New York, January 22, 2016, p. 2.

The Hidden Power of Donald and Bernie

Ted Armison, playing Bernie Sanders on *Saturday Night Live*, mimics: "I am a Jew, an old Jew."

Stephen Colbert, on his late night show on September 18, 2019, asks his guest Bernie Sanders: "How would it feel to be the first socialist to be president?"

Bernie says, "I like the word 'progressive' to describe me," and then goes on to describe what a "progressive" means in exact detail: a $15 an hour minimum wage; a more equitable distribution of the wealth; why does less than 1 percent of the population control 80 percent of the wealth; affordable healthcare for all, etc. "These are things found in all social democratic countries in Europe—Scandinavia, the Netherlands, Germany..."

But Colbert points out, "Ah, the Scandinavian countries...high taxes and high suicide rates."

Yet, overall, Colbert is gentle and fond of Bernie. "Do you feel the Bern?" he asks as the chanting starts from his audience, "Ber-*nie!* Ber-*nie!* Ber-*nie!*" Colbert quips, "Hey, *I'm* supposed to get the chanting, not you."

Colbert then shows a series of clips from mainstream media from CNN to Fox with all the reporters seemingly puzzled how an "old Jewish socialist" is getting not just thousands of people to his rallies, but tens of thousands. They thought the American people had rejected socialism and "radicalism." So, what exactly is Bernie doing that touches the *zeitgeist*? Is he the left equivalent of Donald Trump?

The answer is very simple.

Both have touched a nerve in the masses that says the following: We Americans are afraid of the future. The world is out of control. Wall Street and U.S. corporations have too much control. Deadly viruses are killing us. We have a crazy president. American has lost the respect of the world. And we Americans feel that we are no longer in control of our lives.

But let's look at some details. First, let's see what made Bernie a socialist, and even a socialist-Zionist, especially with his oft-overlooked years on *kibbutz* in Israel in the mid-1960s. We still don't know where he spent those years in Israel. His *kibbutz* is still a mystery. Even his own brother, who lives in England, does not remember the *kibbutz*'s name. What we do know is that it was an extreme Left Zionist *kibbutz* affiliated with the *Hashomer Hatzair* movement. (I was on a milder socialist *kibbutz* affiliated with the *Habonim/Dror* movement also in the '60s—*Kibbutz Gesher Haziv* in western Galilee.)

Now, let's look at Donald Trump and see what gave him such superhuman self-confidence and chutzpah. He was raised as the precocious son of a hard-driving father. Interestingly, we know very little about his mother, but I am sure she was a doting parent who spoiled him miserably.

However, there is a difference between Trump and Bernie. Bernie appeals to our better instincts as Americans: *We can make this a better world if only we will work together and kick the "big boys" out of power, and we can work together—Blacks and whites, Latinos and non-Latinos, gay and straight, Muslims and Jews and Christians united to take control of our lives. But you will need a gentle "uncle" like me to get us to all work together.*

Trump says similar radical things, but instead of love, he uses the whip of xenophobia and misogyny to scare people: *Immigrants and the radical Muslims are taking over America. They are taking either our jobs or our lives. The world has no respect for us anymore. And you need a strong "deal maker" like me to set things straight.*

Both are populists, both are radicals, but one is from the Left and the other from the Right; and it is quite possible they could face each for the U.S. Presidency. What they have in common is that they are outsiders and are thus seen as authentic. People sense that they speak the truth. They are not "bought." They don't need experts. They don't use "sound bytes." They are not scripted and programmed. They are real.

Bernie, since he has always been an outsider, has won on the basis of populist and grassroots support: "I have 450,000 people give me the equivalent of $31.20 each… I don't need, nor do I want, Super PACs."

Trump, because of his own wealth, does not need Super PACs telling him what to do. Nobody, not even the press, tells him what to do. And that is Trump's other "trump card"—people love him for slamming the media and their arrogant or nonsensical questions. People are fed up with the media's dominance of what they see on TV and how they should think. Trump, and to some degree Bernie, both tell them to shove off. *Don't try to trick me. Don't try to stump me. Don't show how smart you are. I'm smarter than all of you combined.*

Ironically, the conservative networks, with their Karl Roves and Koch brothers, had a difficult time with Trump; for so long candidates were in the pocket of the Republican Party, which they thought they could control with the sheer power of their money. Both candidates are showing that these people are paper tigers. Both candidates have shown they don't need to worry about the Koch brothers. In fact, both Rove and Koch are totally impotent in the Trump and Bernie tsunami, totally irrelevant. Perhaps—and I think both Trump and Bernie would agree—that just maybe the Supreme Court decision, that corporations are "people," will be overturned.

Bernie Sanders, on the left, is a socialist, and Donald Trump, on the right, is a man very difficult to pin down politically. Yet each has the charisma to reach out and touch the hearts of millions of Americans. It's turning into one of the most fascinating political years in U.S. history and may just revolutionize this country and its electorate.

When Politics Meets History

The recent controversy at the World Forum on Anti-Semitism memorializing the 75th anniversary of the liberation of Auschwitz in Jerusalem, plus the short film that was shown, was fraught with complex conflicts, ambivalent and confused loyalties, and political propaganda disguised as historical fact. All this confuses the real truth.

As I have written over many decades in books such as *Soviet Partisans of the Soviet Union During World War II* (The Spencer Press, 2016), without the Soviet Union, the Nazis may have "won" the war, or at least would have taken over so much of Europe that the Allies would have lost thousands more soldiers trying to take it back, which they would have done eventually. In the end, they would have used the atomic bomb against Germany as they did against Japan. Only with the help of the Soviet Union did we win the war.

However, the short film shown at the memorial overlooked several contrary historical facts. The controversies began with the Molotov-Ribbentrop Pact of August 23, 1939, the so-called Hitler-Stalin or Nazi-Soviet Pact that allowed Germany to enter Poland and begin World War II. Why did Stalin sign such a pact? It was not his love of Hitler and Germany, but simply that he needed time to build up his army and navy and the armament industry. He was caught off-guard by Germany's rise to power and needed time.

The purges of the Red Army in the 1930s weakened the Soviet Union's defense capacity and contributed to the military disasters of 1941 and 1942, which were mostly caused by their unpreparedness for war. The purges also led to the dismantling of privatized agriculture and its replacement with collectivized agriculture. This in turn left a legacy of chronic agricultural shortages, inefficiencies, and under-production.

Both sides knew that this pact would be short-lived, as was shown on June 22, 1941, when Hitler, having occupied France and neutralized Britain, turned east and attacked the Soviet Union. Vyacheslav Molotov was responsible for telling the Soviet people of the attack when he, instead of Stalin, announced the invasion. Some say that Stalin was so depressed he hid under a bed.

In Operation Barbarossa, Germany invaded the Soviet Union, and the Holocaust began in earnest with the use of the infamous *Einzatzgruppen* A, B, C, and D, whose sole role was to exterminate all Jews, Soviet commissars, gypsies, and criminal/asocial elements in their path.

On August 14, 1939, German Foreign Minister Joachim von Ribbentrop informed the Soviet government that Germany was prepared to improve relations with the Soviet Union and that he was willing to go to Moscow. Speedy negotiations took place in which the Soviet side was represented by the Soviet foreign minister, Vyacheslav Molotov. The two countries signed two agreements: one dealing with economic relations, the other a non-aggression pact that divided Eastern Europe into two spheres of interest. The pact was to be in force for ten years, and they agreed to settle all differences in an amicable way.

The economic agreement provided for an exchange of goods in the value of 200 million Reichsmarks with Germany committed to selling the Soviets machinery and manufactured goods, especially chemical and electrical supplies for oil production and transportation. In return, the Soviet Union would make available to Germany cereals, grain, butter, and other food products. The Baltic states (Estonia, Latvia, and Lithuania) and Bessarabia were to be declared part of the Soviet Union, while Poland would be divided between the two countries by a line consisting of the Narew, Vistula and San Rivers.

The Pact was signed a week before the outbreak of the German-Polish war (September 1, 1939), and, as a result, Poland came to be divided between Germany and the Soviet Union, with Belorussia (Belarus) and western Ukraine (Volynhia—my parents' home state, as well as the location of much partisan activity) annexed to the Soviet Union. This was the area east of the so-called Brest-Litovsk Line; the area to the west was the General Government, where many of the death camps were located. A section of Poland from Lodz to Poznan was also to be annexed by Germany. A northwest rectangular section around Vilna was annexed by Lithuania, and a section of northern Poland from Danzig to Memel became part of East Prussia.

The occupation of Eastern Poland in 1939-1941 was not mentioned in the film. Nor was the infamous Katyn Massacre of 1941, where top Polish officers, intellectuals and commissars were executed in order to destroy Polish leadership and subdue the Polish people. Nor was the cynical role the Soviets played, not only during the Warsaw Ghetto uprising of April-May 1943 by Jewish fighters and partisans such as Mordechai Anielewicz, Antek Zuckerman, Zivia Lubetkin, and Vladka Meed, but also by the Polish Uprisings over a year later in August of 1944.

This non-Jewish Polish uprising broke out at the instigation of the Armia Krajowa, the largest Polish resistance organization, and took its orders from the Polish Government-in-Exile in London. The aim of the uprising was to seize control of Warsaw before the Red Army entered the city, but this was doomed to fail. Aid from the western Allies did not amount to much more than a few arms drops, and the Soviet Union hindered most Allied aid, though they did drop a few supplies in the later stages of the uprising.

The Soviet Army did not lift a finger to help their fellow Communists across the Vistula River but waited until the Germans decapitated the Polish leadership. Once that occurred, the Soviets marched in and took over. None of that was mentioned in the film so as not to upset President Putin. Naturally, Polish President Duda was angry that he would not be able to speak at the conference to counter Soviet propaganda.

He and President Putin have two divergent views of what happened, and Jews are caught in the middle. History is not simple, and it is not cleanly divided between the good guys and the bad guys. While the Soviets must be praised and honored for the great sacrifice of over 20 million soldiers and untold millions of civilians lost in the fight against fascism, they still committed terrible atrocities against the Polish people and subjugated them for decades—not just Poland, but also Ukraine, Hungary, Lithuania, Latvia, Estonia, and other Soviet satellites.

It is ultimately a black eye against Yad Vashem for allowing this film to be shown, but it was inevitable, given the politics of Israel. When Prime Minister Bibi Netanyahu and the Israeli leadership welcomed Putin to Jerusalem, they had to have someone design a film that would not embarrass him.

As I have said, when politics meets history, history loses.

Sources

Dunin-Wasowicz, Krzysztof, "Warsaw Polish Uprising," *Encyclopedia of the Holocaust*, Volume 3. New York: Macmillan, 1990, pp. 1632-1633.

Spector, Shmuel, "Nazi-Hitler Pact," *Encyclopedia of the Holocaust*, Volume 3. New York: Macmillan, 1990, pp. 1040-1042.

XII. The Future of Jewish Radicalism

The Impact of Jewish Radicalism

Jewish radicalism, or the Jewish left, or the Jewish liberation movement (all interchangeable terms) arose from the ashes of the June 1967 Israeli-Arab Six-Day War, but it was nurtured from the ashen memories of the Nazi Holocaust and the fires of Watts, My Lai, Kent State, Jackson State, Berkeley, Columbia, and Wounded Knee.

It arose to fill a spiritual and political vacuum, an emptiness in many middle-class American Jews, an emptiness that organized Judaism—bar and bat mitzvahs, Jewish centers, synagogues, and Hanukkah *gelt*—could not fill. This movement was a "third way" between the secular alienation of the socialist New Left and the bourgeois "lox and bagels" suburban middle class.

It was always a very small movement, never more than a few thousand people, and comprising only a small proportion of Jewish youth and their adult sympathizers. But size, though important, is not essential to the success of a social movement. How many people comprised the early Zionists, the first Hasidim, or the early Civil Rights Movement? Sociology teaches us that it takes only a few dedicated individuals to influence the many.

The active political phase of the movement was surprisingly short-lived, only a few years, from 1968 to 1972. A *Response Magazine* symposium in the fall of 1976 called "Have You Sold Out?" came only four years later. Social movements, like shooting stars, have a very quick but intense life.

I would like to describe five significant changes that were the result of the general American 1960s counterculture and revolution and then insert the Jewish liberation movement into this paradigm. The past few years have seen a flurry of memoirs, "sequels," and histories from an assortment of perspectives, from democratic socialist to neo-conservative. What are these five major changes?

1. *There has been an increased tolerance for diversity.* This zeal for variety was most noticeable in political groupings. One of the strengths (some saw it as a weakness) of the general youth counterculture in its political (New Left) as well as its cultural (hippies) side was its very variety. There was literally an explosion of ideologies, philosophies, and lifestyles. There were Bundists, Zionists of every stripe from revisionist to socialist labor, Diaspora-ists, Yiddishists, secularists, Orthodox, Conservative, Reform, and Reconstructionists. As long as these groups did not infringe on the rights of others, they were not only tolerated but also welcomed. This degree of tolerance has not always existed in Judaism, yet Judaism was never a monolithic religion. There were always schisms. This acceptance of diversity forced Jewish elders to accept youthful diversity, and that is a healthy sign. However, within Israel today, and even America, we see a lack of tolerance for diverse philosophies and opinions, and this is an unhealthy sign.

2. *The acceptance of feeling as being of equal importance to logic and reason.* There are two sides to the brain. The left hemisphere is found to be primarily responsible for processing logic, language, details, mathematical reasoning, and analysis, while the right side deals with rhythm, color, spatial relationships, imagination, and synthesis. Unfortunately, our educational system grooms us from an early age to overemphasize "left-brain" activities, while "right-brain" activities such as daydreaming, imagination, and humor are rarely encouraged in the process of schooling. This acceptance of feelings explains not only the emergence of the sensitivity movement but also the mid-expanding, flowering, touching, ecstatic impulses of the 1960s.

    It underscores the attraction of many Jews to Jewish mysticism, utopianism, communalism, and piety—of Hasidism, the "total high" of *Shabbat* (Sabbath), the ecstasy of song and dance, of nature, of the natural and the supernatural, of the spontaneous and the loving, of the songs of Reb Shlomo Carlebach, the mysticism of

Reb Zalman Schachter, the tales of Elie Wiesel. Modern Judaism on the whole had lost its "soul." It had emphasized too much "left-brain" thinking, too much over-intellectualization and money-making, and not enough elation and openness.

The neo-conservatives of the times, from Sidney Hook and Bruno Bettelheim to Midge Decter and Norman Podhoretz, hated this aspect of the "Left." They mistrusted "right-brain" thinking. These impulses for community and ecstasy deeply touched the Reform and Conservative Jewish movements. People were searching for more "community," more rituals, more joy, more singing, and more involvement in Jewish institutions.

In short, such "left-brain" philosophies as communism and socialism have died out, but Orthodox Judaism, Near-Eastern and Native American religions have flourished.

3. *The rejection of certain pre-1967 values, not the rejection of fundamentals, but an affirmation of belief in them.* These fundamental values included such qualities as love, honesty, ethics, justice, and happiness. Secondary values that were rejected by a vocal minority of middle-class white youth were: (a) the accumulation of wealth; (b) the moral and political correctness of this country; (c) the assumption that all things illegal were also immoral and undesirable; and (d) the unquestioned acceptance of America's and Israel's foreign and internal policy, economic system, and political wisdom.

Within Judaism, many young Jews rejected the authority of the wealthy, the philanthropists, and the community leaders *simply* because they had wealth, title, and credentials. Young Jews wished to judge the person, not the position. They rejected much of Jewishness that was vulgar and ostentatious but accepted the authentic and the fundamental. In some cases, it meant jumping over their parents in order to understand their grandparents. For many it meant a return to tradition and ritual to the utter amazement and even ridicule of their own peers and parents.

4. *A reaffirmation of belief in the individual and in his/her sanctity, importance, and dignity.* In this age of giantism, unfeeling bureaucracy, and impersonal houses of worship, the individual seems lost. Mechanization, automation, technology, and rationality increased these feelings of alienation and anomie.

Religion, too, has become another big business, and not just for tele-evangelists, but also for social directors and PR men for rabbis, and entrepreneurs for community leaders. The Jewish liberation movement began to develop counter-institutions to bring people back in together through *havurot* (communal fellowships), Sabbath gatherings, retreats, and *farbrengen* (joyous gatherings). All were deemed necessary to elevate and exalt the individual in his often lonely search for God, but within the warm framework of fellowship and community, two things lost in this modern world.

5. *We are now, for better or worse, a society strongly influenced by its young—a "prefigurative society," as the late Margaret Mead called it.* In this type of society, unique in history, adults learn from their children rather than the reverse. While today, the pendulum has swung toward a "post-figurative" society, youth today in general still have an important influence on society's values and lifestyles. While the arrogance of the 1960s has mellowed, youth, especially in music, dance, art, movies, and their quest for peace affect us greatly.

Youth's greatest contribution can be more joy, more diversity, more creativity, more openness, more acceptance, more sense of community, more friendship, more tolerance of others, all leading to a saner, safer planet. This is what adults can learn from their children, and perhaps today, in quieter times, maybe children can turn to their parents (who were "children" in the '60s) and learn from them, too.

* * *

A wide range of alternative institutions and activities emerged out of the Jewish liberation movements of the 1960s. Political activism has not totally died out, but it is often done in a quieter, more deliberate way today, whether that is over Soviet Jewry, Palestinian human rights, or Jewish education. At a conference of the North American Jewish Student Network in the early 1970s, Rabbi Arthur Hertzberg asked his audience: "What do you do between demonstrations?" And his answer was that Jews "between pogroms" examined their own lives and became concerned with the *quality* of Jewish life. (Sadly, Rabbi Hertzberg and other scholars have often denied the impact of this movement on the quality of Jewish life. We will correct that in these pages.)

What were some of the activities that improved, even revolutionized, Jewish life? What were some of the developments of the Jewish liberation movement that had such a lasting impact on the Jewish community? There are many:

1. *The resurgence of the Jewish women's movement* was probably the most powerful, longest-lasting impact of all. It led to consciousness—raising groups in all major North American cities and throughout Europe and Israel. In February 1973, a National Conference on Jewish Women was held in New York City, attracting over 400 participants. The effects of this movement were felt in every crevice of the Jewish community. The Reform movement began to ordain women as rabbis; the Conservative movement agreed that women should be counted in the *minyan* (prayer quorum). Even the Orthodox movement has been shaken to its core by the demands of its women in such areas as divorce, wife and child abuse, and ritual participation.

    Many anthologies appeared. Among the first was, as usual, spearheaded by the ubiquitous and highly influential *Response* magazine edited at various times by Alan Mintz, Bill Novak, and Steve Cohen, each one in his own right enormously influential on the movement. A 190-page paperback called *The Jewish Woman: An Anthology* was published by *Response* in the summer of 1973, edited by Bill Novak. It included sections on Jewish women in history, spirituality, *halacha*, the life cycle, ritual, and problems facing women in Israel and the USA. Hailed by former U.S. Congresswoman Bella Abzug as a "wonderful contribution to the women's movement as well as to Jewish life," it was the most definitive study at the time on the subject.

    Jewish homosexuals and lesbians also began to come out of the "closet" both sexually and Jewishly. I recognized that movement in my book *Jewish Radicalism* with an important essay called "Coming Out Jewish" by Robbie Skeist. In it, Skeist combines gay and women's liberation with radical approaches to the Jewish poor, anti-Semitism, Palestinian Arabs, the Vietnam War, and Black-Jewish conflict.

Acceptance has been slow for these minorities within a minority, but much progress has been made. There are gay synagogues and *havurot* in New York, Boston, Montreal, Los Angeles, San Francisco, Chicago, even Tel Aviv, with their own gay rabbis and cantors. The AIDS plague has also increased interest in the role of the Holocaust and the persecution of gays under Nazism.

2. *Jewish media, film, and literature* have been among the most creative aspects of the movement. Yet, ironically, there has been no documentary of the movement itself. The New Jewish Media Project moved from Berkeley to New York City, and such people as Jerry Benjamin, David Kaufman, Eric Goldman, Jay Bender, Buddy Timberg, and Brad Burston (affectionately known as the "Gestetner Rebbe") have produced films, slide shows, and radio programs on such topics as the Holocaust, Jewish youth, Israeli wars, and the Bar Mitzvah, as well as documentaries on Rabbi Shlomo Carlebach and folksinger Bob Dylan (*né* Zimmerman). There has been an upsurge in Jewish expression in poetry, short stories, and novels.

    The Holocaust has been the inspiration for films to many children of Holocaust survivors: *Maus* by Art Spiegelman; *Breaking the Silence* by Eva Fogelman and Edward A. Mason; *Kaddish* by Steven Brand; *The Legacy* by Miriam Rosenbush; *In Dark Places* by Gina Blumenfeld; and *Partisans of Vilna* by Josh Waletzky and Aviva Kempner.

3. *Jewish studies and Holocaust studies* on secular campuses have increased sevenfold in the past twenty years. Courses on some aspect of Jewish life or Hebrew classes are held at over 350 colleges and universities. Yiddish is being taught on at least 17 campuses, including Oxford University. In 80 schools, a student can major in Jewish studies, and over 60 colleges offer advanced degrees. Furthermore, at over 50 campuses, Jewish students organized "Jewish free universities" based on Martin Buber's famous *Judische Lehrhause* in Berlin, which included courses that the more traditional Jewish studies simply would not have allowed in their usual curriculum (this is another influence of the movement); for

example, "Judaism, War, and Conscientious Objection," Jewish Mysticism and Radical Theology," "The Oppression of Jewish Women," "Marxism, Anarchism, and Judaism," "Jewish Cooling," and "Homosexuality and Judaism." Eventually many of these free university courses entered the formal academic world of mainstream courses.

In 1975, there were fewer than a dozen courses on the Holocaust offered in American colleges and universities. Yet by 1985 the Holocaust was the second most widely taught course of Judaic content, exceeded only by courses in the Hebrew Bible. The Holocaust is also taught in many secondary schools. Television programs have proliferated: Gerald Green's *Holocaust* in 1978 was followed by the mini-series on Raoul Wallenberg, John Hersey's *The Wall*, Fania Fenelon's *Playing for Time*, and Richard Rashke's *Escape from Sobibor*. All of these broadcasts attracted major audiences across America, Europe, and Israel.

Furthermore, a new generation of Jewish scholars, badly needed as the European-born scholars died or retired, were trained at the elite schools to carry out long-neglected and needed research. If there is one place where "movement graduates" have found a safe harbor, it has traditionally been within the free air of academia. People who come to mind immediately are sociologists Hillel Levine of Boston University, Steve Cohen of Queens College and Yale, and Jack Nusan Porter of Harvard and formerly of Boston University. Others include Alan Mintz of Brandeis University, Sherman Teichman of Tufts, David Roskies of the Jewish Theological Seminary, and Arthur Green of the Reconstructionist Rabbinical College (RRC) and now Hebrew College. Arthur Waskow was also affiliated with RRC for a time.

4. Spurred on to some degree by the Jewish Defense League as well as influential articles by Paul Cowan in *The Village Voice*, there has been an increased concern with the *Jewish poor and elderly* who too often languished in old-age homes or in dangerous urban dilapidated and dangerous neighborhoods, as personified in the movie *Homicide* by David Mamet. Project Ezra of New York is a good example of an outreach program to these poor Jews. Furthermore, the Jewish poor are often the Jewish Orthodox. Because of large families, private schools, expensive Kosher

food, and low-paying jobs, the urban Orthodox are in serious socioeconomic distress. Also, retired union members—that is, old working-class Jews who were unable to escape to the suburbs, are also caught up in this cycle of poverty. Young Jews made their plight known.

5. *The growth of Jewish fellowships (havurot)* was due to the Jewish liberation movement. Aside from the women's movement, *havurot* are probably the second most important contribution. However, the term "fellowship" should be more fully explained, since there are a wide range of groups that fall under the rubric of fellowship. These include: long-established fellowships, such as the *Havurot Shalom* in Somerville, Massachusetts, an intensive closed group with a great deal of everyday interaction and a wide array of activities; synagogue *havurot*, comprising a few families and individuals who meet at each other's homes for a creative *Shabbat* or festival; non-affiliated groups not connected to a synagogue; neo-Hasidic "communes" that are also open to the public, such as the House of Love and Prayer in San Francisco or the Shabbos House of Rabbi Moshe Blatt of Brighton, Massachusetts; politically active fellowships, such as the Farbrengen Group spearheaded by Arthur Waskow and Robert Agus of Washington, D.C.; Reconstructionist fellowships; and Jewish student houses, such as Kibbutz Langdon in Madison, Wisconsin, and Hebrew House at Oberlin College.

In fact, there are literally hundreds of *havurot* all across North America from Portland, Maine, to Germantown, Pennsylvania, to Los Angeles, California, to Honolulu, Hawaii. No one knows the exact figure, but a loose network and newsletter brings the various strands together in order that this alternative lifestyle will become more widely known. The *havurot* movement is probably one of the most important institutions in the American Jewish community to have emerged out of the Jewish liberation movements of the 1960s.

6. *Neo-Hasidic and other spiritual groups*, as mentioned, are also forming. This blend of Jewish mysticism and Far-Eastern religion has jokingly been called "krishna-mishna," but others may dismiss it as simply "mishna-mish-mash." Some of these fellowships will no doubt amuse more traditional Jews who will be gratified by

the increased interest in Torah Judaism yet wonder why all of the esoteric "trappings" and drugs are necessary.

Some have not been amused. Rabbi Blatt of Boston (who looks a bit like Jesus Christ) was recently attacked and seriously injured by ultra-Orthodox *haredim* in a Jerusalem *mikveh* (ritual bath) when they mistakenly thought he had proclaimed himself Jesus Christ! One Torah group, the Lubavitch Hasidim, have become a major contemporary force in Jewish life today, attempting to bring a "Jewish high" to Jews within a traditional yet missionary framework.

It would be amusing to find out how they would react to the following ad:

OR CHADASH

The Total High of Shabbos

The Mysteries of Torah

The Kabbalah in Daily Practice

The Study of the Holy Language

The Ecstasy of Chasidic Song and Dance

OR CHADASH HOUSE

729 North Spaulding Avenue

Los Angeles, California 90046

Shabbatons, Holiday Celebrations, Free classes in Torah

Mishnah, Gemorah, Midrash, Siddur, Shulchan Aruch.

We also have a House of Prayer, a Jewish Center,

a Library, and a Mountain Retreat.

WE WANT YOU......WE NEED YOU

(All Contributions are Tax Deductible)

This enticing ad should almost be for a "cult," and I am sure Jewish groups are wary of such groups, but the reasons why young people join such religious alternatives, Jewish or otherwise, are still salient today.

7. *Political issues* worldwide have been a major force in Jewish, life. The plight of Soviet Jews were literally forced onto the American agenda by the combined efforts of the Student Struggle for Soviet Jewry and the Jewish Defense League. Other issues that have grabbed the attention of young Jews on campus are the *aliyah* of

Ethiopian Jewry, Arab and Leftist campus propaganda, and South African-Israeli relations.

But it has been the emergence of such peace groups as PROBE, a Boston-based group; *Breira*, a national but New York-based movement; and later, after *Breira's* untimely demise, New Jewish Agenda and Friends of Peace Now, with its Israeli-affiliated counterparts, have not always been effective, but they have been threatening enough to the Jewish establishment. They have been there to keep people honest about human rights and justice for the Palestinian people and the possibility of a two-state solution to the Middle East crisis. These groups are as idealistic as their predecessors were in the 1960s.

Many "graduates" of these movements have made *aliyah* to Israel, and rather than stop all activity there, they have continued their probing and questioning of Israeli society in the areas of civil rights and civil liberties. Some have returned to America but continue their Jewish activism. Two journals that originated out of Jerusalem initially, *Lilith* and *Contact*, appeared to voice concern over war, women's rights, Sephardi equality, Arab human rights, and questions of peace, borders, army life, and related matters.

Challenge, a magazine of the Israeli Left, carries on the struggle today. Irena Klepfisz and her comrades also continue to do important work. Many of these activists are Radical Zionists. They and their distinctive history will be described later in this book. Alliances were made with such earlier splinter groups such as Moked, a coalition of veteran socialists from *Mapam* ranks, Zionist elements of Tel Aviv *Siach*, *Maki*, as well as *kibbutznikim* and young soldiers who have expressed disgust with war mixed with a desire for conciliatory, compromising, and creative political initiatives; a rejection of reliance on military and technological superiority; anti-annexationist; anti-West Bank settlement; and a genuine openness to settling the just grievances of the Palestinian people.

These groups want self-determination for the Palestinians but *not* at the expense of Israel as a Jewish State. These are essentially pro-Zionist alliances. Other parties aligned with American peace groups are the Citizen's Rights Groups of *Shulamit Aloni* and *shinui*. The byzantine politics of breakups and coalitions continue at a dizzying pace in modern-day Israel, and "graduates" of the Jewish liberation movements are often active participants.

8. *Jewish education* has been a major force for social change, and Jewish activists founded one of the foremost institutions of education in North America: the Conference on Alternatives in Jewish Education (CAJE). The first CAJE was sponsored by NETWORK, a national Jewish student coalition, in 1973 and grew into the CAJE. By 1979, the CAJE was already claiming a membership of over 1,500 teachers and educators. Movement people like Cheri Koller-Fox, Jerry Benjamin, and Eduardo Rauch were in the forefront of much educational change and continue to be active in the field of Jewish education and pedagogy.

9. *Democracy in Jewish Life.* On the home front, we have seen a small number of those in the movement entering the established Jewish community—the rabbinate, Jewish communal, defense, and philanthropic organizations, the editorial staffs of Jewish journals and newspapers (a revived English *Forward*, for example), local synagogues, summer camps, and international Jewish groups for, e.g., Holocaust survivors. Rather than "drop out," these people have decided to take the more difficult step of working *within* the system, to have a voice in the formulation of policy, and to make a real impact on adult Jews. This has happened because many Jewish leaders have recognized that these young people are their greatest asset in revivifying the Jewish community of the future.

10. *Creative "Jewing."* Finally, one of the most enduring impacts of the movement has been, on the average, Jews' desire to forge an identity through tradition and creative lifestyles. Hundreds of Jews have been helped by such books as Arthur Kurtzweil's *From Generation to Generation: How to Trace Your Jewish Genealogy and Personal History* in order to find their roots.

The Strassfeld family of colleagues have produced a cottage industry of catalogs, calendars, and how-to books on how to lead a more fulfilling Jewish life. I am talking about the classic three volumes of *The Jewish Catalog* and *The Jewish Family Book*. This "how-to" publishing tradition has been carried out as well by Anita Diamant, Blu Greenberg, and Hayim Donin.

A new Jewish pride is growing again, and Jewish singles and parents want to know how to be authentic Jews again, together with others. Even new "Tzedakah collectives," Jewish charities, have sprung up like The New Israel Find and the creative "mitzvah collectives" of Danny Siegel.

How can one adequately summarize the impact of this movement of radical Zionists, radical Jews, and "new Jews" on the American-Jewish and Israeli communities? It has had its successes and its failures, but the irony is that when a movement is most successful it disappears, like the Civil Rights Movement for Afro-Americans. This movement for Jews has by and large succeeded. It has had enormous success, and important elements of it continue to flourish.

Many historians, both here and in Israel, have ignored or overlooked this movement, and one reason for this book is to reclaim this Jewish movement's rightful place in Jewish history.

About a decade ago, at the Martin Buber Centennial Symposium at Harvard University, I told an Israeli from the Ministry of Education that Buber had an enormous influence on this Jewish student movement and that that movement in turn had a great impact on the American Jewish community. He turned to me and said, "What impact? What movement?" He had hardly, except for the JDL, heard of it, and as for any impact, he thought it was nil.

How quickly memories fade! Or is it simply that knowledge is not passed on? We can't let that happen, either to scholars or to our children!

Led by its young, the American Jewish community went through one of the greatest periods of creativity in Jewish history, rivaling, I believe, the Golden Age of Spain from 1000 to 1492, and the Wilhelmina and Weimar period in German and Austria from 1900 to 1939, but *our* golden age, beginning in 1967, is still growing. We do not know when it will end, but proof of its success has been that many of the movement's contributions have been coopted and absorbed by the established Jewish community: *havurot*, creative prayer, women's and gay rights, Palestinian rights. These are "old hat" to most people today, but where did they originate? Yes, that is the question, and that is what this book is all about—the origins!

Sources and Resources

Jewish Radicalism

There are many sources for this area. Debate over terminology has focused on several sub-groups, at times overlapping. *Jewish Radicals*, with the emphasis on the "Radical," are members of the New Left who happen to be Jewish. They are radicals first, Jews second. People like Mark Rudd in SDS or Abbie Hoffman and Jerry Rubin of the Yippies are Jewish radicals. Radical Jews, however, are Jews first and radicals second. They arose in what was called the radical Jewish movements of the 1960s. These are people like Arthur Waskow, Jack Nusan Porter, and David Twesky. Some like Waskow, Porter, and Michael Lerner were once Jewish radicals and are now radical Jews.

A subset of radical Jews are "radical Zionists," people who are socialists and Zionists with a firm commitment to the *kibbutz* or other communal forms of life. They were, like David Twersky and Jack Nusan Porter, graduates of socialist-Zionist youth movements like *Habonim, Dror,* or *Hashomer Hatzair.* Another subset of the radical Jews, but much more liberal and "spiritually" oriented, are the "New Jews" or "Chavurah Jews." These are rough categories, since people like Arthur Waskow and Michael Lerner overlap into two camps: "Radical Jews" and "Chavurah Jews." In general, radicals and radical Jews have a great distaste for typecasting, generalizing, and labeling, and would dismiss this entire typology, but we need some framework to depict the various groups. And many of our most eminent scholars and intellectuals have spent considerable time analyzing these categories.

For the role of Jews in the New Left, see:

Glazer, Nathan. "The New Left and the Jews." *Jewish Journal of Sociology* (December 1969).

_____. "The Jewish Role in Student Activism." *Fortune* (January 1969).

Glickstein, Gary A. "Religion and the Jewish New Left: 1960 to Date." *American Jewish Archives*, Vol. 26 (April 1974), pp. 23-30.

Porter, Jack Nusan. "Jewish Student Activism." *Jewish Currents* (May 1970).

_____. "The Origins of the Jewish Student Movement: A Personal Reflection." *genesis 2*, Vol. 11 (February 1980), p. 19.

_____, and Peter Dreier. "Introduction," *Jewish Radicalism: A Selected Anthology*. New York: Grove Press and Random House, 1973, pp. xv-liv.

For an analysis of radical Jews and Jewish radicals, see:

Cohen, Percy S. *Jewish Radicals and Radical Jews.* London and New York: Academic Press, 1980.

Jacobs, Paul. *Is Curly Jewish? A Political Self-Portrait.* New York: Vintage Books/Random House, 1973.

Rothman, Stanley, and S. Robert Lichter. *Roots of Radicalism: Jews, Christians, and the New Left.* New York and Oxford: Oxford University Press, 1982.

For an impact of the Vietnam War, see:

Newcomb, Richard F. *A Pictorial History of the Vietnam War*. Garden City, N.Y.: Doubleday & Company, 1987.

Winston, Diane. "Vietnam and the Jews." In Jack Nusan Porter (ed.), *The Sociology of American Jews: A Critical Anthology*. Lanham, Md.: University Press of America, 1978, pp. 189-209.

For the "New Jews," see:

Siegel, Richard, Michael Strassfeld and Sharon Strassfeld. *The Jewish Catalog*. New York: Jewish Publication Society, 1973 and later editions.

Sleeper, James, and Alan L. Mintz (eds.). *The New Jews*. New York: Random House/Vintage Books, 1971.

Waskow, Arthur. *The Freedom Seder*. New York: Holt, Rinehart, 1970.

For other works on the Left, see:

Gitlin, Todd. *The Sixties: Years of Hope, Days of Rage*. New York: Bantam Books, 1987.

Hoffman, Abbie. *The Best of Abbie Hoffman*. New York: Four Walls, Eight Windows, 1989.

Liebman, Arthur. *Jews and the Left*. New York: John Wiley and Sons, 1979.

For the women's days' and lesbians' movements, there are numerous magazines and books. One could start with *Lilith* magazine and the massive bibliography by Jack Nusan Porter in *Sexual Politics in Nazi Germany* (Newton, Mass.: The Spencer Press, 1992).

For videos, see *Eyes on the Prize, Children of the Left*, and *Voices from the Left*, all shown on PBS as specials.

For two views on Leftist Jews, see:

Porter, Jack Nusan, and Arthur Liebman. "Two Views on Leftist Jews." *Jewish Currents*, Vol. 38 (January 1984), pp. 37-40.

See also Robert Wolfe's many writings on Jewish radicals.

Radical Zionism

For historic and classical commentaries on Zionism, socialist or otherwise, see:

Hertzberg, Arthur (ed.). *The Zionist Idea*. New York: Atheneum, 1972.

For an interpretation of American Jewry by a socialist-Zionist, see:

Halpern, Ben. *The American Jew: A Zionist Analysis*. New York: Theodor Herzl Foundation, 1956.

For a theoretical discussion of socialist-Zionism, see:

Gal, Allon. *Socialist-Zionism*. Cambridge, Mass.: Schenckman Publishing Company, 1973.

For a history and overview, see:

Arougheti, Paul J. *If I Am Not for Myself, Who Will Be For Me? The Emergence of the Radical Zionist Movement, 1968-1972.* Unpublished manuscript, 1972.

Katz, Chava Alkon. "Jewish Radical Zionists in the U.S." In Geoffrey Wigoder et al. (eds.), *Encyclopedia Judaica Yearbook 1975/76.* Jerusalem: Keter Publishing House, and New York: The Macmillan Company, 1975, pp. 115-133.

For an analysis of Porter's life, see:

Martindale, Don. "Review Essay: Jack Nusan Porter: Thoughts on Internal and External Peace." *International Journal on World Peace*, April-June 1985, pp. 101-117.

Zionism and Anti-Zionism

For two provocative views on the subject of anti-Zionism and anti-Semitism from two direct and opposite viewpoints, see:

Lerner, Michael. *The Socialism of Fools: Anti-Semitism on the Left.* Oakland, Calif., and Jerusalem: Tikkun books, 1992. This is profoundly pro-Israel and pro-Jewish.

Sharif, Regina. *Non-Jewish Zionism: Its Roots in Western History.* London: Zed Press, 1983. This is profoundly anti-Zionist and anti-Semitic.

See also:

Harkabi, Yehoshofat. *Palestinians and Israel.* Jerusalem: Israel Universities Press, 1974.

Wistrich, Robert S. (ed.). *The Left Against Zion: Communism, Israel, and the Middle East.* London: Vallentine, Mitchell, 1979.

_____. *The Myth of Zionist Racism.* London: Institute for Jewish Affairs, 1976.

_____. *Revolutionary Jews from Marx to Trotsky.* London: Harrap, 1976.

Habonim/Dror/Labor Zionism

For such an important movement, there are surprisingly few analyses. There is quite a bit of primary material in the American Jewish Archives; for examples, journals and leadership manuals like *Furrows* (a monthly for adults); *Haboneh* (a monthly for youth); *HaMadrich* (a publication for youth leaders); and such pamphlets as *Working Together for a Socially Just World: Older Schavot Outline* (May, 1965), published by Ichud Habonim Labor Zionist Youth, 200 Park Ave. South, New York, NY 10003 (old address—the new address is on 27th Street in New York City); *Habonim Leadership Training Seminar* (December 25-29, 1960); *The Impact of Zionist Youth* by Max Langer (August, 1965); and similar material is also very useful for understanding the ideology and action-commitment of *Habonim* youth movements.

Collections of memoirs coming out around the 25th anniversary of *Ichud Habonim* in 1960 that described *Habonim* camping and the history of *Habonim*, are:

Breslau, David (ed.). *Adventure in Pioneering: The Story of 25 Years of Habonim Camping.* New York: The CHAY Commission of the Labor Zionist Movement, 1957.

_____. *Arise and Build: The Story of American Habonim.* New York: Ichud Habonim Labor Zionist Youth, 1961.

See also *The Ideological Development of Habonim*, a pamphlet. For an older perspective from pre-World War II, see the memoirs of Jacob Katzman:

Katzman, Jacob. *Commitment: The Labor Zionist Life-Style in America.* New York: Labor Zionist Letters, 1975.

Such "life-styles" are long dead. They echo a nostalgia that we miss today—a sense of commitment, community, and adherence to movement "ideology," today a taboo word.

The *Jewish Frontier* was also sent to older *chaverim*. A very popular book, published in cooperation with the Reconstructionist Press, was Murray Weingarten (later Moshe Kerem of Gesher Haziv, Israel), *Life in a Kibbutz*, published in 1955, and which sold over 2,000 copies by 1960, a phenomenal figure.

circa 1976

Sources and Resources (added later):

Radical Sociology

These are sources for the section on the making of a radical sociologist at Northwestern University. See:

Dreier, Peter, and Jack Nusan Porter. "Jewish Radicalism in Transition." *Society*, Vol. 12 (January-February 1975), pp. 18-23.

Eisendrath, Craig R., and Thomas J. Cottle. *Out of Discontent: Visions of the Contemporary University.* Boston: Shenkman Publishing Company, 1972.

Kotre, John. *The Best of Times, the Worst of Times: Andrew Greeley & American Catholicism, 1950-1975.* Chicago: Nelson-Hall, 1978.

Ladd, Everett Carl, and Seymour Martin Lipset. *The Divided Academy: Professors and Politics.* New York: McGraw-Hill, 1975.

Morrissey, Joseph P., and Henry J. Steadman. "Practice and Parish? Some Overlooked Career Contingencies for Sociologists in Non-Academic settings." *The American Sociologist*, Vol. 12 (November 1977), pp. 154-162.

Porter, Jack Nusan. "A New Course Proposal: Sociology in Practice." *ASA Footnotes*, Vol. 2 (August 1974), pp. 6-7.

_____. *Student Protest, University Decision-Making, and the Technocratic Society: The Case of ROTC*. Evanston, Ill.: Department of Sociology, Northwestern University, June 1971. The author's dissertation, also available from University Microfilms, Zeeb Road, Ann Arbor, Mich. An abridged version was published by Adams Press, Chicago, in 1973.

_____, and Peter Dreier. *Jewish Radicalism: A Selected Anthology*. New York: Grove Press and Random House, 1973.

Span, Paula. "We Search for the New Campus Leaders." *The Boston Phoenix* (April 6, 1976), pp. 8-10.

Van den Berghe, Peter. *Academic Gamesmanship: How to Make a Ph.D. Pay*. New York: Abelard-Schuman (An Intext Book), 1970.

There are many books on the Chicago Conspiracy Trial and on Lee Weiner. One of the better ones is by co-conspirator Tom Hayden, *Reunion: A Memoir*, New York: Random House, 1988. Hayden's extraordinary life as a radical is described. He had close ties to Milwaukee. He (his Mom) was from Oconomowoc, Wisconsin, which is halfway between Madison and Milwaukee, and he had deep roots in Milwaukee, as did SDS leader Bernadine Dohrn. His grandfather was Thomas Francis Hayden, director of the Northwest Building and Loan Association. His father's family (Haydens and Foleys) included a Mr. James Foley, who was owner of Foley's General Store and Post Office. See also:

Viorst, Milton. *Fire in the Streets: America in the 1960s*. New York: Touchstone Books/Simon & Schuster, 1990.

1990

Jewish Radicalism: A Classic Revisited 50 Years Later

With Peter Dreier, a sociologist, then at the University of Chicago, now at Occidental College in California, I edited a book called *Jewish Radicalism: A Selected Anthology* in 1973. It was actually finished in 1971, but publishing delays made it come out in 1973. An earlier anthology edited by James Sleeper and Alan Mintz, *The New Jews*, came out in 1971 by Random House/Vintage Books. Our book came out through Grove Press and was distributed by Random House. In fact, it even had a number "B-360" when it came out as an Evergreen Black Cat Book with the famous black-faced cat with wide white eyes, in a mass-market paperback edition. The Black Cat series included such giants as Franz Fanon and James Baldwin. The publisher was the renowned Barney Rosset (who passed away recently), and the editor was Fred Jordan.

Those were days when books were actually edited by real human beings, and Jewish and Black "radical" books came out under prestigious labels like Random House Vintage Books, Doubleday Anchor Books, and Grove Press. My, how times have changed.

Jewish Radicalism was, as the outside flap of the hardcover stated, "the first political compendium of philosophies from the Jewish liberation movement [and] serves as an important introduction to the ideas and ideals of Jewish youth and the fears and conflicts of its parents."

It was a time when we were young enough to actually have "parents" and we were told by the media that we were rebelling against them. That was not necessarily true, by the way, but it made good copy. Most sociological studies of the so-called "red-diaper babies" (the offspring of Communist or progressive parents) showed that they were actually *in line* with their parents but took one step further. They were not in rebellion against their parents but against an unfeeling bureaucracy and military complex. In fact, soon, many Jewish leaders saw us as "the future" to a moribund leadership and not as a threat.

The book's back cover lists some of the prime movers and shakers of the '60s and '70s in the Jewish "radical" world, from M.J. Rosenberg and Aviva Cantor Zuckoff to Bill Novak and Danny Siegel to Mary Gendler and Robbie Skeist to Sol Stern and Arthur Waskow to Jerry Kirschen and Everett Gendler to Boris Kochubiyevsky, David Twersky and Sheryl Bacon.

It should be pointed out that the movement was just as diverse as the non-Jewish movements. You had your liberal cultural activists like Bill Novak, editor of *Response Magazine*; radical Socialist-Zionists like Tsvi Bisk and Itzhak Epstein; radical rabbis like Arthur Waskow, Everett Gendler and Stephen Lerner; gay activists like Robbie Skeist; and woman activists like Mary Gendler and Sheryl Baron.

Several made *aliyah* and were active in Israeli politics like David Twersky. Some were political activists; some cultural; some communitarian *havurot*-style activists; and some changed and became quite conservative, people like the cartoonish Jerry Kirschen ("Dry Bones") and most of the Russian refuseniks like Boris Kochubiyevsky.

While Peter disagreed, I felt we needed to include pieces on Rabbi Meir Kahane and a progressive response to him. I felt that "radical" (from the Latin "going to the root of the matter" meant also the radical right as well as the radical left). We needed to understand why young Jews were attracted to the right. In fact, in my several encounters with Rabbi Kahane, he told me, "Jack, if I could have a dozen of you guys (meaning Jewish leftists), I could take over the Jewish world!" He admired the radical activism of leftist Jews.

Being a good sociologist, I made a four-by-four table and made a distinction between radical Jews who were Jews first and radicals second, as our book described, and Jewish radicals like Mark Rudd and Bernadine Dohrn who were radicals first and Jews a distant second. These were two very distinct groups, and the media totally overlooked us. Even American and Israeli scholars overlooked us—in most histories of the New Left (Todd Gitlin, Terry Anderson, David Farber) the Jewish radical movement is not even mentioned. Only one historian wrote a book about it—Arthur

Liebman's *Jews and the Left* (John Wiley, 1979). It remains one of the best books on the subject.

Furthermore, one could divide the movement into the hippies and the political radicals—between countercultural radicals and political radicals. Such dichotomies go back several hundred years. Moses Hess left Karl Marx and his teachings and became a socialist-Zionist, maybe the very first. In his book *Rome and Jerusalem*, he envisions a socialist state in Israel, then known as Palestine. Marx called him a "utopian socialist" and mocked him as a lunatic. Marx and the Marxists also labeled "utopian" all the communitarian communalists like Comte, Saint Simon, Owens and Fourier. It's all there in his *Communist Manifesto.* Who is to say who was more effective in history—Marx and his political radicals, or Hess, Comte, Saint Simon and their followers?

But history moves quickly, especially radical history. To show you how quickly things changed in the '60s and '70s, in 1976, a scant five years after major demonstrations against the war in Vietnam, *Response Magazine* had a special issue called "Have You Sold Out?" But what does that mean?

The true radicals never sold out. They went underground. But these were the Jewish and non-Jewish radicals of the non-Jewish movements (the Weathermen, the Black Panthers). The Jewish component may have "sold out," but the term is fraught with innuendo. Does working for the Jewish "establishment" or even becoming the Jewish "establishment" like John Ruskay being head of the United Jewish Communities or Jerry Benjamin and Bruce Arbit being presidents of the Milwaukee Federation, mean you "sold out" or that you put your ideals into practice? Does writing biographies of famous people like Bill Novak constitute "selling out"? Does going into real estate and making a good living, as I have done, mean "selling out"? I will not judge anyone except someone like David Horowitz, former editor and co-founder of the important '60s journal *Ramparts*, who not only turned conservative but attacked former colleagues and workers.

We all make compromises in life. The youthful radicals of that time got married, had kids, needed to make a living. We couldn't live in a commune our entire life—well, at least most of us. We go through cycles. My wife and I, now in our 50s and 60s, are thinking about moving to Israel and living on a *kibbutz*. Does that mean we have *not* "sold out"?

Jewish Radicalism still resonates. The topics were timeless: the Jewish counterculture, the *havurot*, the Jewish woman, Jewish gays, and the conflict between the right and the left, both in the USA and in Israel.

Overall, I am proud of the book. It stands up over time. I still get calls for it, and I've reprinted it twice. And it's in need of another printing, since Grove Press has let it lapse.

As the teacher and poet Joel Rosenberg wrote in an essay for the book, "Evolution of the Jew as Poet," I think this sums up what it's all about:

> ...I mean cities with drinkable air. I mean countries with open borders. I mean children raised to love their play... I mean cities of students, whole countries that are schools. I mean great-grandfathers at their tents telling ancient tales. I mean mosques with Jews, churches with Muslims, synagogues with Christians. I mean men and women alive as partners, sharing work and sharing birth. I mean the cherishing of silence.

March 2020, but written in 2012

Building a Jewish Radical Movement

At a recent rally and march for Bernie Sanders on February 22, 2020, through downtown Boston, 800 people showed up on a warm Saturday afternoon (ironically on the Sabbath). I might add that this was not an official Bernie rally organized by his re-election committee but by numerous left and democratic socialist groups in the Boston and Eastern Massachusetts area. For a short notice, it was quite a large rally. A week later, 13,000 people showed up at the exact same spot where Bernie spoke. He is a phenomenon. Among their slogans were:

"Our heroes are Martin Luther King, Noam Chomsky, and Howard Zinn."

"Enough already. Silence = complicity. Join me. Speak out."

"We're in a class struggle."

"Workers need to take over their work sites and control their jobs."

"Women need control over their bodies."

And:

"Wow, a Democratic Socialist is winning in California, in New York, in Nevada, and in Massachusetts. Who would have thought that?"

And, of course, no one would have thought it even four years ago. But Bernie's message comes right out of the Jewish radical secular tradition I have been writing about for decades. For some crazy reason, it is reverberating in history today. His message(s) has hit the *zeitgeist*.

But how does one build a movement that is radical and democratic, sensible and acceptable to the American people and in the same breath, how does one build a *Jewish* radical movement that is democratic and relevant?

That is the focus of this essay.

There are already pockets of Jews doing just that: the people around *Jewish Currents* in Brooklyn, New York; the Harvard Jewish Coalition for Peace; etc.

These groups say that Jewish liberation is bound up with the liberation of all people; that the focus will be on fighting anti-Semitism and racism; supporting the safety of Jews and all people through solidarity; creating Jewish spaces and events outside Hillel and conventional Jewish institutions; and engaging with the rich history of radical left and anti-Zionist or non-Zionist Jews. (See Jewish News Service, "Anti-Zionist Jewish group formed by Harvard students," *Jewish Advocate*, February 21, 2020, p. 5.)

These groups tackle very difficult questions surrounding Israel, the rights of Palestinians, Zionism, a "Jewish or a secular democratic state," the Boycott, Divestment, and Sanctions (BDS) movement, and the fight against all forms of oppression including white supremacy, patriarchy, heterosexism, ableism, capitalism, settler-colonialism, and imperialism. In short, they take upon themselves all the "-isms" that we began in the '60s and added new ones, combining sexual, gender, political, climate, disability, and world-domination elements.

What bothers some Jews about this is that they would say—who comes first? Your own Jewish people, or others? Who is more oppressed—Jews, or others? The essays in this book show that we have been grappling with this question for 50 years and longer, back 150 years to the Bundists (non-Zionist socialists) and Socialist-Zionists in Czarist Russia. There is nothing new in all this, except that the schools have failed to teach this history to newer generations.

Yet, while fifty years ago, the Jewish community more or less co-opted many of these 1960s issues (civil rights, Vietnam, poverty, gay and women's rights), today, with more powerful conservative, right-wing, and even fascist forces out there in the USA, Europe and Israel, radical Jewish groups face more powerful opponents, from Trump, from Netanyahu, and from their many supporters both Jewish and non-Jewish.

Bernie is often called a "self-hating Jew," or Bernie "hates Israel." One hears this constantly. Why? Because people fear that he may become the next U.S. president. Alan Dershowitz has vowed to "destroy" Bernie if he is nominated.

However, to answer the critics: Bernie does not hate Israel. He hates certain policies of Israel, especially regarding the occupation of the West Bank and of supporting the rights of Palestinians to a state of their own. Bernie isn't a self-hating Jew but a secular, assimilated "cultural" Jew, not religious and not really a Zionist, but a Diasporist Jew in a long line of Jewish radical traditions going back to the Bund and the Labor Zionists of Eastern Europe, Russia and Ukraine.

Bernie also says that being socialist is really not that radical. There are dozens of socialist countries, including Israel, that have been successful, plus socialism has existed and continues to exist in America in many forms that people don't see as "socialist" or radical anymore: Social Security, the eight-hour working day, the forty-hour working week, childcare. Even subsidies to farmers and to oil and gas producers are socialistic government handouts, yet the Right does not see that.

Furthermore, the specter of socialism and Communism no longer scares off the younger generation who knew not McCarthy.

Jewish radical movements will build on the general radical movements but will help modify the anti-Semitism and anti-Zionism of those movements. True, there is a risk that some of these movements on the Left are dangerous and violent, but for the most part most Americans are sympathetic to democratic socialism. Recent polls have shown that young people between 19 and 28 years of age have a better view of socialism (52%) than of capitalism, which they equate with pollution of our soil, the melting of the ice caps, our oceans filled with plastic and toxic wastes, and the possible extinction of our planet. These young people could carry the day and help Bernie reside in the White House. Still, the label of "socialism" is quite strong and could block Bernie's movement from succeeding. In fact, his own followers have told me that three groups will block them from power: the liberal democratic machine, the media (which are run by the capitalist class), and the capitalist "billionaire" class itself. They will be so threatened that they will try to destroy Bernie's movement. But will they succeed?

March 5, 2020

Conclusion:
Toward a Post-Modern
Radical Jewish Community

We are seeing a radical Jewish movement ascending, but how many of them know their roots? I hope this book will help. There are several possible scenarios for the future. One is by sociologist Steven Windmueller of Los Angeles, a city that is always ahead of its time. Steve gives us ten major trends that are having an impact on the Jewish community:

1. Jews by choice are reshaping American Jewry.
2. Orthodox Jewry is rising in power and numbers, not disappearing (but mostly due to large families rather than through conversions).
3. Millennial and Generation Z Jews are reshaping American Jewry.
4. Islam will replace Judaism as the third major trio of traditional religions—Protestant, Catholic, Jewish.
5. World Jewry is deeply divided over President Trump and over Israel.
6. Are we one community, or multiple communities? Who speaks for Jews?
7. Anti-Semitism is on the rise. "Whiteness" is a tool of anti-Semitism. Our enemies say we are "white" and not "oppressed" anymore.
8. Boutique or startup Jewish associations are replacing or challenging traditional *shuls* and institutions.
9. Independent Jewish finders and family foundations are transforming Jewish philanthropy.

I would add several other factors:

1. Jews have become global citizens, via travel and settlement. You can find Jews in Dubai, Hong Kong, Beijing, Brisbane, Kuala Lumpur, and Kiev (and Chabad is already there).
2. Israel is not the major center of creative Jewish life. It has become a major transformative technological center, but creativity in the arts and humanities is taking place throughout the globe.
3. Jews are leaving America because of the rise of anti-Semitism and are going to Israel. More Jews have been killed in the past three years than in the previous seventy-five.
4. For the first time, a Jewish socialist is on the verge of getting the nomination for the presidency of the United States and could even become president. (I am writing this on February 22, 2020, five months before the Democratic Convention in Milwaukee on July 16-20, 2020, and eight months before the elections on November 5, 2020.)
5. Political correctness has taken over our campuses and other institutions, and it has become difficult for people to be tolerant of adversarial points of view. People are being drowned out or stopped from speaking, whether from the Left or the Right. It is very difficult to teach.
6. Young people (and their parents) are reconsidering college. Rather than spending upward of $70,000 per year, or over a quarter million dollars, for a B.A. degree, they are sending their children (at least temporarily) to trade (fashion, art), real estate, or other "practical" schools that will lead to making money immediately and at a tiny fraction of the cost at a liberal arts college.

A recent article in *The Jewish Week* in 2019 said it all in the title: "Bernie Sanders is 78, and yet he speaks for my generation." Studies have shown that young people, not just Jews, between the ages of 19 and 28 have a more positive view of socialism (52%) than of capitalism (48%). This is due to two factors: (1) Young people blame capitalism for the climate crisis on our planet. (2) People are struggling economically and, despite low unemployment, there is fear for the future. Plus, many jobs are boring, sitting in front of a computer all day. Young people blame capitalism. They feel that, under some form of socialism—meaning more control of your workplace and less alienated labor—you have more say in your work. Young people feel they will be happier and more productive that way.

A second factor is climate change. Young people see that capitalism— profits at all costs, and even amelioration is going at a snail's pace—is the cause of our planet being endangered. They feel a more basic, more natural, even more "hippy" approach to our planet—less waste, less plastic, less paper and cardboard, less pollution, less garbage under some form of communal usage (a form of socialism)—will help our planet survive.

And a third surprise factor is endemic worldwide viruses that have rocked Wall Street, interrupted air travel, and closed schools and companies. The impact on the world, as well as on the 2020 races, will be profound.

Naturally, older adults see this as naïve, that young people don't really know the "real" history of socialism; that they are fooling themselves. True, some forms of socialism morphed into horrible authoritarianism. They point out Russia, as well as Venezuela and Cuba. They are correct. Russia turned into a police-state, and Venezuela and Cuba are economic basket-cases. (Ironically, under capitalistic Putin, Russia is still a police state, though not as murderous as Stalin's, but bad enough.)

I am not speaking of Communism or heavy top-down controlled socialism, but what in Europe is called "democratic socialism" or "social democracy." Ruth Wisse, at a "Jews and Conservatism" conference in New York City on November 10, 2019, called her talk "Jews and Socialism: An Autopsy." I think the death of socialism is a bit premature, Ms. Wisse. As I have shown, we have the next generation. You don't. Young people despise many elements of capitalism and embrace democratic socialism. Yet the modern-day version of "red-baiting" continues. Back in the 1940s and 1950s under McCarthyism, the "bating" was against the Soviet Union and Communism ("Better dead than red"—red was the color of the Communist flag).

Today, it is flung against "radical liberals" or "socialists," but the impact is the same—to marginalize and demonize liberals and leftists and scare people—but it's not working as effectively as it had in the past. Young people are hip. Socialism does not scare them anymore.

This is what I mean by a postmodern radical approach to life and Judaism. The above changes are examples of the structural transformation going on today, and they need to be addressed immediately. Actually, the future of Jewish life, though many conservative or right-wing Jews will disagree, is contained in the platforms of Bernie Sanders, Elizabeth Warren,

Pete Buttigieg, and Amy Klobuchar. It is a progressive politics that emphasizes global warming and climate change, inequality, healthcare for all, the end of student debt, and a tough but cordial attitude toward our allies in Israel, the Middle East, Europe, China, Korea, and Africa.

Bibliography

There are many "sources" and influencers. Here are some books that are good background. I include both pro-radical and anti-radical books:

Arendt, Hannah. *The Jewish Writings*. Jerome Kohn and Ron H. Feldman, eds. New York: Schocken Books, 2007. Arendt dealt with many of these problems decades ago, from anti-Semitism to revolution to the crisis in Zionism.

Carmichael, Stokely, and Charles V. Hamilton. *Black Power: The Politics of Liberation in America*. New York: Vintage Books, 1967. The classic book on Black Power by one of the major leaders of the Black movement, Stokely Carmichael.

Caute, David. *The Great Fear*. New York: Touchstone Books, 1978. On McCarthyism and Red-Baiting in America.

————. *Frantz Fanon*. New York: The Viking Press, 1970. A short biography of the great Black thinker. It should be read along with Fanon's masterful *Black Skin, White Masks* and revolutionary *The Wretched of the Earth*.

Einstein, Albert. *Einstein on Peace*. Otto Nathan and Heinz Norden, eds. Preface by Bertrand Russell. New York: Simon & Schuster, 1960. The great Einstein was highly prolific regarding social and political issues like peace, war, fascism, Nazism, and the need for a "supranational organization" like the United Nations.

Guttmann, Allen. *The Jewish Writer in America*. New York: Oxford University Press, 1971. This book heavily influenced me in uniting literature and politics. Guttmann, a professor of literature at Amherst College, has the "sociological imagination," not just a strong literary sense, as he describes the "insider/outsider" status of Jews in America and their reflection in modern literature.

Liebman, Arthur. *Jews and the Left*. New York: John Wiley, 1979. A classic book.

Lipstadt, Deborah. *Anti-Semitism: Here and Now*. New York: Schocken Books, 2019. There are many books on anti-Semitism, but Prof. Lipstadt has caught the *zeitgeist* with this book. It is a balanced and sober explanation of this mysterious and complex issue.

Neumann, Jonathan. *To Heal the World? How the Jewish Left Corrupts Judaism and Endangers Israel*. New York: St. Martin's Press, 2018. This is a brave book attacking the "political correctness" of the Jewish Left and skewering such leaders as Art Green and

Michael Lerner. I loved it. I may not agree with everything Neumann says, and I am glad he said it. Tikkun Olam has become a cliché in the Jewish world, and Neumann shows how and why.

Newfield, Jack. *A Prophetic Minority.* New York: Signet Books, 1966. One of the first and one of the best books on the radicalism of the Left.

Podhoretz, Norman. *Ex-Friends.* San Francisco: Encounter Books, 2000. He has written several other books about his odyssey from democratic socialist to liberal to Cold Warrior to neo-con to worse, but here he details the painful tales of his falling out with the likes of Allen Ginsberg, Norman Mailer, and Hannah Arendt.

Porter, Jack Nusan, and Peter Dreier. *Jewish Radicalism.* New York: Grove Press and Random House, 1973. The classic movement anthology.

Porter, Jack Nusan. *The Sociology of American Jews: A Critical Anthology.* Second revised edition. Lanham, Md.: University Press of America (Rowman & Littlefield), 1980. By "critical," I mean "socialist," but we had to use euphemisms back then. Contains excellent articles on Vietnam, labor movements, community organizing, and family life, all from a progressive perspective.

Putnam, Robert D. *Bowling Alone.* New York: Simon & Schuster, 2000. This book by a Harvard professor explains so much of why our institutions and organizations are collapsing. People just don't join anymore. It explains the decline in *shul* attendance as well as the collapse of Jewish organizations. So, what can be done about it?

Raider, Mark A. *The Emergence of American Zionism.* New York: New York University Press, 1998.

Troy, Gil. *The Zionist Ideas.* New York: Jewish Publication Society, 2018. This important book is an expansion of Arthur Hertzberg's classic 1959 book *The Zionist Idea.*

Zinn, Howard. *A People's History of the United States.* New York: HarperCollins, 2009. One of the few books mentioned in a Hollywood movie. In *Good Will Hunting* starting Matt Damon and Ben Affleck, Damon uttered the lines.

About the Author

Jack Nusan Porter is considered one of the founders of the field of genocide studies and the sociology of Jewry and the Holocaust: he taught one of the first courses in comparative genocide, at the University of Massachusetts at Lowell in 1977; edited the first anthology in the field, *Genocide and Human Rights: A Global Anthology* in the late 1970s; the first book on Jewish radicals, Jewish Radicalism, in 1973; the first anthology of radical Jewish life (and according to the late Marshall Sklare, first to use the words "the sociology of Jews" in a title), *The Sociology of American Jews: A Critical Anthology* (1978); the first curriculum guide in teaching the sociology of the Holocaust in 1992, *The Sociology of the Holocaust and Genocide* (published by the American Sociological Association, ASA) and works on the *agunah*, *The Chained Wife: On the Agunah*; as well as many article on Jewish culture, politics, and subcultures such as Hasidim, Jewish gays, and radical Jews. He is also a founding member of the Association of the Social Scientific Study of Jewry (ASSJ),

Born in Rovno, Ukraine in December 1944, Porter came to the USA in 1946 after a year in a Displaced Person Camp near Linz, in Bindermichel, Austria, and grew up in Milwaukee, Wisconsin, where he attended the Sherman Elementary School, Steuben Junior High and Washington High School. He has also lived on Kibbutz Gesher Haziv, attended school in Jerusalem at the Machon Institute for Youth Leaders from 1962-1963.

He has been a member of the American Sociological Association for over 50 years since the age of 22, starting at the University of Wisconsin, Milwaukee between 1963-1967, where he obtained his B.A. and became a sociologist under the influence of Karl Flaming, Irwin Rinder, Hugo Engelmann, Don Weast, and Lakshimi Bharadwaj.

He attended graduate school at Northwestern University from 1967-1971, and earned his Ph.D. under Howard S. Becker, Bernie Beck, Janet Abu-Lughod, Alan Schnaiberg, Charlie Moskos, and Richard Schwartz.

He has taught at numerous colleges including Boston University, University of Massachusetts Lowell, Boston College, Northwestern University, De Paul University, the State University of New York—Cortland, and Emerson College, and is presently Research Associate at the Davis Center for Russian and Eurasian Studies at Harvard University.

He was the founder of the *Journal of the History of Sociology* (later called *History of Sociology*), as well as the *Journal of the Sociology of Business*, and has been a contributor to the *Encyclopedia Judaica, Encyclopedia of Genocide*, the *Encyclopedia of Sociology*, and the *Italian-American Experience: An Encyclopedia*. He is the author of such classics as *The Jew as Outsider, Confronting History and Holocaust*, and *Jewish Radicalism*, as well as over 40 books and 700 articles, essays, and reviews.

He is a former vice-president of the International Association of Genocide Scholars (IAGS) and a former research associate at Harvard University's Ukrainian Research Institute (HURI) from 1982-1984. He has won the Robin Williams Award from the ASA's Section on War, Peace, and Social Conflict, and the Lifetime Achievement Award from the History of Sociology section of the ASA.

In 2016, he was nominated for a Nobel Prize for his work on the prevention and prediction of genocide and on the impact of the Holocaust on sexuality and gender.

Porter lives in Newtonville, Massachusetts, not far from his children Gabe and Danielle. His late wife Dr. Raya Evashko was from Kiev, Ukraine. She died in 2017.

Website: www.drjackporter.com

Sources and Permissions

Bona fide attempts have been made to secure permissions from all publishers, but most of the journals and newspapers from the 1960s ceased publication decades ago. In any case, nearly all of my articles and essays have been copyrighted in my name anyway.